CW00819404

# BACKGROUND
# to the BIBLE

**Chris Sinkinson**
**Clive Anderson**
**Brian Edwards**

DayOne

© Day One Publications 2021

ISBN 978-1-84625-702-5

British Library Cataloguing in Publication Data available
Unless otherwise indicated, Scripture quotations are from the Holy Bible New
International Version, (NIV), copyright by Hodder & Stoughton Limited. Used by
permission.

Published by DayOne Publications
Ryelands Road, Leominster, HR6 8NZ, England
TEL 01568 613 740    FAX 01568 611 473
North America  Toll Free 888 329 6630
email–sales@dayone.co.uk
web site–www.dayone.co.uk

Edited by Brian Edwards
Designed by Kathryn Chedgzoy, www.k-c-design.co.uk
Printed by PB Print

# BACKGROUND
# to the BIBLE

**Chris Sinkinson**
**Clive Anderson**
**Brian Edwards (Editor)**

# CONTENTS

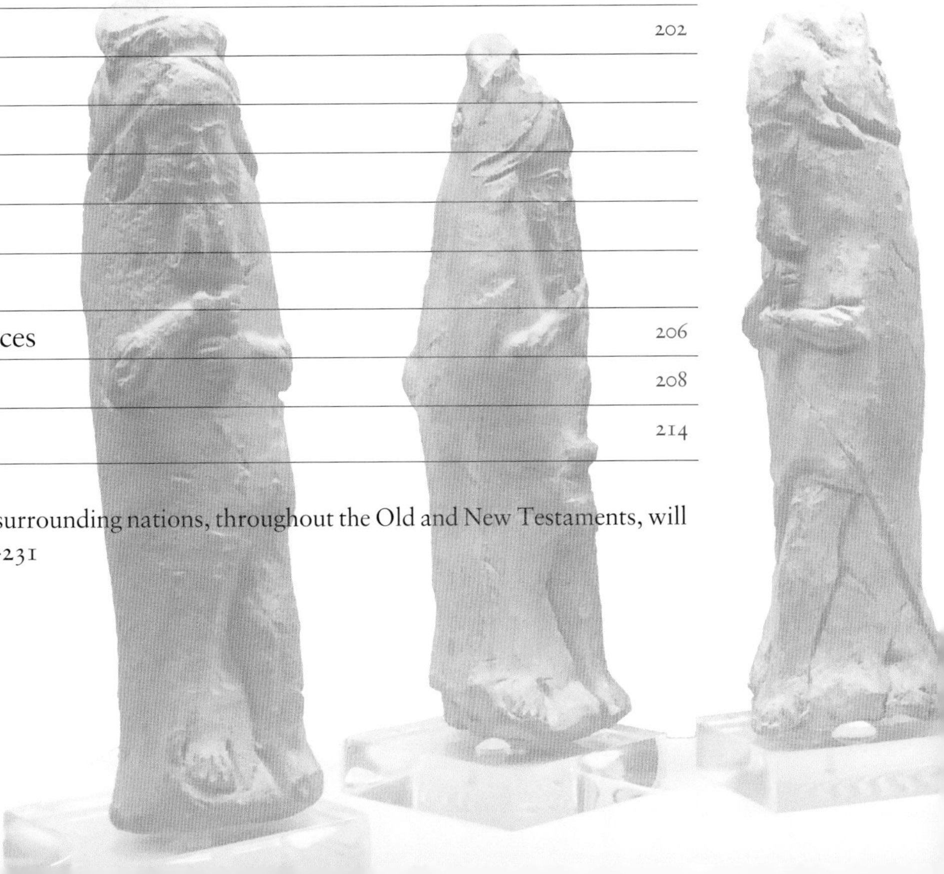

Full timelines of Israel and Judah and the surrounding nations, throughout the Old and New Testaments, will be found in *Evidence for the Bible* pp. 220-231

*Known today as 'Gideon's Spring' it was the 'spring of Harod' where Gideon and his men camped before their defeat of the Midianites (Judges 7:1–8)*

# Background to the Bible

Archaeology is never a static science, and that is especially true for archaeology related to the Bible. Every year, and throughout the year, towns and items are unearthed that throw important light on the background and context of the Bible

*B*ackground to the Bible is intended as a companion to *Evidence for the Bible*. Since its first appearance in 2014, *Evidence* has proved very popular and has been reprinted many times; it is available for purchase in the British Museum and an American edition has also been published. However, there is always so much more testimony from the trowel to illustrate and authenticate the Bible's history, hence *Background to the Bible*.

Unlike most sourcebooks of world religions, the Bible is set in the orderly context of real history.

It contains not only 'stories', but the record of events that really happened from the beginning of creation to the close of the New Testament. This is what makes the Bible a living record of God's plan for restoring a broken world to his perfect fulfilment.

Historical records always have a context: who were the people and what was the age like in which they lived? Who lived around them and how did those people live? What customs and beliefs throw light on the expressions used in the Bible? All these, and much more, are not merely interesting details, but they frequently help us to understand and appreciate the Bible record more fully.

In this companion to *Evidence for the Bible*, we have avoided repetition in the text and only rarely are the same items illustrated. We have frequently referenced where additional information or pictures can be found in *Evidence for the Bible*. Full timelines of Israel and the surrounding empires will be found there also.

The two volumes will sit comfortably together on your coffee table for visitors to enjoy, or in your library as a familiar point of reference.

For serious study or for relaxed and interesting reading, *Background to the Bible* will prove invaluable to all who have an interest in understanding what lies behind and around the events recorded in the Bible.

**Below**
*Chris on a dig near the sea of Galilee and taking it easy on a discarded settee overlooking the Judean wilderness!*

*... so why not sit back comfortably and survey the land with Background to the Bible*

# The miracle of Israel

**Every great empire of the ancient world disappeared under the trash heap of history, only one seemingly insignificant people remarkably survived to the present day**

**Left**
*The 'Broad Wall'. The foundations of the city wall that defied Sennacherib in 701 BC*

When God promised to make the descendants of Abraham 'into a great nation' (Genesis 12:2), it set in train the most remarkable story of any people-group that has covered four millennia. Throughout this time, repeated attempts were made to destroy their very existence.

### First, the Egyptians

When the grandsons of Abraham, the twelve sons of Jacob (Israel), settled in Egypt around 2,000 BC, they were under the protection of a powerful and wealthy nation. However, after four centuries their growing numbers drove them into slavery and finally an attempt was made to destroy them entirely (Exodus 1). The miracle of the Exodus saved them. Later, early in the 13th century, Pharaoh Merneptah left on record his attempt to destroy the people known as Israel.[1] Slowly, Egyptian unity splintered and allowed the Assyrians to take control.

### Second, the Assyrians

By the 8th century BC, the Assyrian empire stretched from Egypt to the Persian Gulf and as far north as modern Turkey.

In 722 BC Sargon of Assyria ended the northern territory of Israel (Samaria, 2 Kings 17).[2] Two decades later Sargon's son, Sennacherib, set out to destroy Judah in the south. The Assyrian field commander taunted the Judaean king Hezekiah in Jerusalem: 'Has the god of any nation ever delivered his land from the hand of the king of Assyria?' (2 Kings 18:33). However, on Sennacherib's own admission, of all the nations he destroyed, Hezekiah was the only king that he never captured; his army was decimated by an unseen hand and he was assassinated in 681 BC.[3]

### Third, the Babylonians

At the battle of Carchemish in 605 BC the power of Assyria was finally broken, and Babylon was the new superpower. In 587 BC, Jerusalem and its temple were destroyed by the Babylonian army of Nebuchadnezzar and its people taken into exile (2 Kings 24:10–13). As a sovereign nation, Israel no longer existed. But the Jews maintained their faith and their unity as a people.[4]

---

1. See The Merneptah Stela in *Evidence for the Bible* p. 32.
2. See *Evidence for the Bible* p. 60.
3. See *Evidence for the Bible* pp. 65–78.
4. See *Evidence for the Bible* pp. 78–93.

## Fourth, the Persians

In 539 BC, the Persian army broke the power of Babylon and Cyrus allowed their captive people, including the Jews, to return home.[5] In spite of local opposition, both Jerusalem and the temple were rebuilt. However, in the time of Xerxes there was a conspiracy in the Persian court to destroy all Jews throughout the empire (Esther 3–7); the courage of the Jewish queen saved them. The extent, power and wealth of the Persian empire exceeded all before them — until Alexander the Great defeated Persia at the Battle of Issus in 333 BC. Alexander's vision of one people, one nation, one language and one currency was almost achieved and the Jews had some respite.

## Fifth, the Syrians

When Alexander died and his empire was broken up, Judah came under the control of Syria and the Seleucid dynasty. In 175 BC, Antiochus IV determined to replace the religion of the Jews by Greek culture and religion. He took the name 'Epiphanes' (God manifest) and claimed to be Zeus incarnate. Judaism was outlawed, the temple treasures plundered, an altar to Zeus was erected in the temple and pigs were sacrificed there. The guerrilla wars of the Maccabees erupted. Although the Maccabees failed to overthrow the Syrians, Antiochus died in 164 BC and the Seleucid kingdom slowly crumbled until defeated by Rome in 63 BC.

## Sixth, the Romans

The Romans arrived in Jerusalem under general Pompey in 63 BC and stayed for three hundred years. Although Israel had some degree of independence, most Jews hated the Roman occupation and rebellion finally led to the entire destruction of Jerusalem and the temple in AD 70 and thousands of Jews were enslaved. The final humiliation was the financing of the Colosseum by the treasures plundered from the temple in Jerusalem.[6] Rome itself was destroyed by the Goths in the 5th century and its empire disintegrated.

## Seventh, a scattered and stateless people

Across the world in the centuries that followed, the Jews held on to their religion, but with no home to call their own. They were variously tolerated, hated and persecuted; only the Allied victory in 1945 saved them from entire extermination. In 1948 the United Nations recognized the State of Israel.

One of the most intriguing phenomena of recorded history is the survival of the Jews during their four thousand years from Abraham to the present day. Was it for their sake only, or for the sake of the whole world?

**Bottom**
'Methuselah', *a date palm tree grown from a cluster of date stones discovered by Yigdal Yadin on Masada in the 1960s; Masada was the final stand against Rome of the Jewish Zealots destroyed in AD 73. 'Methuselah', is a symbol of the survival of the Jewish people*

**Below**
*A coin depicting Antiochus IV Epiphanes, minted between 172 and 164 BC. On the obverse he is shown wearing a diadem; on the reverse, an unnamed goddess is seated on a throne while holding Nike (Victory) in her right hand with the words* Basileus Antiochos (King Antiochus)

5. See *Evidence for the Bible* pp. 96–107.
6. See *Evidence for the Bible* p. 178–180 and page 119 here.

# Israel — a strategic land bridge

**The relatively small size of the land of Canaan should not distract us from its significance on the world stage in Bible times and beyond**

**Left**

*The Fertile Crescent is formed by the Tigris and Euphrates rivers in the east and its western boundary is marked by the Mediterranean Sea. This great arc became known as the cradle of civilization*

**Below**

*When General Edmund Allenby entered Jerusalem in 1917 after the fall of the Ottoman Empire, he was only the latest in a long line of military leaders to lay claim to this strategic region*

The land given to Israel stands at a pivotal site within the broader area of the Fertile Crescent, which includes Canaan and northern Egypt. Canaan was of enormous strategic value for the entire region. It sits on the meeting point of three continents: Africa, Asia and Europe. Far from being an isolated backwater, it was the land bridge of the ancient world for movement between these continents. In the west and east, the Mediterranean Sea and the Arabian desert were significant barriers, whereas an accessible road ran down the length of Canaan.

This 'Way of the Sea' (Isaiah 9:1) was a major trunk road that allowed armies and merchants to move between the empires. This is one reason why the land of the Bible was of strategic interest to so many:

- **Egypt** called the Way of the Sea the 'Way of Horus' and often led military campaigns into Canaan (1 Kings 14:25–26).
- **The Philistines** had come from the Mediterranean Sea and settled the western coastal plain. The Bible sometimes calls the Way of the Sea, the 'Way of the land of the Philistines' (Exodus 13:17).
- **Assyria** laid claim to the north of Canaan and eventually destroyed the northern kingdom of Israel (2 Kings 15:29).
- **Babylon** rose to become the powerful empire that destroyed Jerusalem (2 Kings 24:10–16).
- **Persia** defeated Babylon and established the Achaemenid Empire in which Judah was a province (Ezra 1:1–4).
- **Greece** created an empire stretching east to Persia after the conquests of Alexander the Great, bringing Greek language and culture to the land of Judah.
- **Rome** transformed Judah into its own province of Judea and eventually renamed it Palestine at the time of Emperor Hadrian in order to erase Jewish identity.
- **In the Modern World** nations have continued to fight for control of the land including Napoleon's attempt to conquer Palestine in 1799 and the British Empire taking control of it during the period of the British Mandate (1923–1948).

Significantly, as so many nations came to Judah, it was from here that Jesus commissioned his followers to take the Good News to the ends of the earth (Matthew 28:18–20).

# A Birthplace for archaeology

## In Canaan, the development of civilization has left a wealth of material for modern science to uncover

The two great rivers of the Fertile Crescent were essential to the beginnings of civilization. Sumer and Egypt both developed the earliest civilizations. The biblical reference to Shinar (Genesis 10:10) is probably Sumer. Their innovations in agriculture (including the wheel), mathematics and literature would spread across the world. Bronze and Iron metalworking were both developed in the Fertile Crescent.[1]

Armies crossing the land constructed heavily fortified cities whose walls provided a stable platform for dwellings. When a city was destroyed by war or earthquake, it was rebuilt on top of the ruins; this preserved the artefacts of earlier civilizations and many such *tels* (ruin mounds) still remain. With so much history and covered civilizations, Bible lands were important for the development of biblical archaeology.

- **Helena** (248–330), her interest in the Christian faith, led the mother of Emperor Constantine identifying and excavating biblical sites.

- **Charles Warren** (1840–1927) extensively explored the tunnels and walls of Jerusalem to understand its historical development.

- **Flinders Petrie** (1853–1942) developed a more systematic approach to excavation and honed his skills in Egypt along with many sites in Palestine.

- **John Garstang** (1876–1956) was a pioneer in developing archaeology as a science and keeping extensive photographic records of his excavations. Garstang excavated in Egypt and at Jericho and Ashkelon.

- **William Albright** (1891–1971) identified the Dead Sea Scrolls and developed what became known as 'Biblical Archaeology'. Without believing in the full trustworthiness of the Bible, he claimed archaeology demonstrated that Bible history was generally accurate.

- **Kathleen Kenyon** (1906–1978) became known as the 'mistress of stratigraphy' for her emphasis on careful excavation of the horizontal layers of a site. She developed her skills at Jericho, Samaria and Jerusalem. While her conclusions remain controversial her techniques continue to be valued.[2]

**Right**
*The ruins of Scythopolis from the time of Jesus, and in the background the Tel of Bethshan where the bodies of Saul and Jonathan were taken by the Philistines (1 Samuel 31:8–13). This tel covered 6,000 years and fifteen civilizations*

**Below**
*Excavations at Megiddo reveal twenty different cities built one on top of another, stretching back to the Bronze Age when the circular altar was in use*

.....7....

---

1. Reference to Tubal-Cain (whose name may mean sharpener or hammerer) working in bronze and iron (Genesis 4:22) may refer to a skill later lost, or to the hammering and filing of surface deposits of copper and iron, rather than the later development of smelting.
2. See here pp. 138–148 for more on early archaeologists.

# A well-watered land

**Although only the size of Wales, the land of Canaan (Israel) has a climate and geology for farming and industry which would make it desirable to its larger neighbours**

The distance from north to south—'from Dan to Beersheba' (Judges 20:1)— is around 240km (150mi). In the north, Mount Hermon rises to 2,814m (9232ft), and from here the River Jordan makes its way down the length of the country into the Sea of Galilee; the Hebrew word 'Jordan' means 'to go down'. Galilee is the lowest freshwater lake in the world and its 53km (33mi) circumference sustained a vibrant fishing industry; the surrounding region was ideal for farming wheat and barley.

The central highland ridge is a rugged landscape and was the location for many of the most important Israelite cities including Samaria, Hebron, Bethlehem and Jerusalem. This landscape was suitable for herding sheep and goats. Olive trees grow well here, providing a sustainable crop for food, heating and lighting. The limestone of the ridge provided good stone for construction.

The Jordan river continues to flow south to the lowest point on earth, 1,300 feet below sea level. Water cannot escape the Dead Sea, other than by evaporation, it is therefore devoid of all life. Ancient people knew its value as a source for salt and bitumen.

A wider desert region extends south to the wilderness of Zin and east to the land of Moab. While there is little rainfall in this area, steep gorges, known as wadis, carry run-off rainwater from the highlands through the desert and into the Dead Sea. The biblical text draws attention to 'cisterns' in the highland country (2 Chronicles 26:10) that stored rainfall, whereas in the south 'wells' were essential to find water in the desert territory, deep below ground. Abraham and Isaac dug wells in the Negev desert at the Valley of Gerar and Beersheba (Genesis 26:17–25).

A land 'flowing with milk and honey' (Deuteronomy 31:20) captures this sense of a beautiful land rich in natural resources. Sheep and goats flourished in the mountains and deserts producing milk. The honey probably refers to the sweet date honey which is still widely produced from the date palm trees in the land of Israel.[1]

**Top**
*The Bronze Age Gate at the city of Dan in the north of Israel (18th century BC), then called Laish, is a unique triple arch structure and now protected by a modern canopy*

**Above**
*Archaeological excavations of the city of Beersheba reveal an Old Testament city that thrived in the dry terrain of the south by relying on its system of wells*

1. Though it is noteworthy that in 2005 the only apiary ever excavated in the Ancient Near East was found in northern Israel. Nava Panitz-Cohen, 'To What God?', *Biblical Archaeology Review*, July/August 2008. See also here 'God's Trees' p. 10.

# Seed Time and Harvest

## Understanding the seasons was key to survival and success for the people of Israel

Canaan is marked by two seasons (Genesis 8:22): a rainy season suitable for planting, and a dry season, suitable for harvesting. The rainy season lasts from late October until mid-March. The dry season from April until October. The amount of rainfall in Jerusalem is much the same as London, but it falls over twice the length of time in London. There is snow on the central highlands, including Jerusalem, though it settles only briefly with the warmer desert nearby.

As different crops would be harvested at different times in the dry season, it was important to know when to sow the relevant seeds during the rainy seasons. The Gezer Calendar was a guide to planting seeds from the 10th century BC. Written in an early Hebrew script it was found by archaeologists in 1908 and details when various agricultural activities are to take place and how long they should last.[2]

The barley harvest is first (April), followed by wheat, then grapes, dates and figs. The olive harvest came last at the end of the dry season. Ruth arrived in Bethlehem at the beginning of the barely harvest season (Ruth 1:22), and she was still working the fields at the time of the wheat harvest two months later (Ruth 2:23).

In ancient times trees and wild beasts, were widespread. Among the twenty species of tree mentioned in the Bible are oaks, sycamore and acacia. But the landscape has gradually changed with the impact of farming, overgrazing and soil erosion.

When well-wooded and more sparsely populated, the land could easily sustain such diverse wildlife as aurochs, lions, bears and the wild ass. Along with protecting trees (Deuteronomy 20:19–20), the Old Testament law made provision for the sustaining of wild animals (Exodus 23:11) as well as concern for the welfare of domestic animals (Proverbs 12:10). Such laws are unknown in the ancient world outside of Israel.

**Top**
*A replica of the Tel Gezer calendar at the site where it was found. This is one of the earliest Hebrew texts in existence*

**Above**
*From Mt Arbel overlooking a rich and fertile land and the northern end of the Sea of Galilee*

*A view from Carmel*

2. See *Evidence for the Bible*, p. 31.

# God's trees

**'The LORD God made all kinds of trees grow out of the ground—trees that were pleasing to the eye and good for food' (Genesis 2:9)**

**Above**
*Young women in Ethiopia are reminiscent of the daily task of Israel in the wilderness and the Promised Land*

There are many uses for the vast number of different trees available to us. But, how did the Israelites in the wilderness find all the wood they required for sacrifices, cooking, heating, metalwork and construction?[1]

## Trees in the wilderness

Surveys of communities reliant on wood for all purposes conclude that each person would need 0.3 tonnes per year. Allowing for around thirty-five thousand Israelites (see *Evidence for the Bible* pages 196–197), they would require over ten thousand tonnes of timber each year! One reason why God moved them on regularly. (Numbers 33).

Today Sinai is largely desert, but not in the past. The Egyptologist Flinders Petrie discovered Bronze Age copper mining and smelting, and the consequent huge beds of wood ash, in Western Sinai at the time of the Exodus. See also page 39 for copper mining in Edom.

## Trees for food

Four of seven chief food plants of the promised land are fruit trees (Deuteronomy 8:8): figs, pomegranates, olives, and dates (the desert 'honey'). God prepared the people for their settlement in the Promised Land with sound horticultural advice that a fruit tree should not be harvested in its early years (Leviticus 19:23). He also carefully guarded the ecology of the land by forbidding the destruction of fruit trees even in war (Deuteronomy 20:19–20).

## Trees for medicine

The reference to hyssop and cedar wood in the healing of skin diseases and mildew (Leviticus 14:6) probably refers to the small aromatic juniper tree (*Juniperus phoenicea*) which grows widely in the area and is known to contain many medicinal values; it is still used for cancer and antifungal treatments. In Britain, early editions of *Encyclopaedia Britannica* describe the process of fumigation using the native juniper tree.

## Trees for the Temple

Four trees are used in the building of the Temple: cedar for the beams and panelling, juniper (not 'pine') for the floor, olive and fir for intricate carving of the cherubim and doors (1 Kings 6:14–38). Exactly the right timber for the right job.

1. For a detailed and fascinating presentation of trees in the Bible see *God's Trees*, Julian Evans (Day One Publications, Leominster 2014) from which this material is taken.

# 'A land flowing with milk and honey'

## God promised his people that in the Promised Land they would have a well-balanced diet of protein and carbohydrate

The promise of God in Exodus 3:8 is repeated more than a dozen times from Exodus to Deuteronomy. In ancient times, more significant than bees' honey was date honey; probably the honey referred to in God's promise. The Greek historian Herodotus in the 5th century BC and the Roman writer Pliny in the time of Jesus, both refer to the palm tree producing 'wine and honey'.

Refined sugar was unknown, but the fruit syrup made from crushed or pressed dates was, and still is, commonplace. It is pure carbohydrate, so Moses's reference to milk adds the vital proteins and fats.

The reference by Herodotus and Pliny to 'wine' from palm trees probably refers to the result of piercing the flowers and fermenting the liquid. The Babylonians relished this, and it is probably the 'other fermented drink' referred to in Leviticus 10:9 and Numbers 6:3.

### The palm tree as metaphor and simile

Imagery of the palm tree is found in Psalm 92:12 and Song of Solomon 7:7. The date palm is the tree of the semi-desert, wadis and oases, and in Old Testament times forests of it flourished in the Jordan Valley and in Galilee. It is able to cope with extremes, whether of heat, drought or flooding.

The palm tree provided for almost every aspect of daily life: food and drink, beams, rope, matting, baskets, leaves for roofing and walls, and small ones as 'dusters'; ground date kernels fed livestock. An old saying claimed that the palm tree had as many uses as days in the year.

It is also a tree of great elegance: tall, long-lived and graceful. Its forms decorated the temple (1 Kings 6:29, 32). It was a sign of victory and conquest—hence the waving of their leaves on 'Palm Sunday'. Sennacherib, king of Assyria in the time of Hezekiah, prided himself as 'the Date Palm of Assyria'; and to illustrate his conquest of Jerusalem in AD 70, the Emperor Vespasian issued a coin with a Hebrew woman bowed and weeping beneath a palm and the words: 'Judah Captured'.

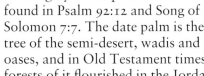

**Right**
*A date palm outside the Church of St Anne by the pool of Bethesda in Jerusalem*

**Inset**
*Vespasian's coin of victory:* Judaea Capta

# Great Ages in Genesis

**The long lifespans mentioned in Genesis has sometimes been read as legend. However, comparison with king lists of the ancient world suggests otherwise**

Most famously Methuselah lived for 969 years (Genesis 5:27). This inspired a name for a large measure of wine (6ltr) and the oldest bristlecone pine tree in the world (nearly 5000 years old)!

Those living before the Flood (Genesis 11) averaged 912 years but from the time of Abraham there is a steep decline to what we would expect today (Psalm 90:10). If Adam was created for eternal life, sin and decay following the Fall would gradually reduce the lifespan and this seems to accelerate after the Flood.

Ancient Sumerian king lists describe even more vast periods over which kings had reigned.[1] The Weld-Blundell Prism (around 1800 BC) provides a list of eight kings who lived prior to 'a great flood'. For example, King Emmenluanna reigned for 43,200 years. The Sumerian King list also refers to a great flood and the reigns of these kings rapidly shrink to more normal lengths after the 'flood'.[2]

Scholars suggest that the numbers used in the Sumerian account probably reflect the 'sexagesimal' (base 60) system of counting which was common across ancient Mesopotamia. Numbers were often multiples of 10 and 60. We use the ancient Babylonian system with our divisions of time (60 minutes in an hour etc.) and geometry (360 degrees to a circle). The origins of this method of counting are found 5000 years ago in ancient Sumer where these king lists were written. When the king lists are read according to this system, the numbers might have a symbolic significance: if we divide the numbers by 60 they are more comparable to those found in Genesis: Enmenluanna's 43,200 reduces to 720 years. Perhaps the Sumerians used their number systems to magnify the greatness of their kings?

Some also see a symbolic significance to all the great ages in Genesis. However, in comparison with other Ancient Near Eastern lists, the Genesis account reads as a sober, historical account of these ancient people.

**Right**
*The Sumerian King List, or Weld-Blundell prism c.1827–1817 BC, describes vast lengths for the kings' reigns*

1. Jacobsen, Thorkild, *The Sumerian King List*, (The University of Chicago Press, 1939).
2. See *Evidence for the Bible* pp. 2–3 for ancient Mesopotamian and Sumerian flood stories

# God and Creation

**The religions of the Ancient Near East saw the divine in various aspects of creation. Many of the gods who were worshipped are identified with the sun, moon and stars**

People have always known that the celestial bodies enable us to understand the passage of time and provide crucial information for agriculture and navigation. The book of Genesis describes them as lights in the sky made by God as 'signs and for seasons, and for days and years' and 'to give light on the earth' (Genesis 1:14).

The stars formed recognizable patterns called constellations, which were known throughout the Ancient Near East (Amos 5:8; Job 9:9; 38:31–32). The Babylonians were the first recorded civilization to develop a system of astrology. Its earliest form connected weather and natural events, such as earthquakes, to the positions of the stars. From about 500 BC, astrological data was codified by the Babylonians to form the twelve Zodiac signs.[3] This system was useful for agriculture; it was only much later that this was considered to have any relevance for predicting events based on when someone was born.

The Israelites used a lunar calendar, basing the start of each month on the appearance of the new moon, which is why a trumpet was blown at the first sighting of the crescent moon (Numbers 10:10; Psalm 81:3). An extra month came to be added every two or three years so that the year remained synchronized with the agricultural and religious calendar (Exodus 12:1–3).

However, ancient people attempted to find deeper meaning in the stars. The Bible warned the Israelites that in their study of the sun, moon and stars beware 'you be drawn away and bow down to them and serve them' (Deuteronomy 4:19). Genesis deliberately avoids Hebrew words for 'sun' and 'moon' which were the names of gods, preferring to call them 'two great lights' (Genesis 1:16). But from the time of the Sumerians these lights were given names and worshipped as representing divine beings.[4] Paul would later observe of Roman society that they 'worshipped and served created things rather than the Creator' (Romans 1:25). By contrast, for the Israelites the heavens 'declare the glory of God' (Psalm 19:1).

3. Ulla Koch-Westenholz, *Mespotamian Astrology,* The Carsten-Niebuhr Institute of Near Eastern Studies, (University of Copenhagen 1995). p. 163.
4. See here pages 14-15, 24, 32-33.

# Abraham left home

## Abraham is one of the most prominent and influential figures of biblical history

Abraham (Abram Genesis 17:5) c.2166 BC is often referred to as 'the father of the faithful' because he believed God (Romans 4:3, 16–17).

Ur of the Chaldeans, the city in Mesopotamia where Abraham's brother Haran (and likely Abraham himself) was born, is identified with Muqaiyir, which is west of the present River Euphrates and some 240km (150mi) southeast of Babylon. Ruins there cover an area about 910 by 730m (3,000 by 2,400ft). It was a centre for worship of the moon-god Sin (Akkadian) or Nanna (Sumerian). The site's most prominent feature is still a temple tower, or ziggurat, some 61m long, 46m wide and 21m high (200 by 150 by 70ft). It is likely that Abraham once worshipped here (Joshua 24:2).[1]

In royal tombs at Ur, excavators found many objects of gold, silver, lapis lazuli, and other costly materials, as well as the evidence of the burial of early Sumerian kings and queens of Ur, together with their retinue of male and female servants.[2] Ruins of what appear to be private houses excavated at Ur show that they were constructed of brick and plastered and whitewashed; some had thirteen or fourteen rooms surrounding a paved courtyard. Among clay tablets found at the site were some

that may have been used to teach cuneiform writing.

It is likely that Abraham's family were wealthy, as later details reveal (Genesis 12:5; 13:5–6). However, by faith the patriarch was looking forward to a better city whose builder and maker is God (Hebrews 11:8–10). The rivers and estuary have now silted up making Ur unprofitable to live in—but could Abraham's family have once been sailors, like some of Jesus disciples?

Although Genesis 12:1 credits Terah with the move from Ur to Haran because he was the family head (11:31), God had spoken to Abraham whilst he was still in Ur (Acts 7:2,4 and Nehemiah 9:7). From Haran, Abraham obeyed God's call to take his wife Sarah and his nephew Lot into Canaan.

**Top left**

*The god Sin shown in this cylinder seal and its impression (bulla) as symbolized by a crescent moon, c. 2100 BC*

**Top right**

*A gold helmet belonging to the king of Ur I Meskalamdug, c.2600–2500 BC, this reveals the wealth of the city of Ur*

**Below**

*Ruins of Ur in Southern Iraq showing the Ziggurat in the background that Saddam Hussain had covered in brick! Inset: as the Ziggurat appeared when discovered in the 1920s. Abraham probably worshipped there in his young days*

1. See *Evidence for the Bible*, p. 4.
2. Sir Leonard Woolley, *Ur of the Chaldees, the final account of the excavations at Ur* (The Herbert Press 1982). p. 51. See also here page 138–139.

# From Sin to Sin

## The moon god, Sin, was worshipped widely across the Ancient Near East, and in Egypt Abraham entered the land of many gods

Sin's chief temple at Ur was named E-gish-shir-gal, 'house of the great light' and a sanctuary at Harran, was named E-hul-hul, 'house of joys'. The cult of the moon-god spread to other centers, and temples to him are found in all the large cities of Babylonia and Assyria. Nabonidus (c.556–539 BC), the last king of Babylon, attempted to elevate Sin to a supreme position within the pantheon.[3]

The region of Haran is referred to variously as Paddan Aram (Genesis 25:20) and Aram Naharaim (Genesis 24:10). Abraham lived there until he was seventy-five years old, before continuing to Canaan in response to the command of God, (Genesis 12:4). Although Abraham's nephew, Lot, accompanied Abraham to Canaan, Terah and the rest of the family remained in Paddan Aram (Haran). Which is why Abraham's grandson Jacob fled there when escaping from his brother Esau (Genesis 28).

How did Abraham and Jacob find their way? One of the earliest known kings of the Ancient Near East is Sargon I (c.2334–2279 BC),[4] whose empire is thought to have included most of Mesopotamia. Sargon ruled from his (archaeologically as yet unidentified) capital, Akkad (also Agade), a little before Abraham, and he established routes across the empire for both protection and trade. Abraham probably left Ur during the rule of Shulgi (c.2095–2047 BC) and followed these trade routes.

A Neo-Assyrian text from the 7th century BC claiming to be Sargon's autobiography, asserts that the great king was the illegitimate son of a priestess. He wrote: 'My high priestess mother conceived me, in secret she bore me. She set me in a basket of rushes; with bitumen she sealed my lid. She cast me into the river which rose over me.'[5] What history lies behind this 'legend' is disputed. It is erroneously assumed by some that this is the origin of the account of Moses! See also page 34 and loan words on pages 18–19.

.15.

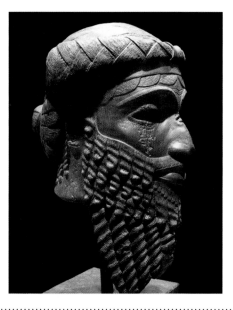

**Above**
*Ruins of the mosque in the ancient Mesopotamian city of Harran in SE Turkey. The mosque also incorporates far older remnants, perhaps belonging to the renowned Sin temple that would have been standing when Abraham emigrated to Harran*

**Left**
*A bronze head of Sargon I, discovered in Nineveh in 1931*

3. See *Evidence for the Bible*, p. 92.
4. This is not the Sargon II of Assyria (722–705 BC) referred to in Isaiah 20:1.
5. Piotr Bienkowski and Alan Millard *Dictionary of the Ancient Near East* (The Trustees of the British Museum 2002). p. 252.

# Camels and critics

**It is frequently suggested that camels were not domesticated in Israel before the 10th century BC; therefore, references to camels in Genesis are evidence that it was written much later than the time of Moses** [1]

**Above**
*A 'petroglyph' (rock-art) in Saudi Arabia depicting a four-spoke chariot with two horses. A camel is tethered to one of the horses. Late Bronze Age to Early Iron Age (1550 to 1000 BC). 'Al Musharafa Chariot', Saudi Arabia*

Perhaps the critics are looking in the wrong place.

First, archaeologists work mostly in urban excavations, but camels are animals for long wilderness journeys and their remains are less likely to be found in the towns.

Second, Abraham (around 2000 BC) did not come from Israel but from Mesopotamia (today including Iraq and parts of Iran, Syria and Turkey) and for this area there **is** evidence that the camel was being used well before the time of Abraham and Moses.

Besides, the absence of evidence is never evidence of absence.

We do not know whether Abraham owned Dromedary (one hump) or Bactrian (two hump) camels, but there are inscriptions, older than Abraham, that refer to the use of camels. For example:

- Around 2500 BC, a list of animals from the city of Shuruppak in Sumer (Mesopotamia) includes one called *am.si.harran*, a word literally translated as 'four-legged humped of the road' i.e. used as a beast for transport. [2]

- The same word is used in a Babylonian love song (between 2000 and 1600 BC) from Nippur (modern Niffer in SE Iraq): 'O Dumuzi make the milk of the camel yellow for me…the milk of the camel is sweet… its buttermilk is sweet'. Significantly, Dumuzi is the god of domesticated herds [3].

- The town of Alalakh, also in Mesopotamia and close to the hometown of Abraham at Haran, offers a 17th-century BC list of animals that required food for a royal journey—it included camels: 'the donkey of the sea' [4].

- A plaque dated around the same time from Eshnunna in Sumer (the earliest known civilization in southern Mesopotamia) shows a rider on a Dromedary.

- An 18th-century BC cylinder seal from Mesopotamia pictures a two humped Bactrian camel with two riders [5].

1. The 19th century biblical archaeologist William F Albright, and more recently Lidar Sapir-Hen, Erez Ben-Yosef and Mairav Zonszein for example.
2. Wayne Horowitz, '"Sweeter Than Camel's Milk": The Camel in Sumerian, The Bactrian Camel in Genesis?' The Hebrew University of Jerusalem. Bible Lands e-Review 2014/S3. For a more accessible article see 'Did Abraham ride a camel?' Mark W Chavalas in *Biblical Archaeological Review* Nov/Dec 2018.
3. Martin Heidi, 'The Domestication of the Camel'. Phillipps University, Marburg 2011 p 356.
4. Martin Heide p. 359.
5. See *Evidence for the Bible* p. 4 for a picture of this.

# Camels in peace and war

## The evidence for the early use of camels may be sparse in archaeology and inscriptions but the many incidental references to the camel in Genesis are unlikely to be later insertions

When Abraham arrived in Egypt (Genesis 12:14–16) the reference to his ownership of camels may be a deliberate indication of his wealth since the camel was not common in Mesopotamia at that time. And so with Jacob (30:43). When Rebekah came to Isaac she (literally) 'fell down' from the camel (24:64), which implies that, unlike Eleazar (24:11), she did not yet know how to make a camel kneel! The reference in Genesis 32:15 to (literally) 'thirty milking camels and their colts', is an important fact since no other 'milking' females are referred to in the list. Camel milk was a delicacy at that time, but not later. [6] Abraham not only rode camels, but he also drank their milk.

The reference to the Midianite and Ishmaelite traders using camel caravans around 1900 BC (37:25) need be no surprise since these came from southern Judah and Arabia.

Camels were included in the fifth plague on Egypt in Exodus 9:3, and are among the forbidden food in Leviticus 11:4. Job, considered among the earliest books of the Bible (see here page 38), owned 3,000 camels. Camels are referred to in the time of Saul (1050 BC) and David, and at the arrival of the Queen of Sheba (from North Africa?) in the time of Solomon (970–930 BC. 1 Kings 10:2). The later historical books and the

**Above**
*The panel on the* Black Obelisk, *below that of Jehu, shows the tribute brought to Shalmanezeer III by the unknown king Musri.* See *Evidence for the Bible p. 52. for the full Obelisk*

prophets (eg. Ezra 2:67; Isaiah 60:6) made frequent reference to the camel as a domesticated animal.

The first known record of camels used in warfare outside the Bible, is found on the stela of the Assyrian king Shalmaneser III. When Ahab of Israel joined a coalition of twelve kings to oppose this ruler, it included 1,000 'camel riders' belonging to 'Gindibu of Arabia'.[7]

Here also, an unknown king from Musri (possibly Egypt?) brought tribute to Shalmaneser including 'seven camels whose humps are two'.

However, according to Judges 6:3–5 and 7:12, much earlier around 1200 BC, the Midianites and Amalekites and 'other eastern peoples' marshalled huge herds of camels for battle.

17.

6. Martin Heide p. 366.
7. The inscription on the stela of Shalmanezer III recording the battle of Qarqar in 853 BC. Heide pp. 348–349. See the stela in *Evidence for the Bible* p. 51.

# Egyptian words in the Old Testament

**To read of 'sidewalks' or 'pavements', 'freeways' or 'motorways' reveals the setting of the book. The Old Testament also has clues to its setting in the words used**

**Left**
*Ay, one of Pharaoh Akhenaten's advisors, receiving the 'Gold of Honour', reminiscent of Genesis 41:42. c.14th century BC*

**Below**
*A cartouche bearing the name Ramesses, meaning born of God, which is transliterated into Hebrew in Genesis 47:11 as the name of the region where the family of Jacob settled*

Much of the early books of the Bible is set in the context of Egypt; that is the land of Moses' upbringing. The accounts of the Israelites in Egypt and in the wilderness include many 'loanwords' from Egyptian.[1]

For example, the Egyptian word for a 'seal' or 'ring' appears in Genesis in exactly the form it had around 2000–1300 BC. Egyptian names are abundant in Genesis including Potiphar ('he whom Ra has given'), Asenath (probably 'she belongs to Neith'), and even the name of Moses (a common element in Egyptian names, such as Pharaoh Thutmose, from a verb meaning 'to give birth').[2] Egyptian loanwords from Genesis to Deuteronomy

include words for objects like pole, linen, cup, magician, items of clothing, the Nile, and titles like Pharaoh. Even the ark in which Moses was laid (Exodus 2:3) is described using the Egyptian word for a 'chest'.

One short section, Genesis 41:41–45, has many Egyptian cultural references. The greeting given to Joseph, '*Abrek!*' (v.43), is not a Hebrew word at all, but probably renders an Egyptian greeting. Joseph is also given an Egyptian name (v.45) and the 'gold necklace' placed around his neck (v.42) was an Egyptian custom from around 1600 BC. Known as the 'Gold of Honour' it was given to high ranking officials in ancient Egypt.[3]

The presence of so many loanwords was not a common feature of ancient writing [4] and their use reveal a personal acquaintance with Egypt around the time of the events described. No later writer would know these details.

1. R. D. Wilson, *A Scientific Investigation of the Old Testament,* (The Sunday School Times Company: Philadelphia, 1937).
2. James K. Hoffmeier, *Israel in Egypt: The Evidence for the Authenticity of the Exodus Tradition*, Oxford University Press: Oxford, 1996, pp. 84–88, 140–142.
3. Susanne Binder, *The Gold of Honour in New Kingdom Egypt*, (Aris and Phillips: Indiana University, 2008).
4. Benjamin J. Noonan, *Non-Semitic Loanwords in the Hebrew Bible: A Lexicon of Language Contact*, University Park, Pennsylvania: Eisenbrauns, 2019, p. 62.

# Persian influence

## In later books of the Old Testament, these Egyptian 'loanwords' drop away and instead, we find words that have been borrowed from Persia

When Persia defeated the Babylonians in 539 BC some Jews began to return to Jerusalem. Bible books (Ezra, Daniel, Nehemiah, Esther and Chronicles), reveal that they were written at this Persian period by the presence of many Persian loanwords. Persian words are practically absent in the Pentateuch, but they are common in these later books. For example, in Esther: 'There are no Greek words used in the text at all, a fact that clearly points to it being composed before the Hellenistic [Greek] era.' [5]

The Persian Empire (modern Iran) dominated the region from 539 to 333 BC. Their administration and culture came to influence the entire fertile crescent. Some of their loanwords 'describe items, institutions, and concepts that were introduced by the Persian administration and did not have a ready equivalent in Hebrew.' [6] But other words did have Hebrew equivalents and the use of Persian alternatives reflects a writing style appropriate for the time.

Ezra was a Persian teacher (Ezra 7:6), while Nehemiah, as cupbearer to the King, was able to converse with Persian royalty (Nehemiah 2:3).[7] This explains the familiarity with Persian vocabulary among the Hebrews.

- **Satraps**: (Esther 3:12; Ezra 8:36; Daniel 6:1) These were the governors of Persian provinces. A Persian political word for **Governor** (*Tirshatha*) is also used at this time (Ezra 2:63; Nehemiah 10:1).

- **Law**: (Esther 1:13) The Persian word (*dat*) appears nineteen times in Esther despite Hebrew already having a common word for law, *Torah*.

- **Paradise**: (Nehemiah 2:8 'royal park') '*Pardes*' reflects the walled botanical gardens or parks of Persian royalty. As the word entered Hebrew it would be used to describe the paradise of God's dwelling.

- **Darics**: (Ezra 2:69; Nehemiah 7:70) The Persians introduced coinage to the Hebrews and the Daric was a pure, gold coin. The reference in 1 Chronicles 29:7 is to its value as a weight, rather than a coin, but demonstrates that the book was written in the Persian period.

**Below**
*The 'Frieze of Archers' from the palace walls of Susa and no doubt part of the description given in Esther 1:6*

.19..

**Inset**
*A Persian gold Daric bearing the image of an armed King. Introduced by Cyrus the Persian, they were no longer in use after the time of Alexander the Great, c.330 BC*

5. *Ancient Civilisations in the Middle East*, Thames and Hudson, 2008, p. 238.
6. Aren Wilson-Wright, 'From Persepolis to Jerusalem: A Reevaluation of Old Persian-Hebrew Contact in the Achaemenid Period', *Vetus Testamentum* Vol. 65:1; p. 158.
7. *Evidence for the Bible*, pp. 96–97.

# Semites in Goshen

## The presence of foreign settlers in Egypt from the time of Joseph to Moses is supported by the archaeological record

Many of these settlers are from Canaan, and scholars identify them as 'Semitic' because of their cultural practices and language (Hebrew and Aramaic). 'Semitic' is derived from Shem in Genesis 5:32. Semitic settlers had been arriving in the Nile Delta region of North East Egypt since the earliest times of Egyptian history.

During the Second Intermediate Period (from about 1782 to 1550 BC) the Nile Delta region of Egypt was governed by foreign rulers called the Hyksos. Manetho, the third century BC Egyptian historian, used the name 'Hyksos' which is now understood to mean 'Rulers of Foreign Lands.' This period saw an influx of Semitic settlers bringing new inventions with them including bows, chariots, metalwork and horses.

Goshen is in this region of North East Egypt and was assigned to Jacob and his extended family who arrived around 1876 BC (Genesis 45:10). It was here that the Israelites worked on the great store cities of Pithom and Rameses (Exodus 1:11).[1]

While direct evidence for the Hebrews in Goshen is limited, there is good evidence for settlers from Canaan bringing their own customs and culture into this region.

- The Brooklyn Papyrus from the 18th century BC lists ninety-five servants, many have Semitic names and some are specifically Hebrew; for example 'Shiphrah' is also the name of one of the midwives at the time of the Exodus (Exodus 1:15).[2]

- Burials in the area of Goshen follow a style known from Canaan and not Egypt, and Canaanite storage jars and weapons are found in the graves.

- At Tell el-Yehudiyeh (Arabic for 'mound of the Jew') there is evidence of settlement by Semitic shepherds and a distinctive style of pottery that originated in Palestine c.1700 BC.

Egyptologist Professor Hoffmeier concludes that from 1800 to 1450 BC: 'Egypt was an attractive place for the Semitic-speaking people of western Asia to migrate'.[3] This was the time of the Patriarchs.

**Left**
*A juglet from Tell el-Yahudiya, c.1640–1550 BC, a Semitic style of pottery found in the region of Goshen in Egypt but also common in Canaan*

1. This has been taken as evidence for a late date of the Exodus because Egyptian records refer to these cities being built in the 13th century; however, there were already substantial store cities in the region long before this time.
2. See also *Evidence for the Bible* p. 16. Papyrus Brooklyn 35.1446. Generally dated to about 1740 BC. See Hershel Shanks, 'First Person', *Biblical Archaeology Review* 24:01, 1998.
3. James K. Hoffmeier, *Israel In Egypt*, (Oxford University Press, 1996) p. 68.

# Building in Brick

By 1570 BC the Hyksos were overthrown and nationalist Egyptians regained control of Lower Egypt. What had been a land of refuge for the Patriarchs became hostile to such foreigners

**Left**
*Semite and Nubian slaves making bricks for the Egyptians. From the tomb of Rekhmire*

The Hebrews were regarded as potential traitors in Egypt and put to work making mud bricks (Exodus 1). A great deal is known about brickmaking at this period of Egyptian history and the Bible provides many references that demonstrate its authenticity.[4]

The tomb of Rekhmire, an advisor to Pharaoh (c.1445 BC), provides a wall illustration of Semitic slaves, among others, at work making bricks for a temple in Thebes. Many details match what we read in the Bible. The Israelites were enlisted as 'slave labour' with task masters over them (Exodus 1:11). The tomb of Rekhmire shows armed Egyptian slave-masters watching over the slaves. The Hebrews were put to work making 'brick and mortar' (Exodus 1:14). The tomb illustration shows the process of baking bricks with the use of clay, water, and straw. The straw helped to bind the clay together so that it did not break in the process of baking.

Moses appealed for Pharaoh to release the people in order to celebrate a religious festival (Exodus 5:1). References to workmen being permitted time off to celebrate religious festivals include a limestone ostracon from Deir el-Medina, near Thebes, which gives various reasons for absence including 'offering to (his) god.'

In response to the demand of Moses, Pharaoh makes conditions worse for the Israelites by making them find their own straw while continuing to impose the same daily quota (Exodus 5:8). Papyrus Anastasi III from the time of Pharaoh Merneptah (c.1220 BC) refers to the 'daily quota of bricks' and Papyrus Anastasi IV includes a complaint about the lack of straw.

All of these details help to confirm that the biblical text is describing real conditions for the Hebrews at this time in Egyptian history.[5]

---

4. See Evidence for the Bible p. 17.
5. K A Kitchen, *On the Reliability of the Old Testament*, (Eerdmans Publishing Company. 2003) pp. 247–248.

# Semites in the Sinai

Ancient Egypt prized the precious stone turquoise. A large-scale mining operation was discovered in southern Sinai at Serabit el-Khadeim and archaeologists have found intriguing evidence for the presence of Semitic workers

**Left**
*Remains of the Temple of Hathor at Serabit el-Khadeim in the Sinai*

Archaeologist Flinders Petrie excavated here and found both the camps of the miners and a significant Egyptian temple to the goddess Hathor. The temple was built during the twelfth dynasty of Egypt (c.1875 BC) and remained in use for 800 years.

Hathor was a goddess associated with turquoise and revered at this location. However, the workers themselves included Semitic people from Canaan and Goshen. There are many upright monuments (stelae)

at the site bearing inscriptions that testify to their presence.

The goddess Hathor was often depicted as a cow and imagery shows her wearing a headdress of cow horns. Given the location of the temple in the Sinai this may help explain why the Israelites cast a bronze calf to worship as they waited for Moses (Exodus 32).

However, one of the most intriguing discoveries by Flinders Petrie and his wife was a series of inscriptions using simple hieroglyphs dating to around

1500 BC. The inscriptions were not typical hieroglyphs and Petrie realised that they represented some form of alphabetic script.

What the Petrie's had noticed is considered by some to be the birthplace of the alphabet that would be developed by the Hebrews and continues to be in use as our English alphabet to this day.[1] It also represents clear evidence for the foreign workers who laboured in the Sinai during this period of Egyptian history.

1. Orly Goldwasser, 'How the Alphabet was born from Hieroglyphs', *Biblical Archaeology Review* March/April 2010, pp. 36–74.

# The invention of the alphabet

## The Hebrew and English alphabets look very different at first glance, but on examination, they share a common ancestor

Latin and all European languages, including Greek, plus Arabic and Hebrew have all developed a common set of signs. We now know this 'alphabetic' system arose with Semitic settlers living in ancient Egypt.

The 'Hieroglyphic' script of Egypt involved over seven hundred characters which function in various ways and can be written in different directions. To use them, a scribe would need significant training!

At Serabit el-Khadeim evidence emerges for a new way of using a few simple signs. This is called the 'Proto-Sinaitic' script and it uses only twenty-seven signs and employs them only for their 'sound value'. For example, the letter '*a*' is represented by the head of an ox and is the first letter of the word for ox (*aleph*). The sign for a house (a rectangle with a door) was used, not to represent a house, but to represent the sound '*b*' which is the first letter of the word for house (*beth*).

So, this system is called the 'alphabet' (*aleph – beth*), from the first two letters of the script. This simple idea allows any word in any language to be recorded using only a few letters that anyone can remember.

Examples of the alphabet from Serabit el-Khadeim include a sandstone sphinx that has a dedication in Egyptian hieroglyphs to the goddess Hathor. But on the base of the sphinx there is another dedication using the alphabetic script. While it is not possible to determine a precise date, it certainly belongs to the period when the Hebrews were in Egypt before the Exodus.

Further examples of the early alphabetic script were found at a site in Egypt, near Luxor, called Wadi el-Hol. John Darnell suggests that these date as early as 1900 BC and attributes them to Asiatic mercenaries working for the Egyptians.[2]

From Egypt, this alphabetic system spread throughout Canaan and was developed by the Hebrews, Arameans and Phoenicians. It proved so successful, in later modified forms, that it has remained to this day. Unlike the complicated hieroglyphic script, these few simple characters allowed it to be used by common workers. The Hebrews reduced it to twenty-two letters which the Greeks would later supplement with vowels.

**Above**
*Sandstone sphinx from Serabit el-Khadeim in the Sinai bearing inscriptions in hieroglyphics on the shoulder and the early alphabetic script on the base*

2. John Coleman Darnell, 'Two Early Alphabetic Inscriptions from the Wadi el-Hol: New Evidence for the Origin of the Alphabet from the Western Desert of Egypt', *The Annual of ASOR* 59, 2005, pp. 67–124. See also *Evidence for the Bible* pp. 7–9.

# The Bull 'gods' of Egypt

**Throughout the Ancient Near East the bull was revered as a symbol of strength and power. It also became an object of worship**

Early records show that in ancient Egypt the **Apis bull** was regarded as a sacred incarnation of Osiris. One of the earliest images from Egypt is the Narmer Palette (c.3100 BC) which includes an image of the goddess Hathor depicted as a cow. Worship of a god represented by a bull was also widespread in Canaan from earliest times. [1]

Tragically, throughout the Old Testament, the Israelites were drawn to this form of religion. While waiting for Moses on Mount Sinai, they cast a golden calf (Exodus 32:1–35). This reflected the religious influence of Egypt. Many years later, when God's people divided into a northern and southern kingdom, the northern king, under Jeroboam, cast two calf idols for worship (2 Kings 17:16–23). [2] During the reforms of Jehu (c. 841–814 BC) an attempt was made to demolish the idols associated with Baal, yet the 'golden calves of Bethel and Dan' were not destroyed (2 Kings 10:25–29).

The Phoenicians lived in the coastal region, and **Astarte** was their god symbolized by a bull, as was **Baal** for the Canaanites. Statues of bulls were common across Assyria, Babylon and Persia. Apart from its strength, a bull (or the now extinct Aurochs that once roamed this part of the world) may have been revered for the crescent shape of its horns which resembled the crescent moon. [3] Both the sun and the moon were worshipped as divine beings.

The Bible uses the horn only as a symbol of strength (Psalm 18:2) and altars were built with horns as a place of refuge (1 Kings 1:50). However, God could not be identified with any earthly image, and the sun, moon and stars are described only as 'lights' to mark the seasons (Genesis 1:14–15); they were never to be worshipped (Deuteronomy 4:19).

The Bible uses many analogies from creation in order to describe God's strength, faithfulness and mercy, but the prophets continually warned the Israelites not to confuse the Creator with his creation. Hosea reminds them: 'This calf – a metalworker has made it; it is not God' (Hosea 8:6), and Isaiah mocks the worship of wood (Isaiah 44:12–20).

**Top**
*An 8th century BC stela from Bethsaida with image of a bull warrior. Note the disc shaped horns*

**Middle**
*The Narmer Palette has images of the goddess Hathor, depicted as a cow at the top of each side*

**Bottom**
*Egyptian Stela showing worship of an Apis bull with a moon disc between its horns (c.644 BC)*

1. The widespread worship of the bull is explained in John Day, *Yahweh and the Gods and Goddesses of Canaan,* (Sheffield Academic Press: London, 2002). pp. 34–41.
2. See *Evidence for the Bible* p. 46 for Jeroboam's altar at Tel Dan.
3. For the relationship between the bull and the moon in the Bethsaida stela see Othmar Keel, *Goddesses and Trees, New Moon and Yahweh: Ancient Near Eastern Art and the Hebrew Bible*, pp. 115–121.

# 'gods' of Canaan

**The ancient world was polytheistic, and gods were adopted by different nations as their own. The Old Testament is consistent in referring to the correct gods of each nation**

The bewildering number of gods in the Old Testament reflect the confusion of ancient religion. The monotheism of Israel was unique and in striking contrast with its absolute conviction that worship should be devoted to one God alone (Deuteronomy 6:4–5).

**Baal.** The Semitic word *ba'al* simply means 'Lord' but it came to identify a particular god commonly worshipped among the Canaanites (Judges 8:33). Considered Lord of the earth, he was responsible for fertility and identified with storm and rain. 1 Kings 18 records Elijah's contest with the prophets of Baal. Baal, often as part of a place or person's name, occurs one hundred and forty times in the Old Testament.

**Hadad.** Also known as Adad by the Assyrians, Hadad was often portrayed with the headdress of a bull. He was worshipped by the people of Aram-Damascus (Syria) who were neighbours to Israel and their kings are often named Ben-Hadad (Son of Hadad) in the Bible (1 Kings 20:26; 2 Kings 6:24).

**Asherah.** As the gods were considered a family, they were male and female in form. Asherah was a mother goddess. The Israelites were to destroy her shrines, represented by a pole (Exodus 34:13). Jeremiah called her the 'Queen of Heaven'

(Jeremiah 7:16–18) because she was identified with the moon. When Manasseh, King of Judah, erected an Asherah pole for worship he is described as worshipping the 'starry host' (2 Kings 21:3).

**Dagon.** The Philistines worshipped Dagon (Judges 16:23) and built a temple to him (1 Samuel 5:2). Once thought to be associated with the fish, ancient sources outside the Bible describe him as a Canaanite god of the crops.

**Chemosh** and **Molech.** The Moabites worshipped Chemosh while the Ammonites worshipped Molech (1 Kings 11:7). The important Moabite Stone c. 840 BC is dedicated to Chemosh.[4] Molech is a corruption of the Hebrew word 'king' and associated with child sacrifice.[5] These references in the Bible accurately describe the worship of surrounding nations.

.25.

**Top**
*A typical figurine of the Canaanite storm god Baal found at Ugarit, Syria c.1200 BC*

**Bottom**
*A colossal statue of the god Hadad, in a style associated with the Hittites, c.775 BC*

4. See *Evidence for the Bible* p. 36.
5. See *Evidence for the Bible* p. 55 and this book p. 45.

# Magic men in Egypt

## Who were the 'Egyptian magicians' who tried to copy the miracles of Aaron and Moses?

**Left**
*A frieze on a wall in the tomb of Pharaoh Horemheb, showing the gods Osiris, Anubis, and Horus*

**Right**
*The Shabaka Stone.*

Paul, referring to the plagues upon Egypt, gave the magicians names, but just who were Jannes and Jambres (2 Timothy 3:8)? Although mentioned in Jewish literature and Tacitus, little is known for certain about them. Paul is simply using the legendary names without commenting on the authenticity of the names. As significant sorcerer-priests they fashioned or mimicked what Aaron and Moses were doing up to the plague of frogs. At that point they must have convinced Pharaoh of their skill, but they could go no further.

They were probably the foremost sorcerer-priests at that time. The ancient Egyptian word for magic is *heka*, considered to be one of the forces used to make and maintain creation. Any person who seemed able to utilize magic was considered special.

In the Execration texts from 1900 to 1800 BC ('execrate' means to curse or denounce), occurs an interesting perspective about Egyptian political fears. Kings saw reason to dread other nations and tried to ward off danger by magical formulae. The enemy's names were inscribed on bowls and figurines which were then ritually smashed, in order to bring calamity and confusion upon them.

The Shabaka Stone in the British Museum, from Pharaoh Shabaka who reigned from 716 to 702 BC, recalls that he was inspecting a temple and came across a papyrus 'a work of the ancestors which was worm-eaten' and could not be understood from the beginning to end. Shabaka ordered the text to be copied in a more permanent form, and that is what appears on this stone. At some point the Shabaka Stone was re-used as a millstone, with much of its text in the center being destroyed. On it is an account of creation:

'Then Horus [god of kingship and sky] stood over the land. He is the uniter of this land, proclaimed in the great name Ta-tenen, south of his Wall, Lord of eternity. *Then he sprouted the two Great Magicians upon his head.* He is Horus, who arose as king of Upper and Lower Egypt, who united the Two Lands in the Nome of the Wall, the place in which the Two Lands were united' [1]

1. Miriam Lichtheim, *Ancient Egyptian Literature. The Old and Middle Kingdoms.* (University of California Press 2006). p. 53.

# The gods and the plagues of Egypt

**The magicians served over 2,000 gods in Ancient Egypt, many were considered to be influential at the time of the Plagues**

The plagues were brought upon Egypt so that the Pharaoh would know Israel's God was the only true God (Exodus 7:3–5; 12:12; Romans 9:17).[2] The ancient Egyptians had a ten-day week and the ten plagues deliberately challenged many of the gods and the whole of their life. The seven-day-week principle of Genesis 2:3 had to be reinstated at Sinai (Exodus 20:8–11). Note also further challenges in Exodus 7:12; 14:12.

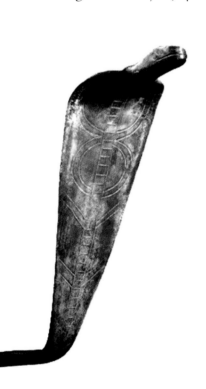

**Above**
*An Egyptian magic staff or wand*

| Plague | Some of the gods involved |
|---|---|
| 1. Blood | *Khnum*, ram god, creator of life the guardian of the Nile's sources.<br>*Hapi*, god of the Nile spirit of Nile.<br>*Osiris*, god of the underworld, whose bloodstream was the Nile.<br>*Sobek*, crocodile god, called the god of water. |
| 2. Frogs | *Hapi*, god of the Nile its dynamic essence.<br>*Hekat*, goddess of fertility and childbirth. |
| 3. Gnats | *Priests*, ministers of Egypt's gods, who threw dust on their heads to symbolize contrition and humility. |
| 4. Flies | *Horus*, falcon god of the air, which was now inundated with flies.<br>*Kheprer*, symbolized as the flying beetle.<br>*Golden flies* were given to a soldier who had done well in combat, persistently 'stinging' the enemy'. |
| 5. Livestock | *Apis, Buchis, Mnevis*, Bull gods.<br>*Hathor, Heset, Mehet-Weret, Shentayat*, cow goddesses.<br>*Amun, Kherty, Khnum*, the ram gods. |
| 6. Boils | *Imhotep*, the Healer.<br>*Sekhmet*, goddess of creating epidemics and bring them to an end. |
| 7. Hail | *Nut*, the sky goddess.<br>*Osiris*, a god intimately connected to grain. |
| 8. Locusts | *Min*, the god of fertility.<br>*Geb, the* earth god who provides the nourishment and fruits of the earth. |
| 9. Darkness | *Ra*, in his many manifestations considered the supreme deity.<br>*Shu*, the god of sunlight and air. |
| 10. Firstborn | *Heir*, who represented special qualities of life and strength especially for the succession. This was a great blow against Pharaoh who, as Ra's son on earth, was himself a god. |

27

2. For a more detailed presentation of the Egyptian gods see Clive and Amanda Anderson, *Egypt Land of Moses, monuments and mummies* (Day One Publications, Leominster 2009). p. 68.

# The Egyptian *Book of the Dead*

## The Ancient Egyptians had a complex version of the afterlife and believed that the dead had the opportunity to be reborn there, provided they fulfilled certain criteria

Mummification and a burial complete with rituals were indispensable, and the living were therefore required to fulfil these things on behalf of the dead.[1] Among the essentials that were required and prepared in advance were texts and a tomb—if you could afford it. Ordinary people were buried in a common pit.

Mummification and the ritual texts, which are known as the Pyramid Texts, reveal something of the journey that had to be undertaken. The texts include the books of breathing and the books of the sky, but especially the most famous known as the *Book of the Dead*. It is not strictly a book, because the text was written on papyrus and tomb walls. See Oxyrhynchus here on page 124–125.

There were several versions of *The Book of the Dead* (also known as the Book of the Two Ways); it showed access to the happy land 'located somewhere in the Far West'. However, reaching that depended on leading a virtuous life on earth as well as fulfilling certain tasks in the afterlife. Between the time when the new-born soul left the tomb and the moment it settled down amid the comforts provided for it in the Land of Eternity, it had a long and dangerous journey.[2]

The journey to the afterlife began with proper preparations and rituals being completed before the deceased had to pass through a series of ordeals: the Ferry-man must be persuaded to take the dead across the River of Death, and then came the twelve gates guarded by fearful serpents. Amulets and a copy of the *Book of the Dead*— with relevant spells and a map to work out how to pass the many dangers—were buried with the dead. At the Lake of Fire, forty-two Assessors read out a list of sins and wrong-doings and the deceased had to swear that he was innocent of them all. If that test was passed, he was admitted to the judgement hall of Osiris, where the heart was weighed against the Feather of Truth.

**Above**
*Inside the tomb of Nefertari, one the Royal Wives of Ramesses II showing Khepri, who has the head of a scarab beetle. The tomb is decorated with text from* The Book of the Dead

**Right**
*Nefertari holds out two round nemset jars above an altar piled high with fruit, vegetables, cuts of meat, and loaves of bread. Ready to receive her offerings, are three goddesses Isis and, not shown here, her sister Nephthys and Ma'at*

1. Eric Hornung, *The Ancient Egyptian books of the afterlife* (Cornell University Press 1997).
2. Barbara Mertz, *Red Land Black Land* (William Morrow 2008). p. 377.

# Preparation for the afterlife

## The tombs were prepared and mummification carried out by skilful workers

The tomb was an essential part of enabling the right things to be in place before the afterlife. The most famous are the Pyramids and the royal burials in the Valley of the Kings and the Valley of the Queens. Inside these monumental structures the walls are adorned with colourful illustrations. Other tombs were prepared for the nobles and the wealthy.

Mummification was essential because it was believed that the preservation of the body enabled the spirit to find sustenance for the afterlife; without a body the spirit would go hungry. Mummification probably began with the burial customs of the Predynastic period (c.4,000 BC), when the dead were placed in shallow graves in the sand and became naturally preserved and were still recognisable. Animals disturbed the graves, particularly the jackal, who became Anubis the god of mummification.

The embalmer's skill is seen in the intricate wrappings preserving the bodies. Believing the West was the way to the afterlife, the embalmers' workshops were located on the west bank of the River Nile.[3]

Jacob and Joseph were prepared in this way. Jacob was buried in solemn pomp (Genesis 50:1–14), and Joseph, after being embalmed and coffined, was carried through the

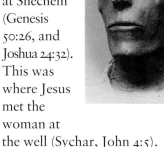

wilderness for forty years and was buried at Shechem (Genesis 50:26, and Joshua 24:32). This was where Jesus met the woman at the well (Sychar, John 4:5).

Sometimes an inscribed scarab beetle (see next page) was placed over the heart of a mummy with the words: 'My heart does not testify against me at the judgement'. If the life had been virtuous, the deceased could join the ancestors in the kingdom of the West.

The body was placed in the tomb and after being sealed it was essential that offerings were left outside for the spirit of the deceased to go out and spiritually partake of them; to enable this, a false door was constructed (or painted). Royal false doors were made out of red granite.[4]

But this was only the start of the journey!

**Above left**

*The carefully mummified head of Pharaoh Seti I (1294–1279 BC). He probably reigned during the period of the Judges in Israel*

**Above right**

*A wooden coffin from Egypt with a guide for the deceased to the underworld*

29

**Right**

*An example of an embalmer's skill from the Ptolemaic period in Egypt 305 – 30 BC*

---

3. For details of embalming see Clive and Amanda Anderson, *Travel Through Egypt* (Day One Publications, Leominster 2009). p. 54.
4. Vivian Davies and Renee Friedman, *Egypt* (The British Museum Press 1998). p. 80.

# The Ancient Egyptian
## negative confession

### How can anyone have peace of mind beyond death?

The heart scarab was placed on the mummy of the deceased as well as the Negative Confession (also known as The Declaration of Innocence). This formed part of Spell 125 of the *Book of the Dead*. It is a list of forty-two sins which the soul of the deceased could honestly say it had never committed. The deceased would recite this when they entered the Hall of Judgement and stood face to face, first of all with Osiris (god of the underworld), and then Osiris backed up by a further forty-two other divine judges, all of whom the deceased had to name. The deceased then asserted their purity and worthiness as their heart was weighed against the Feather of Maat, the goddess of truth. Rather than boasting about their good actions, this was a negative statement of what they had not been guilty of.[1] Clearly no one could honestly declare that they had never done anything wrong, so their hope was filled with misgiving. How could anyone be sure if their appeal would be accepted?

When Job presented his case to God, he too declared his innocence (Job 31). However, the context of Job is that his false friends suggest that his calamity is God punishing him for sins and Job defends himself against that charge. He is not claiming sinlessness, but he is not guilty of those things they would accuse him of. For example, he was not guilty of lust, cheating, or adultery; he was not an unjust employer, greedy or ignoring the poor; he was not idolatrous or vindictive. Whatever faults Job had, there were some things God could not be punishing him for. With this, God himself agreed (1:8, 22). He

**Above**
*Hunefer, a Royal Scribe of Pharaoh Seti I (1294–1279) clothed in white linen in the judgement hall, is led before the god Osiris on his throne. A section of the* Book of the Dead *prepared especially for Hunefer*

longs to be exonerated before God (v.35) and had a firm expectation for life beyond death (19:25–27).

Because of Jesus' death and resurrection, the New Testament does not require us to declare our 'righteousness', but to confess our sins. And then offers the promise: 'If we confess our sins, he is faithful and just and will forgive our sins and purify us from all unrighteousness.' (1 John 1:9). A promise wholly unknown to the Ancient Egyptians.

1. R.O. Faulkner, *The Ancient Egyptian Book of the Dead* (University of Texas Press 1972). p. 29.

# A standard list of the Laws of Maat

## The 42 Negative Confessions

1. I have not done wrong.
2. I am not a man of violence.
3. I am not evil minded.
4. I am not greedy.
5. I am not a slayer of men.
6. I am not fraudulent in measures of grain.
7. I commit no fraud.
8. I am not a robber of sacred property.
9. I am not a teller of lies.
10. I am not a robber of food.
11. I am not sluggish.
12. I am not a transgressor.
13. I have not slaughtered the sacred animals.
14. I have not made anyone cry.
15. I am not a land-grabber.
16. I am not an eaves-dropper.
17. I have not caused terror.
18. I trouble myself only with my own affairs.
19. I commit not adultery with another's wife.
20. I am chaste with anyone.
21. I do not cause terrors.
22. I am not a transgressor.
23. I am not hot of speech.
24. I have not acted with insolence.
25. I have not avenged myself.
26. I am not the cause of weeping to any.
27. I am not given to unnatural lust.
28. I indulge not in anger.

**Above and below**
*A Heart Scarab of Hatnefer (1492–1473 BC). The scarab's base is engraved with a version of the* Book of the Dead *chapter 30A*

**Left**
*A Heart Scarab of the Divine Father Hori in the shape of a heart (c.1539–1075 BC)*

29. I am not given to cursing.
30. I am not of aggressive hand.
31. I am not one of inconstant mind.
32. I do not kill the sacred animals.
33. I am not noisy in my speech.
34. I am neither a harmer nor a doer of mischief.
35. I do not curse the King.
36. I put no check upon the water in its flow.
37. I am not one of loud voice.
38. I curse not a god.
39. I am not swollen with pride.
40. I have no unjust preferences.
41. I have no strong desire except for my own property.
42. I do not offend the god of my domain.

The elaborate details in respect to death and the afterlife are astonishing, especially as no one knew if it all worked. Moses, instead of speaking about the *Book of the Dead* refers to God's book (Exodus 32:32–33). Psalm 69:28 calls it the Book of Life, and in Revelation 21:27 it is the Lamb's Book of Life, for all who have put their trust in the Lord Jesus Christ.

# Praying to the gods

**The nations surrounding Israel provide many examples of sincere and emotional prayers to the gods—but they are very different from the Psalms**

**Left**
*The (poor quality) relief of the Hittite King Hattusilis III and his wife Pudu-hepas, considered one of the most influential women known from the Ancient Near East. Hattusilis was the king who established a peace treaty with the Egyptians in 1259 BC* [1]

**B**ewilderment. It was generally assumed that illness must be the result of offending the gods. One long, sad prayer from a bewildered Sumerian worshipper addresses his petition to any god and no god in particular, since he does not know why he is suffering or what god/goddess he has/has not offended: 'May the God whom I know or do not know be quieted towards me.' He longs for his sin, if there was any, to be removed, but he has no assurance that it will be (391–392).[2] A similar Hittite prayer at a time of plague, is mystified why there is no response because 'I worshipped all the gods, I never preferred one temple to another' (394–395).

**Bargain**. A Hittite queen (Pudu-hepas) prays earnestly for the King Hattusilis who is ill, to the 'Sun-goddess of Arinna', who is married to the Storm-god and has influence over all the other gods. The goddess is promised that she will 'enjoy the reverent worship of my family'. Apparently, the physicians 'spoke charms' over the king, but the queen is taking no chances and separately prays also to the son and the daughter and the grand-daughter of the Sun-goddess! (393–394). They are all promised gifts if the king recovers.

The emphasis is frequently to bring the gods into a good frame of mind by the petitioner who promises to complete their religious ritual properly or make restitution if that is needed. The gods are reminded that the Hittites provide for them daily, clean their images regularly, pay careful attention to the ritual sacrifices and festivals, and will improve if necessary—'So stand by us!' (399–400).

**Flattery**. Whichever god the petitioner addresses, they frequently let them know that they are chief among all the gods: 'O Telepinus, there is no other deity more noble and mighty than thou' (397). For Ashurbanipal of Assyria, when the Sun-god (Shamash) rises, all the gods assemble and bow down (387); he is all-knowing, merciful and righteous, shining over the whole earth.

Whilst the prayers to the gods often use similar exalted language as the biblical psalms, the psalms reflect a warm and personal relationship with the one true God of Israel to the exclusion of all others. This is wholly unknown outside Israel.

---

1. See *Evidence for the Bible* pp. 20, 33, 226.
2. Page numbers in brackets refer to the full texts for these prayers in James Pritchard *Ancient Near Eastern Texts* (Princeton University Press 1969, orig 1950).

# Pharaoh Akhenaten and Psalm 104

**Some critics suggest that Akhenaten was the founder of monotheism and left a pattern for the Old Testament to follow!**

Amenhotep IV was tenth ruler in the eighteenth dynasty of Egypt (c.1352–1336 BC). He became known as the 'Heretic King' because he worshipped only the Aten, or sun god, outlawed all other gods and closed their temples.[3] He renamed himself Akhenaten ('of great value to Aten'), moved his capital from Thebes to Amarna and renamed it Akhetaten ('the horizon of Aten'). He married the beautiful Egyptian Nefertiti, and was the father of Tutankhamun (though not by Nefertiti).

However, the Pentateuch, written by Moses before 1400 BC, precedes Akhenaten. It is more feasible to suggest that the pharaoh was influenced by the God of Israel since he would have heard of the Exodus.

Was **Psalm 104** modelled on Akhenaten's *Hymn to the Aten*. Here is the contrast between *Hymn to the Aten* and Psalm 104.[4]

- Akhenaten's god Aten is identified with the sun itself.

*'Thou living Aten, the beginning of life! When thou art risen on the eastern horizon, thou hast filled every land with thy beauty... Thy rays encompass the lands to the limit of all that thou hast made... When thou settest in the western horizon, the land is in darkness... At daybreak thou arisest on the horizon...'*

**Right**
*Pharaoh Akhenaten (left) with Queen Nefertiti and three of their daughters under the rays of the sun god Aten*

**Background**
*Akenhaten*

**In Psalm 104** God is the creator of all things—the sun is only part of his creation: 'The moon marks off the seasons, and the sun knows when to go down' (v.19 cf. Psalm 19:4–5).

- Akhenaten is the only one who knows the Aten.

*'Thou art in my heart, and there is no other that knows thee, save thy son Akhenaten.'*

**Psalm 104** is a very personal psalm, but like all the other psalms there is no indication that the writer alone knows God.

- All creation is made for Akhenaten and Nefertiti, who were gods.

*'Everything is made to flourish for the King since thou didst found the earth and raise them up for thy son, who came forth from thy body... And Nefertiti.'*

The biblical psalmist is only a humble worshipper.

The religion of Akhenaten was never popular and was reversed on his death.

Throughout their history, the Hebrews were alone in the Ancient Near East, in believing in only one God.

---

3. See also *Evidence for the Bible* p. 29.
4. For the text see Pritchard, *Ancient Near Eastern Texts*. pp. 369–371.

# Joseph, a 'borrowed' story?

## It is suggested that some Old Testament narratives were invented in the sixth century BC and borrowed the storyline from neighbouring histories or legends

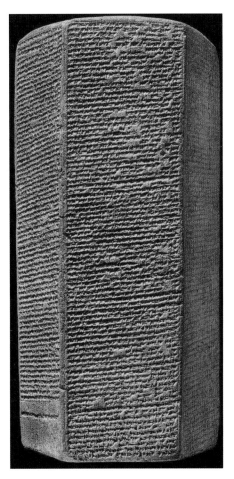

**Above**
*The Esarhaddon prism describing the early events of his reign*

**C**omparing the narrative of Joseph with that of **Esarhaddon of Assyria,** one scholar assumes 'almost all scholars now agree that the Joseph story is not a faithful historical account.'[1] Joseph, and the jealousy of his ten brothers, is well known. That of Esarhaddon less so.

Sennacherib of Assyria (704–681 BC) designated Esarhaddon his heir, confirmed by divination, though he was not the eldest son. His brothers were angry and plotted and slandered against him. Esarhaddon escaped to a safe place where the gods 'spread their sweet protecting shadow over me.' The brothers quarrelled among themselves and defied the gods. Esarhaddon returned to Nineveh with an army, scattered the enemy, 'meted out a grievous punishment' on his brothers, destroying their descendants, and took the throne. [2]

Other parallels? Both Joseph and Esarhaddon were not the firstborn of their father's second wife who is not the mother of the other brothers. Haran and Egypt appear in both accounts. However, phrases by the critics such as 'even though there is no proof, these parallels suggest', the account 'may have circulated more widely', 'one can easily imagine' and 'it seems feasible' hardly establish certainty! A careful comparison of the accounts reveal the striking dissimilarities.

It has also been suggested that the **seven years of famine in Egypt** (Genesis 41) is 'possibly' derived from an Egyptian Stela dated 332/331 BC which refers to seven years of drought and famine 2300 years earlier. However, since the Egyptian inscription is dated long *after* the Joseph story was supposedly invented, it assumes the Jewish scribes in the 6th century had knowledge of an Egyptian legend that predated them by almost 2000 years and of which we have no other evidence than the 4th century Egyptian Stela!

Another suggestion is that the account of **Moses' infancy** was based on the discovery of the great Sargon I who ruled the Akkadian Empire c. 2334–2279 BC. Legend claimed that a gardener found him floating in a basket on the river, took him home and adopted him as his own son. That is where the similarities with Moses end!

Almost any event of history can find a rough parallel somewhere, but that can never by itself invalidate the genuineness of a subsequent sober account.

1. Such a comparison was made by Eckart Frahm 'Surprising parallels between Joseph and King Esarhaddon', *Biblical Archaeology Review* May/June 2016.
2. For the full text of Esarhaddon see Pritchard *Ancient Near Eastern Texts* (Princeton University Press, 1969), pp. 289–290.

# The Flood, a 'borrowed' story?

**It is frequently assumed that the Flood account in Genesis 6–9 was borrowed from the Epic of Gilgamesh which is the most complete of all the Akkadian (Ancient Near East) flood stories** [3]

Among this and the other Akkadian accounts the contrasts with the Old Testament are clear (224–268). [4]

- The Gilgamesh Epic gives no clear reason for the flood. We are reliant upon the Atrahasis epic to learn that the cause was the din caused by humans on earth.[5] In Genesis it is God's righteous judgement upon sin.

- The hero, Utnapishtim, is seeking immortality and his rescue was a reward.

- The announcement of the flood, the dimensions of the ark (Utnapishtim built a six storey cube), the occupants (Utnapishtim included the craftsmen), the length of time for the flood and the details of birds sent out, are entirely different from the biblical account.

- There is no warning to the nations, it was a secret held only by Utnapishtim who encouraged the people to believe that when the rains came it was a sign of blessing. Noah warned for 120 years.

- In the Epic there is no covenantal relationship with God through the rainbow.

- The gods quarrel and lie, are terrified at the severity of the flood and finally 'gather over the sacrifice like a swarm of hungry flies' (268).

Clearly the Flood was deeply embedded in the legends of nations, but the biblical account shows no dependency on the legends and bears the mark of divine revelation.

**In all Akkadian literature even** the gods could die (137). Death was prior to creation, and mankind, created by the blood of the evil god Kingu, was sinful from the start and therefore sin and death were natural (139). At death, the deceased were provided with food and implements for their future (151). The realm of the dead had its own pantheon of gods (182). Only the gods had a clear expectation of resurrection; for example, Tammuz died in the summer and rose again in the spring (207). This, and much more, is in stark contrast to the Old Testament understanding of creation, sin, death and the afterlife. See for example Job 19 :25–27; Psalm 17:15; Daniel 12:2; Isaiah 26:19.

Almost the only agreement is the inevitability of death followed by some form of judgement—both common observations in every time and culture.

*Most of the flood legends from the Ancient Near East are broken and incomplete. The fullest accounts, though different from each other, are the Gilgamesh (above) and Atrahasis (below)*

3. See *Evidence for the Bible* for the Gilgamesh tablet and its story p. 2. The Gilgamesh Epic is a lengthy legend which includes twelve separate tablets that have no biblical connection. The flood legend is Tablet XI. The full text can be read in Pritchard *Ancient Near Eastern Texts* (Princeton University Press, 1869) pp. 96–97.

4. For a scholarly and detailed comparison between the Akkadian myths and the Old Testament see Alexander Heidel, *The Gilgamesh Epic and Old Testament Parallels* (University of Chicago Press, 1946). The page numbers here in brackets refer to Heidel's monogram.

5. See *Evidence for the Bible* p. 3 for the Atrahasis account.

# Genealogies and an invented history?

## Some believe that Jewish scribes 'invented' Israel's history around the 6th century BC to boost the morale of the Babylonian and Persian exiles

The significance of genealogies is often overlooked in responding to those who suggest much of the Old Testament is an invented story

That claim has long been challenged by recent discoveries and the fact that the biblical records fit accurately what we know of the periods they describe.[1] However, there are many other reasons to trust the accuracy of Old Testament history—and the genealogies is one.

Lengthy genealogies occur in Genesis, Numbers, Ezra and Nehemiah; the first nine chapters of 1 Chronicles contain little more than the records of a few thousand men and women. To assume these were invented, is to completely misunderstand the importance of genealogies. They established the right of service (Ezra 2:59,62) and entitlement to land (Numbers 1). They were recorded accurately and stored carefully. Reliable men were specifically entrusted 'to deal with genealogies' (2 Chronicles 12:15).[2] This is why the genealogies of Jesus in Matthew 1 and Luke 3 are so significant. Scribes did not 'invent' genealogies. If those in the Bible are dismissed as forgeries, then all ancient genealogies must suffer the same fate.

One genealogy in particular is significantly detailed. In a thorough and scholarly defence of the obvious literal reading of a genealogy, Jeremy Sexton concludes, 'Gen 5 and 11 specify the age of each patriarch at the birth of his descendant, unlike any other genealogies in Scripture or in extant Ancient Near Eastern writings.'[3]

The biblical lists are also unique having a wider inclusion of wives, daughters, concubines, and incidental details. In ANE genealogies, only the royal family line was preserved for more than a few generations.[4]

- In Jacob's genealogy (Genesis 46), we have the names of the mothers of each of the grandchildren. One was a 'son of a Canaanite woman' (v.10), two 'died in the land of Canaan' (v.12), three were born to Leah 'in Paddan Aram' along with their sister Dinah (v. 5), another group includes their sister Serah (v.17).

- In 1 Chronicles 26:10, the chronicler carefully notes that Hoash had a number of sons and although Shimri was not the firstborn 'his father appointed

him the first.' Evidently the chronicler guarded against the suggestion that he had made a mistake.

These details are evidence of a carefully recorded and authentic record.

**Above**
*A clay tablet of the genealogy of the Babylonian King Hammurabi. Ancient genealogies are important for historians and are generally accepted as reliable*

1. See *Evidence for the Bible*. pp. 4, 6, 36–45.
2. For further details see *Nothing but the Truth*. pp. 123–126.
3. Jeremy Sexton, 'Who Was Born When Enosh Was 90?: A Semantic Reevaluation of William Henry Green's Chronological Gaps.' (*The Westminster Theological Journal* 77, no. 2 September 2015). pp. 193–218.
4. For a comparison of biblical and contemporary genealogies see Abraham Malamat 'King lists of the Old Babylonian period and biblical genealogies' (*Journal of the American Oriental Society* Vol. 88, No.1 Jan- Mar, 1968). pp. 163–173.

# Authentic detail

**Some details may seem entirely irrelevant for us, but it was not the practice of ancient writers to invent details simply to give the appearance of an authentic record**

Numbers 33 lists fifty place names for the route of the Exodus. The fact that many are unknown today is hardly surprising after 3,500 years! However, a writer in the 6th century BC would have 'invented' names well known to us.

Occasionally, details appear irrelevant. For example:

- In the list of Esau's descendants, the Edomites, we read 'This is the Anah who discovered the hot springs in the desert while he was grazing the donkeys of his father Zibeon' (Genesis 36:24). Presumably, the writer expected his contemporary readers to know exactly what 'hot springs' he was referring to and where they would be found.

- After a reference to the land of Moab, we are informed: 'The Emites used to live there—a people strong and numerous, and as tall as the Anakites. Like the Anakites, they too were considered Rephaites, but the Moabites called them Emites. Horites used to live in Seir, but the descendants of Esau drove them out. They destroyed the Horites from before them and settled in their place, just as Israel did in the land the LORD gave them as their possession' (Deuteronomy 2:10–12). For what purpose would this detail be invented?

- 1 Chronicles 7:21–22 introduces a spat between two sons of Ephraim and the 'native-born men of Gath.' This led to the death of the sons, the comfort of the neighbours to the grieving father, the birth and naming of his next born son, and even the record of his daughter who was in the construction industry! This is evidence of an accurate historical record.

### Some details are even amusing

- Deuteronomy 3:11 informs us that Og king of Bashan slept on a super king-size bed made of iron; it was 4m (13ft) long and 1.8m (6ft) wide and could still be seen in Rabbah of the Ammonites!

### Authentic honesty

In the ancient world, 'origin' stories only described the good in their ancestors. Israel's origin

**Above**

*The meticulous detail of Israel's Tabernacle in the wilderness (Exodus 26–40) would be irrelevant in the 6th century BC. By then the Tabernacle had long been replaced by a magnificent Temple—which itself had been destroyed. The claim that the detail was 'Just as the Lord commanded Moses' (39:32) would be considered blasphemy if invented. (A model of the Tabernacle in Timna Park, Israel)*

includes slavery and rebellion against God. Their first king, Saul, was a tragic disaster, David was guilty of adultery, murder and mismanagement, and Solomon turned to the gods of his many wives. How would such 'invented' detail boost the morale of exiles? Unlike the surrounding nations, the Old Testament is scrupulously honest.

# Job an Edomite?

**The phrase 'Job's comforters' is well known, but was he merely a legendary character?**

To dismiss his story as legend because of the conversation between Satan and God in chapters 1 and 2 reveals only the critic's unbelief in the supernatural.

**The purpose of the book** is to encourage selfless trust and worship of God even in the most desperate circumstances. Valued examples of courage, loyalty or love must come from real people, not make-believe. The book of Job begins with a phrase commonly introducing Hebrew history: 'There was a man…'.

**The book is set early in the history of Israel**, perhaps even around the time of Abraham.

- Like Noah and Abraham, Job offered sacrifices before the priesthood was established in the time of Moses (compare Genesis 8:20 and 22:13 with Job 1:5); like Abraham, Job's wealth was judged by his herds, flocks and servants (compare Genesis 24:35 with Job 1:3; 42:12).

- Significantly, although Job lived outside the land of Israel (1:3 ), like Enosh and Jacob (Genesis 4:26; 28:16), he was aware of the covenant name *Yahweh* ('the LORD'), although not its full meaning (Job 1:21). The character of God as 'Almighty' (*Shaddai*) first revealed to Abraham in Genesis 17:1, occurs more often in Job than any other book in the Bible (eg. Job 5:17; 40:2).

## The book refers to known places from the ancient world

- The Sabeans and Chaldeans (1:15,17) are known to history. See also Isaiah (45:14), Ezekiel (23:42) and Joel (3:8).

- Eliphaz came from Teman (2:11), a town in Edom mentioned often in the Old Testament (eg. Jeremiah 49:20).

- The land of Uz (1:1) descended from Shem (Genesis 10:22–23); the prophet Jeremiah included Uz among places well-known (Jeremiah 25:19–26), and he identified it with Edom (Lamentations 4:21). Therefore, Job came from Edom, the descendants of Esau (Genesis 36:10), who were constant enemies of Israel.

**Elsewhere in the Bible** Job is associated with real people. Ezekiel linked Job with Noah and Daniel (Ezekiel 14:12–14); James referred to 'Job's perseverance' and to the end of his story: 'You have seen what the Lord finally brought about' (James 5:11).

There are many suggestions who wrote the book, but it is likely that it was Job himself. It is magnificent poetry with a timeless message of resolute trust responding to the often-mysterious providence of God.

Thomas Carlyle, a renowned historian, counted Job as one of the great men of history, adding (perhaps extravagantly) that nothing written in the Bible or out of it is 'of equal literary merit' as the book of Job. [1]

**Left**
*A small (5 cm) 9th century metal figurine from Edom's Khirbat en-Nahas. Possibly a king or a god, it was found in one of the gate's guardrooms*

1. *On Heroes, Hero-worship, & the Heroic in History*, Thomas Carlyle (Appleton & Co, New York 1941 p.34).

# Edom a strong kingdom?

**For years, some claimed there was no evidence before the 7th century BC that the Edomites were anything more than scattered 'pastoral nomads'** [2]

However, the Bible claims that as early as Israel's Exodus from Egypt (around 1450 BC) the Edomites refused to allow Israel to pass through their territory and threatened them with significant force (Numbers 20:14–21). Later, Saul, David and Solomon each fought against the Edomites, who were a strong people with their own king and army (1 Samuel 14:47; 2 Samuel 8:13–14; 1 Kings 11:14). All this was dismissed as fiction.

By the time of the prophet Jeremiah (626–587 BC) it is agreed the Edomites had their own king and were firmly settled in the Highlands east of Judah. Around 640 BC Jeremiah vividly warned Edom that they could not escape God's judgement (Jeremiah 49:7–22). But were they a strong organised kingdom almost a thousand years earlier?

Archaeological research from 1997 to 2006 at Khirbat en–Nahas, between the Dead Sea and the Gulf of Aqaba in modern Jordan, discovered that in the lowlands of Edom copper production was a major industry at least between 1200 and 900 BC. Scores of copper mines were discovered, some penetrating 65m (200ft) into the hillside. Slag waste and ash beds (as much as half a metre deep) were evidence of smelting. A huge four-chamber city gate was also uncovered, the single entrance into a large fortress 73m (240ft) square. Pottery and carbon dating of the charcoal, confirmed a date around the time of David and Solomon and that Edom was capable of strong city fortifications and large-scale copper production.[3] All hardly evidence of scattered 'pastoral nomads'!

Job vividly described this mining that he was familiar with (Job 28:1–11). It also confirms the biblical fact that Edom had their own king long before Israel: 'These were the kings who reigned in Edom before any Israelite king reigned…' (Genesis 36:31–43).

**Above**
*The gatehouse controlled the only entrance into the massive tenth-century Iron Age fortress at Khirbat en-Nahas in Edom. Only two of the four chambers have so far been excavated*

**Below**
*Mounds of black slag, the waste from copper smelting at Khirbat en-Nahas. Radiocarbon dating proves that widespread copper production was carried on here from 12th to 9th centuries BC*

2. *The Bible Unearthed*, Israel Finkelstein and Neil Asher Silberman (Free Press, New York 2002).
3. 'Copper, the emergence of ancient Israel's rival', Thomas E Levy and Mohammed Najjar (*Biblical Archaeological Review* July/August 2006).

# The Egyptian scarab

**The Egyptian scarab was widely used as a religious emblem in all periods of Egyptian history from about 2345 to 30 BC, but there is no unambiguous mention of it in the Old Testament**

**Far left**
*A cartouche of Tuthmosis III at Karnak Temple (Egypt) showing the scarab beetle with the Sun disk at the top*

**Top right**
*A monumental Scarab 90cm high, 153cm long and 119cm wide*

**Left**
*A Gold and Inlaid Stone Pectoral with Lapis Scarab from the tomb of Tutankhamun (1336–1326 BC)*

In ancient Egyptian religion, the scarab was an important symbol in the form of the dung beetle (*Scarabaeus sacer*). At night the beetle burrows into the sand or soil and, when warmed by the morning sun, emerges, and so came to symbolise resurrection. It was associated with the divine manifestation of the early morning sun, Khepri, who was believed to roll the disk of the morning sun over the eastern horizon.

The beetle rolls animal dung into balls and lays its eggs inside. As seeds and eggs germinate it represented new birth and new life.

The scarab also referred variously to the ideas of existence, manifestation, development, growth, and effectiveness. It was a common Egyptian amulet, seal, or ring, and portrayed frequently on mummies and monuments.[1]

On mummies, the most important amulet was the heart scarab, placed to prevent the heart from incriminating its owner in the underworld's hall of judgement. These are bigger than usual and, according to the magical texts, they ought to be made from a dark green stone—green being the colour of the god Osiris. The scarab would be used to convey a message on the flat base, and often there was a short inscription from the *Book of the Dead*, and/or a royal name.

Historically, the most valuable class of scarabs is that which bears royal names; these ranged in date 2134–1991 BC to 30 BC.

The Mesopotamian cylinder seal (see here p. 67) never became popular in Egypt, partly because the Egyptians rarely wrote on clay tablets; however, during the third millennium BC, the stamp seal was introduced from Canaan. Later, the Egyptians adapted it into the scarab shape, which then became dominant.

1. Lorna Oates and Lucia Ghalin, *The mysteries of ancient Egypt*. (Anness Publishing 2004). p. 287.

# Scarabs in the East

**Given their religious significance for the Egyptians it is surprising that over three thousand scarab seals from the ancient world have been documented in Israel**

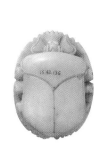

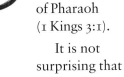
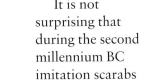

Scholars have long known of the enormous influence of Egypt on what is sometimes called the Levant (from a French word referring to where the sun rises in the east). This is the entire eastern seaboard of the Mediterranean. In ancient times the Egyptians considered this under their influence. Many of the people who lived in the Levant traded with Egypt and would have wanted to be on good terms with them. Even

Solomon married a daughter of Pharaoh (1 Kings 3:1).

It is not surprising that during the second millennium BC imitation scarabs became popular in Canaan. Some were imported but many were manufactured locally. The Phoenicians developed their own 'Egyptianised' style of scarabs. They are identifiable because though they use Egyptian images and hieroglyphs the style is often crude and the inscriptions make little sense.

Because of their religious significance, it is possible that some of the idols referred to in the Old Testament are scarabs (Deuteronomy 29:17; Ezekiel 14:4). One scholar points out

that the Hebrew word *gillulim*, used to describe a religious ritual object that had been brought from Egypt (Ezekiel 20:8 'idols') is related to the Hebrew word used for dung (*gelalim*).[2] No wonder the Israelites were to throw away such 'worthless' objects despite the apparent value of the precious stones they were carved from!

In view of the fact that the scarab in various forms pervaded so much of Egyptian religious symbolism, it is significant that the exact word does not appear in the Old Testament, and it was never used in connection with Israel's true worship. Since the godly Judean king Hezekiah portrayed a scarab on a seal, perhaps it often lost is religious significance.

The faith of Israel was certainly not copied from Egypt.

**Top left**
*Carved Scarab beetles from Egypt's Middle Kingdom period (2030–1650), used as amulets and seals*

**Far left**
*An 11th century BC 'Egyptianised' scarab found on an archaeological excavation near the Sea of Galilee*

**Left**
*This seal portraying a scarab reads: 'Belonging to Hezekiah [son of] Ahaz, king of Judah'*

2. Zohar Amar 'The Scarab: The Idol that Rolls in Dung', *Biblical Archaeology Review*, (Summer 2020 46:3). pp. 52–55.

# Sealed with a Stone

**The names of many people and places from the ancient world are found on documents left behind in their ruins. Most striking are tiny clay impressions that once sealed important documents**

The Babylonians commonly used cylinder seals which were rolled out on wet clay to leave an impression behind.[1] Among the Egyptians, Israelites, and in Canaan generally, the seal stone was common.

A cheap seal could be made of limestone, but for those who could afford it a gem, such as amethyst, would be used. The engraver might include an image and sometimes a personal name. The seal could be hung from a necklace or set in a ring. They were used to authenticate ownership of an object or document (1 Kings 21:8). In the Bible it is used as a powerful metaphor for a binding relationship (Song of Songs 8:6). The clay impression left by a seal stone is called a *bulla* (pl.*bullae*) and, though fragile, these have also been recovered in excavations.[2]

Two stone seals have been identified bearing the names of servants of King Uzziah (Azariah c.767–740 BC). One reads 'belonging to Abiyau, servant of Uzziah' and the other, 'Belonging to Shebnayau (Shebnayahu), servant of Uzziah'.[3] They each include an image of a man along with the text. While these stones were not discovered on archaeological excavations they were found long before forgers were aware of the authentic details that date them.[4]

Excavations in Jerusalem have recovered bullae bearing biblical names. One is of Gemariah, son of Shaphan (Jeremiah 36:10). Shaphan was a chief scribe at the time of King Josiah (2 Kings 22). Another records the name of Azariah, son of Hilkiah (1 Chronicles 6:13). Hilkiah was a High Priest in the Temple of Solomon.

More recently, two bullae have been excavated that refer to two individuals named in the same Bible verse (Jeremiah 38:1). One reads 'Gedaliah son of Pashhur' while the other reads 'Jukal, son of Shelemiah.'[5]

**Left**
*The unprovenanced seal of Shebnayau, servant of Uzziah with its corresponding impression (bulla)*

1. See the cylinder seal here on p. 67.
2. More seals can be seen in *Evidence for the Bible*, pp. 69,86,87.
3. See *Evidence for the Bible*, p. 69.
4. 'Identifications of Biblical Persons', Lawrence J. Mykytiuk, in Meir Lubetski and Edith Lubetski (editors), *New Inscriptions and Seal Relating to the Biblical World* (Society of Biblical Literature: Atlanta: Georgia, 2012). p. 47.
5. Eliat Mazar, 'Did I Find King David's Palace?' (*Biblical Archaeology Review*, January/February 2006). See also *Evidence for the Bible*, p. 86.

# Fingerprints of Kings

**Some bullae and seals include the names of kings from Israel, testifying to their real existence. Some of the images on these seals raise interesting questions**

**Above**
*The Hezekiah Bulla and broken Isaiah Bulla . Note the distinctive winged sun disk on Hezekiah's Bulla*

**Below**
*The now lost seal of Shema, servant of Jeroboam II (below), from Megiddo with an image of a roaring lion. The discovery of a clay bulla (bottom), bearing a very similar image to the seal, was announced in 2020*

In 1905, Gottlieb Schumacher discovered at Megiddo the seal of Shema, a royal servant to Jeroboam II (2 Kings 14:23; c.782–753 BC). It includes the emblem of a roaring lion. Though drawings (and replicas) exist of this seal, Schumacher sent the seal to the Turkish Sultan in Constantinople where it disappeared. However, in December 2020 experts authenticated a stamped clay bulla of Jeroboam II bearing an almost identical image.[6]

In 2015 Eliat Mazar discovered in Jerusalem a bulla bearing King Hezekiah's name. Other examples of Hezekiah bullae have been found, but this was the first from an archaeological excavation.[7] It was in a collection of thirty-three bullae from excavations near the Temple Mount, and among them was one that, though broken, has text that might be read 'Isaiah, the prophet'. It certainly belongs to the correct historical layer for the period of Hezekiah and Isaiah.

Unlike Egyptian or Phoenician seals, Hebrew seals are generally without imagery and only bear text; this may reflect the biblical commandment against making graven images.[8] However, there are exceptions on the seals of biblical kings. A roaring lion on the seal of Jeroboam seems suitable (Hosea 11:10). But some Israelite seals bear pagan Egyptian icons, including the winged scarab beetle, spitting cobra and ankh symbol. Perhaps this is what the prophets warned against (Ezekiel 20:8). The winged sun disk, a typical Egyptian motif for the god Re, used by Hezekiah is particularly puzzling given that the Bible describes him as a faithful king. However, in the ancient world the Assyrians used the winged sun disk to represent their god Ashur and the Babylonians to represent Marduk. Perhaps Hezekiah took this common image for divinity to represent Yahweh.[9] Unwise, but not an indication of paganism.

6. '2700 years ago, tiny clay piece sealed deal for Bible's King Jeroboam II', *Times of Israel*, 10 December 2020.
7. See *Evidence for the Bible*. p. 69.
8. Alan Millard, *Discoveries from Bible Times*, (Lion: Oxford, 1997). p. 113.
9. Boyd Seevers, 'Seals in Ancient Israel and the Near East: Their Manufacture, Use, and Apparent Paradox of Pagan Symbolism', *Near East Archaeological Society Bulletin*, 61 (2016). pp. 11–12.

# The conquest of Canaan

**When the Israelites entered their Promised Land, they began a relentless and merciless policy of total extermination of the local tribes**

**Left**
*A 'tophet' (possibly meaning 'a place of burning') in ancient Carthage outside Tunis today—a burial site including those of child sacrifices. It is one of many tophets across North Africa*

This was God's command (Deuteronomy 7:1–11; 12:29–31) and Joshua obeyed (Joshua 10–11). Men, women and children were slaughtered without pity.[1] Why?

**God loves compassion, truth and righteousness.** But he hates cruelty, deceit and sin. He is holy and expects his people to be holy (Deuteronomy 10:12–13). He is also a forgiving God where there is repentance (Psalm 86:5). God warned Israel against the debased pagan worship of Canaan and their shameless fertility cults, human sacrifices, and terrifying sorcery, witchcraft and spiritism (Deuteronomy 18:9–13). Pagan worship was not an innocent alternative, it involved extreme evil and cruelty.

**It is God alone who defines sin** (Romans 7:7) not our 'instinctive values'. 'Instinctive values' led Stalin and Hitler to massacre millions for their ideology. Even today, it encourages vicious persecution, enslaves more people than ever, applauds the most obscene relationships and lifestyles, and affirms the killing of millions of healthy unborn children for convenience.

**Sin must be punished or it will be applauded.** Extreme sin requires extreme judgement.

God punished sin at the beginning (Genesis 3:16–19) and later destroyed almost the whole of humanity in a worldwide Flood (Genesis 6–8). The command to cleanse Canaan was to keep Israel pure as an example of holiness. It was *moral* cleansing, not ethnic cleansing. No nation ever again has the authority from God to practice this extreme moral cleansing.

It was an example of God's hatred of evil and its tragic human consequences. It is also a warning of an even more terrifying judgement that will come at the close of time (2 Thessalonians 1:8–9).

**Tragically, God's command was broken almost immediately** (Judges 3:5–6; 10:6). Later, both Israel and Judah adopted Asherah and Baal which involved gross immorality and the live sacrifice of children (2 Kings 17:16–17; 2 Chronicles 28:2–3; 33:6). Jeremiah and Ezekiel accused Judah of building 'the high places of Topheth in the valley of Ben Hinnom to burn their sons and daughters in the fire' (Jeremiah 7:30–32; 19:1–6 and Ezekiel 23:39).

1. See also *Evidence for the Bible* pages 27–29 for the conquest and page 55 for child sacrifice.

# Child sacrifice — 'the blood of the innocents'

## In spite of attempts to prove otherwise, there is no serious doubt that this cruel practice existed in the ancient world

### The record of ancient texts

The Greek historian Diodorus Siculus (died 30 BC) refers to the practice at the siege of Carthage in 310 BC. And the 2nd century AD historian Justin, records that the Persian ruler Darius I forbade child sacrifice in the 5th century BC. It was practiced in ancient Rome until outlawed by the Senate in 97 BC. No one bans a ritual that doesn't exist![2][3]

In AD 197, Tertullian, the church leader at Carthage, wrote 'Children were openly sacrificed in Africa to Saturn as lately as the proconsulship of Tiberius [c.AD 14] … And even now that sacred crime still continues to be done in secret'. Tertullian expressed the Christian concern for all life: 'We may not destroy even the foetus in the womb… nor does it matter whether you take away a life that is born, or destroy one that is coming to the birth… It is child murder.'[4]

Some consider that the sacrifice of infants and children took place only in times of extreme danger or disaster. See for example 2 Kings 3:27. However, the evidence is that it was tragically more common than that.

### The record of archaeology

Gravestones (*stelae*) at Carthage, above urns containing the cremated remains of children, include inscriptions indicating the children were given as a live sacrifice: 'To Tanit [Tophet], the face of Ba'al, and to our lord, to Ba'al Hammon'. Baal and Molech are identified in child sacrifice in Jeremiah 32:35.

One inscription from Carthage records a man named Tuscus giving Baal his mute son in the hope that he would later receive a healthy child in exchange.

A 10th century BC inscription set up by an Aramaean king warns those who would vandalise his memorial: 'May he burn seven of his sons before Adad. May he release seven of his daughters to be cult prostitutes for Isthar.' The practice had long spread by Phoenician settlers to Canaan where child sacrifice became horrendously prevalent.

Across the ancient world, both in the Bible and therefore in the history of Judaism and Christianity, abortion and infanticide became synonymous with murder.

**Right**
*In the Tophet at Carthage, many of the more than 20,000 buried urns containing the cremated remains of infants were marked by a stela (a stone pillar) with an inscription indicating their offering to the gods*

2. 'Child Sacrifice at the Tophet', Andrew Cross, The Hebrew University in Jerusalem 2012
3. 'Canaanite Child Sacrifice, Abortion, and the Bible' Henry B. Smith, Jr. Associates for Biblical Research, *The Journal of Ministry and Theology*. Autumn 2013.
4. Tertullian *Apologeticus* IX.25. If possible, read the whole of this section in *Apologeticus* to understand the sordid practices as late as the 2nd century AD.

# Joshua on Mount Ebal

'Joshua built on Mount Ebal an altar to the LORD, the God of Israel' (Joshua 8:30)

When Adam Zertal excavated a site on Mount Ebal in the 1980s he found a significant ancient altar with thousands of pottery shards that dated around 1200 BC. The 9m by 14m (29ft by 46ft) structure was built of uncut stones and had a ramp 7m (23ft) long that allowed access to the top. This is not found at altars excavated at Megiddo or Dan which both have steps.

The main structure was built of uncut stones. It was hollow inside and filled with dirt, ash and over three thousand animal bones. The bones showed evidence of having been butchered and burnt and were primarily of animals considered pure according to the law of Moses: cattle, sheep and goats.

Two scarabs (an Egyptian god-emblem in the form of the dung beetle) had also been deliberately buried here, one of which bears the name of Pharaoh Thutmose III who reigned from 1479–1425 BC and is possibly the Pharaoh of the Exodus;[1] although the style of the scarab fits more with the form that they took in the 13th century.

The entire site was abandoned around 1140 BC and covered in stones, probably in order to protect it. There is also evidence of an even earlier round altar formed from uncut stone which had been

**Above**
*The altar of uncut stones on Mt Ebal, of unknown origin*

modified over time. Archaeologists have been divided over the significance of Zertal's excavations. Some deny any religious significance and suggest other interpretations of the structure such as a watchtower.

However, the use of uncut stones (exactly as described in Joshua 8:31 and unlike other Israelite altars at Dan and Beersheba), the access ramp rather than a staircase (explicitly required for the modesty of the priests) and the presence of bones from animals considered ritually clean for sacrifice, all fit perfectly the altar described in Exodus 20:25–26.

Unlike the altar on Mt Ebal, the altars for the tabernacle were made of acacia wood—which is 'durable, hard and strong' and plentiful in the Sinai desert [2]—to be portable; they were overlaid with gold or bronze (Exodus 30:1–3; 38:1–2).

1. See *Evidence for the Bible*, pp. 22–23.
2. Julian Evans, *God's Trees*, p. 25.

# Horned Altars

**God gave Israel specific instructions how to build an altar and the purpose they would serve. Discoveries in the land of Israel reveal both their construction and their corruption**

Some altars were to be constructed from uncut stone, packed with earth and having a horn at each top corner (Exodus 29:12; Leviticus 4:7). Blood of sacrifice was sprinkled on the altar and the horns of an altar had the additional function of being a means for a fugitive to claim sanctuary (Exodus 21:14; 1 Kings 2:28).

**Beersheba.** A four horned altar was found here in secondary use as part of a wall. The stones have been cut with shaped corner horns and a simple image of a serpent engraved on one side. Standing 1.5m high (3 royal cubits), it matches the dimensions of the tabernacle altar (Exodus 27:1). Some archaeologists suggest it may have been destroyed during King Hezekiah's religious reforms and then reused in an 8th century BC wall (2 Kings 18:22).[3]

**Dan.** Archaeologists have found parts of a large altar including one of the corner horns and its access steps. This altar belongs to the period of King Jeroboam I who, in 930 BC, built it as a rival place of worship to Jerusalem (1 Kings 12:29–31).[4] Remains of an earlier sacrificial altar reflect the Danites long history of corrupt religion (Judges 18:27–31).

**Megiddo.** Three small limestone altars with horns at each corner

Left & below
*The altar found at Beersheba was first (incorrectly) reassembled on site in 1973. Below, in its finished reconstruction at the Israel Museum*

47

date to the time of King Solomon. These were probably used to burn incense or make grain offerings to the Lord (Exodus 30). Similar examples have been found at Arad, Dothan, Ekron and Jerusalem.[5]

**Shiloh.** In 2019 three altar horns were discovered at the site where the tabernacle once stood. Evidence for sacrificial activity was found associated with an Iron Age monumental building (c.1177–980 BC)

including a large quantity of animal bones considered clean for Israelite sacrifice.

The altar at Mt Ebal was of unhewn stone (as Exodus 20:25); however, there are many altars made of cut stone. Perhaps there was more than one type of altar, but the abundance of various horned altars testifies to religious corruption.

3. *Biblical Archaeology Review*, 1:1, 1975, 9.
4. See *Evidence for the Bible* p. 63.
5. Seymour Gitin, 'The Four-horned Altar and Sacred Space: An Archaeological Perspective', in *Sacred Time, Sacred Place: Archaeology and the Religion of Israel* (ed. Barry M. Gittlen). pp. 95–123.

# A Healthy nation

**Many of our common rules for health and safety have their foundation in God's concern for the health and hygiene of Israel**

## Hand washing!

As recently as the 19th century, almost half the women admitted to a 'lying-in hospital' died soon after giving birth. A Hungarian physician, Ignaz Philipp Semmelweis (1818–1865), suggested that puerperal fever ('childbed fever') was caused by the doctors transferring infection from patient to patient. He insisted on handwashing with a solution of chlorinated lime between patient examinations. This reduced mortality to less than one percent, but he was ridiculed and certified insane. After his death, Louis Pasteur confirmed the theory of germs and Joseph Lister identified the value of antiseptics.

Not only were the Levitical priests to make good use of the large bronze bowl of water when they performed their sacrificial duties (Exodus 30:17–21), but God also instructed his people that touching an unclean animal would make them unclean. He also ordered that any material onto which a carcass, however small, had fallen must be washed and any receptacle into which it fell must be broken (Leviticus 11:29–35). Drastic measures, but housewives would quickly learn to keep containers covered.

## Sanitary care

God gave specific instructions to maintain cleanliness among the Israelites, and sanitary rules were of fundamental importance. Dysentery and cholera, caused by poor sanitation, was one of the greatest causes of death for both soldiers and civilians until modern times. It was only in 1854 that Dr John Snow associated water contaminated with human excrement with the outbreak of cholera in Soho, London.

The potential for this among the Israelite encampment in the wilderness was obvious. But God had the answer.

His instructions were simple, well adapted to the climate and their situation, and enforced by the highest motives (Deuteronomy 23:12–14). God instructed that the sewage be removed from the camp, and buried—'have something to dig with'.

**Above**

*Across the world there are eleven statues or busts of Ignaz Philipp Semmelweis , the 'patron saint of handwashing'. This marble sculpture by Alajos Stróbl (1906) is in Budapest, Hungary*

**Left**

*A replica of the pump in Broad Street, Soho, London where, in 1854, Dr John Snow associated cholera with contaminated water. When the pump handle was removed, the outbreak subsided. The well had been dug only 1m from a disused cesspit*

# Rules for health and safety

**God expected Israel to apply his detailed regulations to the broader principles of life in a community**

## Food regulations

Long before anyone understood the health dangers of animal fat, God forbade Israel to eat it (Leviticus 7:22–24). They would obtain all the necessary fat for their health from normal meat and milk, fruit and nuts, without tucking into the fatty fat.

God has much more to say on food hygiene. In the list of allowed and forbidden animals for food, a general rule was that carnivorous animals or those that lived off carrion where forbidden (Leviticus 11:1–28). Our modern society follows the same rule.

## Marriage relationships

Before they understood the significance of hereditary diseases and weak genes, God gave Israel a clear list of unlawful marriage relationships to avoid this and to maintain harmony and decency among 'close relatives' (Leviticus 18). Such a precise list is found nowhere else among the often promiscuous societies of the ancient world.

## Skin diseases and boils, mildew and mould

The detailed care for various forms of infectious diseases (Leviticus 13–14) may appear irksome, but it prevented the spread of disease among a close-knit community. Any form of bodily

discharge was also covered by God's detailed laws for cleansing (Leviticus 15:1–33)

## Circumcision

Although debate continues over the health advantages of circumcision,[1] there is little doubt that it was more than a symbol of Jewishness (Leviticus 12:3). The Egyptians practiced it for 'cleanliness sake' according to Herodotus.[2] Their priests had to be circumcised and shaven. Circumcision as a sign of the Covenant with Abraham long pre-dates Israel's time in Egypt.

## Safety and public liability

The principles of guarding against accidents and taking responsibility for neglect that caused harm to others, are clear from Deuteronomy 22:8 and Exodus 21:28–36).[3]

## Ecology and animal husbandry

The instruction to take the eggs of a wild bird but to leave the hen (Deuteronomy 22:6) was intended to prepare Israel to care for the land they would shortly enter by maintaining a balanced ecology. The thoughtful welfare of farm animals was a lesson in good animal husbandry (Deuteronomy 6:14; 22:10).

**Top**
*Even today Israel is careful to bury their dead outside the city walls. This is the Mount of Olives outside the old city walls of Jerusalem*

**Above**
*King Piye's victory stela This claims that to enter the Pharaoh's presence, a man had to be circumcised, clean [ ie shaven], and a non-fish eater!*

49

1. For example, the protection against cervical cancer in women.
2. The Greek Historian Herodotus (b. 484 BC) *History* II:37.
3. Some of these laws are reflected in ancient law codes; for example the Code of Hammurabi 251 for the ox that gores someone. See *Evidence for the Bible* p. 24 for Hammurabi Code.

# Moses and the Ebers Papyrus

**Possibly the oldest medical document on record gives us an insight into the primitive medicine of the Ancient Near East at the time of Moses**

The Egyptian Ebers Papyrus is dated around 1550 BC, but thought to be a copy of one much older.[1] With some 700 to 800 remedies, it is a mixture of diagnoses, treatment and surgical procedures. Subjects include cataracts and 'crocodile bites', contraception and abortion, blindness and baldness, heart conditions and ear discharge. Many of the treatments use natural remedies from plants, herbs and fruits, whilst others included cat and wasp dung, human excrement and urine.

Eye complaints were common. For cataracts, Goose-grease and honey was tried as a poultice. For other eye problems, ass's tooth mixed in water and applied round the eyes would 'ensure that he recovers quickly'. Treating a wound included the use of human excrement, and for burns, a frog or head of an electric eel warmed in oil. Failing this, an incantation to the god Horus is recommended!

Withdrawing a splinter had a few possible solutions: worms blood, cooked and crushed in oil; a mole, killed, cooked and drained in oil; or ass's dung cooked in fresh milk.

For a lady's spotty face (if the natural remedies fail) bullock's

bile and whipped up ostrich egg. For a man's baldness, ointment of equal parts of lion, hippopotamus, crocodile, goose, serpent, and ibex fats — or others more disgusting!

**Moses was familiar with these remedies in Egypt,** and had he used this knowledge, Leviticus would have been a very different book! There is none of the Levitical wisdom of health and safety principles in the Ebers Papyrus. And there are none of the Ebers remedies in Leviticus; in fact there are no remedies at all. However, there are ceremonies to pronounce religious cleanness after healing and these included careful washing (eg. Leviticus 14:1–57).

Leviticus was not Moses' invention but God's revelation. The regulations had a ceremonial and religious context because God wanted his people to be an example to the surrounding nations: 'consecrate yourselves and be holy, because I am holy' (Leviticus 11:44).

**Above**
*The Ebers Papyrus, an Egyptian medical document from about 1500 BC, describes combining animal and vegetable oils with alkaline salts to form a soap-like material used for treating skin diseases, as well as for washing*

---

1. It is thought to have been found in a mummy. It came into the possession of Edwin Smith in 1862, who sold it to George Ebers in 1872. It is now in the University of Leipzig. There are other similar medical directories from the ancient world.

# Illness in the ancient world

**Many in the ancient world believed that all illnesses were a result of evil taking possession of a person's body with the gods indifferent or supporting**

One clay tablet found in King Ashurbanipal's library at Nineveh begins:

> 'The evil curse fixes a man
> A raging voice over him is fixed
> The evil curse is a great calamity
> That man the evil curse slaughters like a lamb
> His god from over him departs
> His goddess stands angry at his side
> The raging voice like a cloak covers him and bears him away.'[2]

In an attempt to combat disease and infection, Asclepieons (healing centres) were developed across the ancient Greek-speaking world. Two of the most famous were at Epidaurus in Greece and Pergamum in Turkey.

Pergamum (Revelation 2:12–17) has been described as the 'Lourdes' of the ancient world. People came from all over to be healed by the god Asclepius, the divine physician in Greek mythology and a son of Apollo. On arrival people took cleansing baths (purgation), and then had a cleansing diet for several days. Sleeping in special chambers, the sufferer hoped Asclepius would come in a dream, which, when interpreted, would lead to a cure being prescribed. Asclepius was

**Below left**
*Asclepius with his serpent-entwined staff.*

**Below right**
*'Diviner's Manual' from the Library of the last Assyrian king, Ashurbanipal (668–627BC)*

identified by the symbol used for medicine, the snake entwined staff; this was possibly influenced by the healing in Numbers 21:8 which is the earliest account of the snake/pole coimbination. Even today, thousands of people travel to ancient Asclepieon's in the hopes of being healed.

The most famous physician, surgeon and philosopher from Pergamum was Galen (AD 129–210) who collected all the significant Greek and Roman medical thought and added his own discoveries and theories. He had a profound influence on medicine until the Renaissance in the 14th century.

Luke, the travel companion of Paul and compiler of the Gospel and Acts, was a medical doctor (Colossians 4:14).

51

2. Philip Matyszak, *Ancient Magic—A practitioners guide to the supernatural in Greece and Rome* (Thames and Hudson 2019). p. 156.

# Sickness and healing in the ancient world

**Sickness and disease was common in Bible times and no one was immune—from the poorest beggar to the wealthiest king**

Living to an old age was a mixed blessing. Pharaoh Ramesses II (c.1303–1213 BC) lived to be ninety. His mummy revealed that he was suffering from severe dental problems, arthritis and hardening of the arteries. Mummies from ancient Egypt have revealed terrible tooth decay, osteoarthritis, gangrene, and heart disease; one study revealed that more than half of those aged over forty suffered from atherosclerosis (a blockage in the arteries).[1]

The Bible does not define medical conditions in any detail, therefore the sicknesses it describes are not always entirely clear. Dysentery would have been common where sanitation was poor. The death of Jehoram (2 Chronicles 21:19) and the illness of the father of Publius (Acts 28:8) are examples of this chronic infection.

Plagues have been common throughout history. There are a number of Hebrew words that may be translated 'plague' in the Old Testament. Sometimes it refers to a multiplication of pests, such as some of the plagues on Egypt, but at other times it describes something closer to Bubonic plague, such as the bodily swellings experienced by the Philistines

**Left**
*The Mummy of Ramesses II now in the National Museum of Egyptian Civilization in Cairo*

**Below**
*Surgical Instruments including forceps, scalpels and curettes. From a wall relief on the Egyptian temple at Kom Ombo c.100 BC*

(1 Samuel 5–6). God can bring about such plagues as a means of sudden judgement (2 Samuel 24:10–17).

Skin diseases are often referred to in the Bible. The Hebrew and Greek words traditionally translated 'leprosy' could refer to a range of skin conditions. In fact, many of the descriptions suggest that these conditions were not Hansen's disease at all. The lesions are often described as white and the skin flaky (Exodus 4:6; Numbers 12:10; 2 Kings 5:27) which are not indications of leprosy. A range of skin infections described in Leviticus 13:2–12 show that the Israelites were aware of many different causes.

The worldview of the Biblical writers saw suffering and death as an interruption of God's original

purpose for a good creation (Genesis 1–3); the result of living in a fallen world which awaits redemption (Romans 8:21). However, sometimes suffering could be a result of not living God's way with proper sanitation and diet. Only occasionally it was God's judgement on an individual as seen in 2 Chronicles 26:16–21.

1. Emma Young, 'Ancient Afflictions: Mummies Got Heart Disease Too', *New Scientist* 6 November 2013.

# The Balm of Gilead

## The biblical law made provision to protect the health of the nation through diet and sanitation

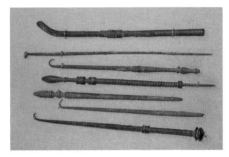

**Far left**
*The tombstone of Jason, a 2nd Century AD doctor, seated on a stool examining a child with a swollen stomach. An egg-shaped object to hand was probably designed to be heated and used to draw blood*

**Left and above**
*Luke would have been familiar with surgical instruments, some of which, like the forceps, have changed little since his time!*

The Old Testament law placed emphasis on purity and cleanliness.[2] The need to clean wounds and apply bandages was well known (Isaiah 1:6; Luke 10:34). Wine was used medicinally (1 Timothy 5:23) and the Israelites knew the importance of mental health to physical well-being (Psalm 104:14–15; Proverbs 17:22). For his skin infection, Hezekiah was told to prepare a 'poultice of figs and apply it to the boil' (Isaiah 38:21). Figs were commonly used in the ancient world for their medicinal value. Jeremiah referred to the balm of Gilead (Jeremiah 8:22); this was made from the resin of a tree and could bring pain relief and healing particularly to skin abrasions. It was probably imported from the spice traders that travelled on the King's Highway (Genesis 37:25).

Jesus encountered many sicknesses (Mark 1:32–34). Some were natural, like a woman suffering menstrual bleeding (Mark 5:25–29), the man blind from birth (John 9:1) and those with skin infections (Luke 17:11–19). Others, were supernatural, reflecting demonic influence (Mark 5:1–20). In each case Jesus brought healing, though in varied ways. He was not giving us a pattern to follow.

There are a number of incidents where Jesus used his own saliva in a healing (Mark 7:33; Mark 8:23; John 9:6). The Jewish Talmud refers to the healing properties of saliva, particularly in relation to blindness. Tacitus, the Roman historian, records that Emperor Vespasian claimed to have healed a blind man with his spittle as a way of demonstrating divine power; however, Tacitus plainly did not believe it.[3] The healings performed by Jesus are credible and multiple. His emphasis on compassion and healing would motivate Christians to continue to develop medical solutions for our suffering.

Luke himself was a doctor (Colossians 4:14),[4] and the gospel he wrote includes references to the role of physicians not found in other gospels (Luke 4:23; Luke 5:31). While other gospel writers describe a sick woman only getting worse through the advice of doctors (Mark 5:26), Luke put them in a somewhat better light only highlighting that no one had helped her get better (Luke 8:43)!

2. See here pages 48–49.
3. William Lane Craig and J. P. Moreland, *The Blackwell Companion to Natural Theology*, Wiley-Blackwell: Oxford, 2009, p. 655.
4. See also *Evidence for the Bible*, pp. 127 and 151.

# Women in Hebrew life

## A thoughtful reading of the Old Testament reveals the true value and dignity of a wife in Hebrew society

**M**ale and female were created equally 'in the image of God' (Genesis 1:27). Eve was a 'compatible companion' to Adam (the meaning of Genesis 2:20). Unlike our modern contempt for chastity and faithfulness, marriage was a sacred and binding covenant (Malachi 2:14; Ezekiel 16:8) and portrayed with true affection (Song of Solomon 4:10; 1 Samuel 1:4–5); the wife's happiness was important (Deuteronomy 24:5). Wives were a vital and valued part of an integrated household; a good wife was *honoured* above all, not simply valued (Proverbs 31:10–11, 28–31). In society there must be order and leadership. Husbands were expected to provide spiritual and temporal leadership. Responsibility and accountability did not mean domination or female inferiority and slavish subservience.

Many Old Testament and Ancient Near Eastern (ANE) laws were designed for the protection of women and girls against male mistreatment.

- Women could inherit, own and manage property (Numbers 27 and 36: Joshua 17:3–4; Ruth 4:3; Genesis 31:14–17).

- Not all marriages were 'arranged'. Zelophehad's daughters were free to 'marry anyone they please' (Numbers 36:6). In Genesis 24:58 Rebekah was given a choice.

**Right and inset**
*Part of the column containing the laws of the ancient Babylonian king, Hammurabi. It includes many protections for women, including death as the punishment for raping an engaged girl* [1]

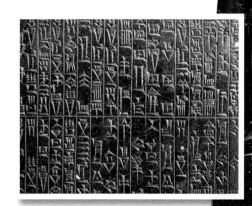

- Men were held accountable for raping a woman, whether slave or free (Deuteronomy 22:23–29).

- A wife was protected from casual divorce (Deuteronomy 22:13–19). In some ANE laws she received half the property.

- The unusual test for adultery in Numbers 5:11–31 was not 'magic' but divine intervention to avoid male prejudice.

- Both Hebrew and ANE laws provided for the care of widows (eg Deuteronomy 24:19–22; Isaiah 1:17).

There are many examples of excellent women on centre stage:

Sarah, a mother to Israel (Genesis 21:1–7).

Hannah, a woman of faith and prayer (1 Samuel 1).

Abigail, a peacemaker between violent men (1 Samuel 25).

Deborah, a bold prophetess and leader (Judges 4).

Ruth, a devoted daughter-in-law (Ruth).

Esther, an example of brave loyalty (Esther).

'Hebrew and Ancient Near Eastern laws provide compelling evidence that women had a more central role in ancient society, were held in higher esteem, and were granted more rights than is commonly recognised.'[2]

1. See *Evidence for the Bible* p. 24 for the Hammurabi code.
2. Carol Pratt Bradley in *Women in Hebrew and Ancient Near Eastern Law*, (Studia Antiqua 2003. Vol.3 No.1). A balanced presentation comparing the Hebrew and Ancient Near East position of women. See also Carol Meyers in *Families in Ancient Israel* (Westminister John Knox, Louisville KY 1997).

# Women in the world and the church

**In the time of the apostles, women could own property, run successful businesses and reach prominence in society** [3]

In Acts 13:50; 17:4,12 'prominent' means influential and wealthy. Although the Jewish historian Josephus reflected the general attitude to women: 'Let not the testimony of women be admitted, on account of the levity and boldness of their sex',[4] God allowed women to be the first to report the resurrection of Jesus and Jesus showed thoughtful care for three despised and sinful women in John 4, 8 and Luke 7.

**Lydia** was in the fashionable designer trade. She owned property, and the 'members of her household' almost certainly included domestic slaves. Whether widowed or divorced (a Roman free-woman could divorce her husband, compare Mark 10:11–12), Lydia's house was sufficiently large to entertain Paul and Silas and provide a meeting place (Acts 16:13–16, 40).

Around AD 43, Junia Theodora was commended by the citizens of Corinth for her hospitality and generosity; and in AD 79, Eumachia controlled a brick making company in Pompeii and was also a priestess of a temple.

Paul commends eight women who were members of the church in Rome for their hard work (Romans 16). **Phoebe** was a businesswoman who carried the letter from Corinth to Rome. She is described as a 'servant' (*diakonon*) of the church in Cenchreae, and her 'great help' (*prostatis*) meant she gave assistance from her own resources.

Roman class-structure was jealously guarded, but Phoebe came as a 'sister' to all believers whether slave or free.

Although **Euodia and Syntyche** are gently reprimanded by Paul, he appreciated the faithful support he received from them (Philippians 4:2–3), and **Priscilla and Aquilla** (mentioned seven times) are commended for their hospitality and Christian service.

The respect and submission the apostle encourages the wife to give to her husband is balanced by a husband's love which is as purposeful and selfless as that of Christ for the church (Ephesians 5:22–33). Peter similarly balances submission and love in a marriage (1 Peter 3:1–7).

In 1st century Rome, women were rebelling against male domination where it was allowed (even expected) that husbands would be adulterous. A woman's dress betrayed who she was, and the lavish adornment described in 1 Timothy 2:9 was that of the 'respectable' prostitute. Married women wore a head covering in public and not to do so was a sign of that rebellion.[5]

**Above**

*A 2nd century AD Roman marriage ceremony 'The joining of hands', displayed on a marble sarcophagus*

3. See *The Book of Acts in its first century setting—Graeco-Roman setting*, ed Gill and Gempf (The Paternoster Press, Carlisle 1994).
4. Josephus *Antiquities* Book IV chapter 8:15.
5. For a full treatment of women in Roman society Bruce W Winter *Roman Wives, Roman Widows* (Eerdmans Publishing 2003). Also, Lindsay Allaston-Jones, *Women in Roman Britain* (British Museum Press 1989).

# Children and adoption

**In the ancient world, a child was immediately part of the economic life of the *bet ab* ('father's house')**

**Above**
*A 12.7cm (5inch) footprint of Ba'ala-bia aged two years. The contract accompanying it relinquished her parents' rights, and that of her two younger brothers sold with her. From Syria in the 13th century BC*

Two or three generations plus servants/slaves lived as one economic unit.[1] In the Bible there are many records of the young life of its main characters: eg. Isaac, Joseph, David, Josiah. Samuel was taken to the tabernacle after he was weaned (1 Samuel 1:24, possibly at the age of three), but the word 'boy' (*naar*) in v.25 refers to a young lad shaking himself free. Childhood, as we understand it, was unknown.

In Ancient Near Eastern (ANE) literature there are references to wet nurse contracts, adoptions, inheritance, and slave purchase. The ancient law of the Babylonian king Hammurabi, soon after the time of Abraham, guarded the care of adopted sons in detail (laws 185–193), allowing them, under certain circumstances, to return to their natural parents. The adoptive parents had full responsibility for their welfare, and often the adopted boy would be first in line for inheritance unless another son was born. Adopted children were expected to play a full part in family economy, including caring for the adoptive parents in their old age.

Poverty or debt was often a reason why a child was sold into adoption, or slavery, from birth. Moses was adopted by Pharaoh's daughter and a wet nurse (Moses' mother) was hired. He belonged to Pharaoh's daughter and was therefore trained and educated as an Egyptian.

Adopted girls would sometimes come as part of the dowry and would belong to the wife. Although Exodus 21:7–11 allows a man to sell his daughter, her future welfare is carefully guarded.

However, the bond between parent and child is evident in the many Hebrew words to describe its development: *yeled*, the baby in the womb (Exodus 21:22 as ESV) and newborn (Isaiah 9:6). *yoneq*, the suckling child (Isaiah 11:8). *olel*, the child in need of protection (Lamentations 2:19). *gamul*, the weaned child (Isaiah 28:9). *taph*, often the youngest member of the family (Deuteronomy 1:39). *elem,* a young man under twenty years, neither ready for marriage nor war (1 Samuel 17:56). *naar*, youth shaking free (Genesis 22:5; 1 Samuel 2:26). *bachur*, the adult youth, ready for life (1 Samuel 9:2; Psalm 148:12).[2]

This is reflected in the New Testament where we have children playing (Matthew 11:16–17) and Jesus' tender care of them used as an illustration of simplicity of faith (18:1–6; 19:13).

1. A useful article on this subject: Kristine Henriken Garroway 'Children in the Ancient Near East' *Biblical Archaeology Review*, November/December 2018.
2. Alfred Edersheim *Sketches of Jewish Social Life in the Days of Christ*. Chapter 7 'The upbringing of Jewish children'. These words are not always used so specifically, and their meaning cannot always be brought out in an English translation.

# Surrogate mothers

## Abraham's use of Hagar as a surrogate mother to produce an heir was common in the Ancient Near East. This places the account two thousand years BC

An heir was vitally important to continue the family line and retain family and tribal property. When Abraham and Sara were childless, Eliezar, the household servant and a foreigner, was likely to be his adoptive heir; this was something Abraham lamented (Genesis 15:2,3). One solution was adoption. Another was to take a surrogate woman to provide an heir (16:1–4). It was often one of the household slaves, and this was the option Sarah suggested. She was following local custom, not the promise of God.

There are many surviving marriage contracts that allow for this, and ANE laws that controlled the treatment of such offspring. If subsequent children are born to the husband and wife, the surrogate child and its mother must be adequately cared for. The code of Hammurabi specifically guarded against the sale or dismissal of a surrogate mother (law 146) and if an adopted son was dismissed, he was entitled to one third share of the family inheritance (law 191). On the death of the father, 'the children of the first wife and the children of the slave shall share equally' in the inheritance, though the first born will have a preferential share (law 170).

A document from Mari, the capital of the Amorites at the time of Abraham, specifically stated that if the parents had more children, the adoptive son would be 'senior heir' with a double share of the inheritance and the other brothers to share the rest.

Abraham's reluctance for Sarah simply to dismiss Hagar and Ishmael was because he knew that he would be acting against custom (Genesis 21:8–11). He needed divine permission, and God would care for the mother and child (21:12–21). The narrative of Jacob, Rachel and Leah using Bilhah and Zilpah as surrogate mothers shows how common this practice was (Genesis 30).

This may seem strange to us, but 'The past is a foreign country; they do things differently there' [3]— but not necessarily as inappropriately as we imagine. In a different culture, the surrogate mother might consider it an honour, and in the best household would be well treated.

**Below**

*An Assyrian marriage contract, dated c. 2000 BC, between Laqipum and Hatala. The contract stipulates that if the couple cannot produce a child within the first two years of marriage, they will appoint a female slave as a surrogate*

57

---

3. The first line of L P Hartley's novel, *The Go-Between*.

# Musical Instruments in the Bible

**Archaeologists have found the remains of over four hundred individual instruments from ancient Israel which help us understand what they looked like and how they were played** [1]

Many different instruments are mentioned in the Bible and not all can be identified with certainty. Wind instruments were common, from the simple hollow bone used as a flute, to the mighty trumpet (*shofar*) which could be the hollow horn of a ram blown as a call to worship.

The flute was a simple instrument first mentioned in Genesis (Genesis 4:21) and eleven examples have been found from ancient Israel. What is called a 'pipe' may have been a flute with a reed. [2]

A trumpet was an important instrument used on the battlefield. Rather than modern brass instruments with valves, ancient trumpets were simple tubes of hammered metal. A number were found in the tomb of Tutankhamun by Howard Carter. See here page 141.

An important trumpet for ancient Israel was the shofar. This was a ram's horn blown as a call to worship (Leviticus 25:9). The priests would use this trumpet at the temple in Jerusalem (2 Chronicles 29:26). Archaeologists found the remains of a 'trumpeting stone' from the Herodian walls around the Temple from where instructions indicate a priest was to blow the shofar.

Percussion instruments include the tambourine, which Miriam played at the crossing of the Red

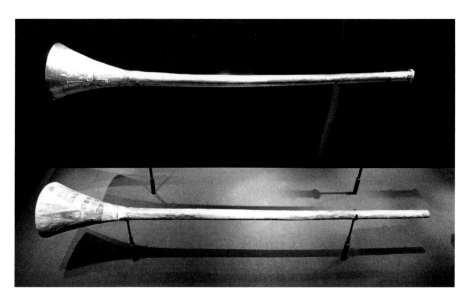

Sea (Exodus 15:20). The timbrel or tambourine was a hand-held frame drum. None of the ancient images show them with any metal bells or cymbals attached so that was probably a later development. A single reference in 2 Samuel 6:5 may be a 'sistrum' or could be a clay rattle of which many have been found in ancient Israel.

**Above**
*A silver trumpet from the Tomb of Tutankhamun along with a wooden core used to modulate the sound*

**Below**
*The large stone from the south west corner of the Temple Mount bearing a Hebrew inscription indicating that it was placed at the point where the priests would have blown the shofar*

1. Lawrence, Paul J. N., *Egg Whites or Turnips? Archaeology and Bible Translation* (Eugene, Oregon: Wipf & Stock). pp. 26–37.
2. Braun J., *Music in Ancient Israel/Palestine*, (Grand Rapids, MI: Eerdmans). p. 14.

# Make a Joyful Noise

**David is known as the 'sweet harpist of Israel' and stringed instruments were widely used across the ancient world**

Stringed instruments include the lyre (Genesis 4:21) and harp (1 Samuel 10:5). At the Royal Cemetery of Ur (see here page 138–139) nine lyres and three harps were recovered and these date to 2500 BC. In the Old Testament the Sea of Galilee is called the 'Kinneret' (Numbers 34:11).[3] This is thought to be related to the Hebrew word for a harp (*kinnor*) as the shape of the Sea of Galilee resembles this ancient instrument. This kind of 'harp' is probably just one form of lyre.

Lyres are depicted with different numbers of strings. The Royal Standard of Ur from 2500 BC shows a lyre with eleven strings, while the Beni Hasan tomb scene from 1800 BC depicts Semitic settlers arriving in Egypt with an eight-string lyre.

The lute was another form of stringed instrument. A clay plaque found at the Canaanite levels of Tel Dan show a dancing musician playing a lute.[4] It dates to the 14th century BC. An entire band is evident on a stand recovered from Philistine Ashdod. Clay figurines attached to it represent musicians playing double pipes, lyre, cymbals and tambourine.

Lists of instruments are found in 1 Chronicles 15:28 and Daniel 3:5 but some of these require translators to make educated guesses as to their identity.[5] Reference to 'bagpipes' in some translations of Daniel 3:5 is thought by some to be a kettle drum. David is described as having musical instruments made for temple worship (2 Chronicles 7:6) which may imply his personal involvement in their manufacture. Whatever forms they took, the diversity of instruments reflected the diversity of creation itself in bringing praise to God (Psalm 150).

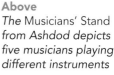

**Above**
*The* Musicians' Stand *from Ashdod depicts five musicians playing different instruments*

**Left**
*The Royal Standard of Ur includes a court musician playing a lyre c.2500 BC*

**Below left**
*Sennacherib's relief of the fall of Lachish includes Jewish prisoners playing on their lyres as they are taken into captivity. It is suggestive of the later captivity of the Jews in Babylon where their captors demanded that they play their harps for them (Psalm 137)*

3. In the New Testament this lies behind the Greek word, 'Gennesaret' (Luke 5:1).
4. Avraham Biran, 'The Dancer from Dan', *Near Eastern Archaeology*, Vol. 66: 3, Sep. 2003. pp. 128–133.
5. Paul J. N. Lawrence, *Egg Whites or Turnips? Archaeology and Bible Translation*, (Eugene, Oregon: Wipf & Stock). p. 26.

# Pilgrim Festivals

**The Jewish feasts and festivals of today have their origins in great events of the Old Testament and were fixed points in the annual calendar**

The three great pilgrim festivals in the Jewish calendar required a journey to Jerusalem to celebrate a significant moment in the story of the Exodus.

**The festival of Passover** (Hebrew *pesah*) was also known as the feast of unleavened bread and commemorates the time when God passed over the homes of the Israelites in Egypt but brought death to the firstborn in the land (Exodus 12). The event was so important that the month of Aviv, when Passover occurred, would be considered the first month of a new year. Aviv means 'ripening' and always coincides with spring when the barley was ready for harvest.

Fifty days after Passover came **the festival of Weeks** (*Shavuot* in Hebrew); it marked the time when the Israelites received the Ten Commandments in the wilderness. It would also coincide with the wheat harvest (Exodus 34:22). In Greek this festival is called Pentecost. Jesus was crucified at the time of Passover (Luke 22:7–8) and the Holy Spirit was poured out at the time of Pentecost (Acts 2:1).

After the grain harvests came the harvests of fruit and the last of these coincided with the **feast of Tabernacles** (*Sukkot* in Hebrew) which occurs around September/October. This commemorated the Israelites' time in the wilderness when they had to make shelters in the desert (Leviticus 23:42–43). In John 7:2 Jesus celebrated this festival.

Among the other festivals in the Jewish calendar were the **feast of Purim** (Assyrian *puru*), during February to March, which commemorated the protection of the people at the time of Esther, and the **festival of Lights** or Feast of Dedication in December (*Hanukkah* in Hebrew). Hanukkah commemorates an event that took place between the Old and New Testaments and is found in the historical books of Maccabees (in the *Apocrypha*) when the Jews rededicated the Temple to the Lord c.165 BC. Candles are lit at this time in remembrance of the menorah lampstand in the Temple. The New Testament records Jesus going to the Temple to celebrate this festival (John 10:22–23).

For Christian festivals see page 94.

**Above**
*The Magdala stone, discovered in 2009 in a 1st century synagogue, includes one of the earliest images of the Menorah which was associated with the Temple and Hanukkah*

**Below**
*Among the Elephantine Papyri is this earliest reference outside of the Bible to the instructions for the Passover meal. Dating to 419 BC it was discovered in Egypt in 1907*

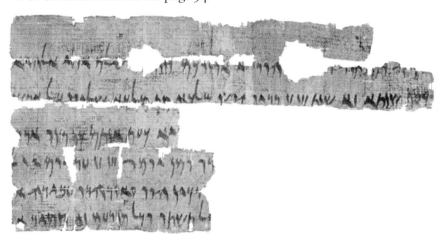

# Passover and the Lord's Supper

Christians continue to celebrate the Lord's Supper which has its origins in a Passover meal that Jesus shared with his disciples

**Left**
*A Roman period Triclinium, suitable for reclining guests at a banquet; this is possibly how Jesus was seated with his friends for the Last Supper (John 13:25). From a mosaic floor at Sepphoris, a significant city in 1st century Galilee*

All four gospels record Jesus sharing a last meal with his disciples before his arrest. Mark describes it as taking place 'On the first day of Unleavened Bread, when it was customary to sacrifice the Passover lamb' (Mark 14:12). The traditional view is that the Last Supper took place on Thursday evening, and some recognize a number of features of the meal that are at least reminiscent of a Jewish Passover—Joachim Jeremias notes fourteen parallels.[1]

However, the Gospel of John records that the crucifixion took place on the 'day of preparation of the Passover' (John 19:14), which suggests the last supper had taken place the evening before Passover.

Therefore, some suggest that the Last Supper was not a Passover meal and was held before this festival had begun.

The apparent discrepancy may be a result of two distinct religious calendars in use by the Jews. John, following the official calendar in Jerusalem, places the Last Supper before the Passover had begun. Matthew, Mark and Luke, following an older Jewish calendar that was still in use in Galilee and elsewhere, describe it as a Passover meal according to their calendar.[2] There is therefore no inconsistency if they are using different calendars.

Some, however, believe that the meal Jesus shared was deliberately held a day before the lambs would

be sacrificed. They notice that lamb, an essential element of a Passover meal, is not mentioned at the Last Supper, and that Jesus died at the very time the lambs were being sacrificed (John 19:31). Therefore, the Passover that Jesus shared with his friends was held 'the day *before* Passover was scheduled to be eaten, namely from sundown Thursday to sundown Friday.'[3]

Whatever and whenever the Last Supper was, it used elements of the traditional Passover meal. When Jesus spoke of his disciples eating his flesh and drinking his blood (John 6:54) it was a metaphor pointing to his role as the true Passover lamb (John 1:29).[4]

1. Joachim Jeremias, *The Eucharistic Words of Jesus*. (SCM Press, London:1967). pp. 41–62.
2. See *Evidence for the Bible* pp. 205–207 for a summary of the significant conclusions of Colin J. Humphreys, *The Mystery of the Last Supper*. (Cambridge University Press, 2011).
3. Ben Witherington III, *Making a Meal of It: Rethinking the Theology of the Lord's Supper*. (Baylor University Press, Waco, Texas 2007).
4. John Jacobs, *Around the Table of the King--Meditations on the communion service from a Jewish perspective* (Day One Publications 2021).

# The significance of Salt

**Salt was a valuable commodity in Bible times, and it is mentioned on over fifty occasions. It was more than simply a seasoning to flavour tasteless food**

**Left**
*The salt cliffs stretch up to seven miles along the coast of the Dead Sea and can reach 18m (60ft) in height*

Israel had a plentiful supply of rock salt from the cliffs to the south-west of the Dead Sea, an area associated with the judgement on Lot's wife (Genesis 19:26). Sometimes referred to as the 'Salt Sea' (Genesis 14:3; Deuteronomy 3:17), it is the deepest and saltiest salt lake in the world at 304m (997ft), and lies 430m (1,412ft) below sea level. It is approximately one third salt which is almost ten times as salty as the oceans. 1ltr (1.75pints) of water produces 250gr (0.55lbs) of salt.

Because of its preservative qualities (even new born infants were rubbed with salt–Ezekiel 16:4) it became a symbol for incorruptibility and purity. Salt was mixed with the sacrifices as a token of the pure and lasting covenant between God and his people Israel (Leviticus 2:13; Numbers 18:19; Ezekiel 43:24). A 'covenant of salt' referred to an enduring bond (2 Chronicles 13:5). This led rise to the phrase the 'salt of the covenant'; and 'to eat of his salt' was a sign of enduring friendship and peace. The literal phrase in Ezra 4:14 is 'because we eat the salt of the Palace'(ESV); it expressed a bond of loyalty to the king.

- In the Gospels, salt is used as a metaphor. It is a symbol of preservation from corruption, and Jesus warns his disciples against becoming tainted with the tastelessness and corruption of the world (Matthew 5:13).

- In the context of the disciples squabbling over who was the greatest, Jesus' reference to 'have salt in yourselves, and be at peace with one another' (Mark 9:50) refers to the need for humility and true friendship. A failure here means they lose their saltiness.

- The reference to being 'salted with fire' (Mark 9:49) refers back to the sacrifices which were accompanied with salt. The application is likely to refer to the necessity of sacrifice on the part of disciples (see vs 42–47).

- In the Greek and Latin world of Paul's day, salt (*sales*) was used metaphorically to refer to intellectual humour and sparkling wit that gave pleasure to life. [1] This easily degenerated into vulgar speech. In Colossians 4:6, Paul lifts it to a higher level of spiritual wisdom and Christian grace in place of pagan wit (compare Ephesians 5:4).

1. *Dictionary of the Apostolic Church*, ed. J Hastings (T and Clark, Edinburgh 1918) Vol.II p. 442.

# Unleavened bread

**The presence or absence of leaven (yeast) in bread-making was a significant part of the ceremonial worship of Israel and became a symbol of the spread of either evil or good**

Leaven was fermented dough (sour dough) that is used to infiltrate the whole batch as a raising agent for bread. It consists of minute living organisms of the yeast-fungi and was made from bran, barley or from certain plants; mixed with water it was left to turn sour. A small amount of this yeast was sufficient to permeate the whole batch. This was 'leavened' bread.

The week commencing the Passover was called 'the days of unleavened bread' (Matthew 26:17) and is based on the command in Exodus 12:8, 17–20; 23:15 and Leviticus 23:6. All leaven was removed from their homes, and during the week of the Passover only cakes of unleavened bread could be used.

This was a perpetual reminder of the haste with which Israel left slavery in Egypt, with no time to prepare their bread and carrying their kneading bowls with them (Exodus 12:34). But because leaven was the result of decay, it was not used in the blood sacrifices (Leviticus 10:12), although, as one of God's good gifts, it was included in the thank offerings (Leviticus 7:13; 23:16–17; Amos 4:5).

The fermentation process was regarded as a form of decay. Plutarch, the Greek philosopher born around AD 40 wrote: 'Yeast is itself also the product of corruption, and produces corruption in the dough with which it is mixed... altogether the process of leavening seems to be one of putrefaction.'[2] This, together with its permeation of the whole dough, explains Jesus expression 'leaven of the Pharisees and Sadducees'—a reference to their corrupt teaching and hypocrisy (Matthew 16:6–12; Luke 12:1), and similarly of Herod (Mark 8:15).

Paul twice quotes a popular saying 'a little yeast works through the whole batch of dough' (Galatians 5:9), and in 1 Corinthians 5:6–8 Christians are encouraged to celebrate Christ their Passover lamb by replacing the leaven of 'malice and wickedness' with the unleavened bread 'of sincerity and truth'.

Positively, in Matthew 13:33 Jesus compares the permeating effect of yeast to the influence of the Kingdom of God upon the whole of society.

**Above**
*Today Jews eat the Matzah (unleavened bread) in their annual Passover celebration*

2. Plutarch *Quaestiones Romanae* (Roman Questions) 109. ed. Frank Cole Babbitt.

# 'To this day'

**The critical view that the entire 'story' of Israel from Genesis to the division of the monarchy under Rehoboam (1 Kings 12) was invented to give the Jews a 'history', lacks any credible evidence**

**Left**
*Rachel's tomb in the 1930s. It has been restored today, but there is little certainty that it is the correct site; the earliest record identifying it comes from the early 4th century AD*

On the contrary, there are many indications that the records were written close to the time of the events described.[1] The expression 'to this day' occurs around fifty times in the Old Testament and refers to something that was still present at the time of writing. For example:

- Rahab, rewarded with her life and that of her family after the fall of Jericho, 'has lived in Israel *to this day*' (Joshua 6:25). Possibly as early as 1400 BC.

- About the same time, Joshua 15:63 records that the tribe of Judah could not dislodge the Jebusites from Jerusalem and that '*to this day* the Jebusites live there with the people of Judah.' This must have been recorded before 1004 BC when David made Jerusalem his capital (2 Samuel 5:6–9 and 1 Chronicles 11:4–8).

- When Solomon housed the Ark of the Covenant in the temple, the carrying poles that fitted into the four corner rings were so long that their ends could be seen protruding from the Holy Place in front of the inner sanctuary. The detail 'and *they are still there today*' (1 Kings 8:8) could never have been added after 587 BC when the Babylonians totally destroyed the temple in Jerusalem, after which nothing more is known for certain of the Ark.[2]

- In 1 Kings 12:19 we read that from the division of the monarchy in the time of Rehoboam (930 BC), 'Israel has been in rebellion against the house of David *to this day*.' This must have been recorded before the year 722 BC when the northern territory of Israel was conquered by Assyria and ceased to exist as a separate nation—two hundred years before the supposed scribal forger in the mid-sixth century.

Either these details are the work of brilliant forgers, unlike any known ancient writer of history, or they are the careful records of contemporary events.

---

1. See also here pages 18–19 for Egyptian and Persian loan words demonstrating the same point.

# Monuments

**There are at least nine monuments for sites of significance in Israel that were still visible in the writers' day**

**Monuments with meaning**
Rachel's tomb (Genesis 35:20); the monument for crossing the River Jordan (Joshua 4:9); the pile of stones over Achan's burial (Joshua 7:26); the cave of the five entombed kings (Joshua 10:27); Gideon's altar at Ophrah (Judges 6:24); the rock commemorating the return of the Ark (1 Samuel 6:18); Absalom's monument to himself (2 Samuel 18:18); the Field of Blood (Matthew 27:8); and the tomb of David (Acts 2:29). None of these can be certainly identified today but they must have been clearly visible at the time the records were written.

Eight hundred years later these monuments would have long disappeared. We know how quickly whole cities of the past were buried under the sands. The vast city of Nineveh was destroyed by Babylon in 612 BC. The 'palace without equal'—with over 70 rooms, library of some 30,000 clay tablets and almost eight miles miles of city walls—all crumbled into the desert. Within two hundred years virtually nothing above ground was visible. It remained like this until the archaeologist, Austen Henry Layard, discovered it in 1847.

In addition, there are some fifteen changed place names where the new name is still used 'to this day'. Each one is an example of a near-contemporary recording of the events.

**The destruction of Ai**
Joshua destroyed the city of Ai and intended it to be 'a permanent heap of ruins, a desolate place *to this day*' (Joshua 8:28). However, by the time of the Babylonian conquest eight hundred years later, the city had been rebuilt because Jeremiah warned of its destruction yet again (Jeremiah 49:3). No sixth century scribe would have invented Joshua 8:28 when he knew that the city had been rebuilt.

**A monument of nonsense?**
Amusing, and apparently irrelevant, is the comment in Deuteronomy 3:11 that Og king of Bashan slept on a super king-size bed made of iron; it was 4 m (13 ft) long and 1.8 m (6 ft) wide and 'is still in Rabbah of the Ammonites'! Its relevance is precisely to authenticate a contemporary record. At the time it was a humorous marvel that was talked about far and wide. However, half a millennium later who would either know or care about Og's bed?

**Right**
*Nineveh was uncovered in 1847 by Austen Henry Layard and this picture shows how entirely a great city can soon be lost*

# Light on the detail

**Through the Bible there are many incidental references that may not transfer meaning to a modern reader**

**B**oundaries and battles
'Do not move your neighbour's boundary stone set up by your predecessors...' (Deuteronomy 19:14).

The boundary stone is referred to on at least six occasions in the Old Testament. It marked the boundary of the owner's land, and to move it was an act of theft. Deuteronomy 27:17 pronounces a curse on anyone who moves a boundary stone. Most ancient boundary stones, like the one here, have been discovered in temples, the bank vault of the day, and they too call vengeance from the gods on this theft. Possibly the site was marked with a cheaper terracotta copy.

'As soon as David returned from killing the Philistine, Abner took him and brought him before Saul, with David still holding the Philistine's head' (1 Samuel 17:57).

This is not simply a grizzly addition to spice up the account. In ancient warfare the only way to identify a defeated warrior was to present his head. There are other references to this, for example 1 Samuel 31:9 and 2 Samuel 20:21. The image from ancient Nineveh shows an Assyrian soldier rewarded for his success in battle, proved by the heads of his slain

The Philistines were constant enemies of Israel: '**In still another battle, which took place at Gath, there was a huge man with six fingers on each hand and six toes on each foot**' (2 Samuel 21:20). Unusual? Interestingly this coffin lid from Philistine territory in the time of the Judges, around the 13th century BC, shows a Philistine with six fingers on his left hand!

'Joshua, summoned all the men of Israel and said to the army commanders who had come with him, "Come here and put your feet on the necks of these kings"' (Joshua 10:24).

A common act of a triumphant commander or king was to stand with his feet on the neck of his defeated enemy. In this wall relief of Tiglath Pileser III of Assyria (744–727 BC) his foot is on the neck of King Hanunu of Gaz.

'Taking one of the stones there, Jacob put it under his head and lay down to sleep' (Genesis 28:11).

In a hot and dry climate, keeping the head off the ground would allow a free circulation of air and also keep the ears and hair free from insects. There are many examples from the ancient world made from wood, ivory and stone.

## Bricks, bullae, and beds

'You are no longer to supply the people with straw for making bricks; let them go and gather their own straw' (Exodus 5:7).

Bricks made with mud from the River Nile or desert clay were the primary building material for houses throughout Egyptian history; they were also used alongside stone in tombs and temples. Straw was essential to bind the mud together and the bricks were left in the sun to bake hard. Mud bricks were economical, easy to use and could be incredibly long lasting. Some of the oldest in Egypt are found at the royal burial sites at Abydos where massive mudbrick walls date to 3,000 BC.

Bricks like these from Luxor are still used today and show the straw binding the mud together.

'Your seal and its cord, and the staff in your hand' (Genesis 38:18).

A common seal in the ancient world was carved onto a stone and pressed into soft clay to create the impression. The impression is known as a *bulla* (pl. *bullae*).[1] A seal was similar to the ID or visa card of today. Another form was carved onto a cylinder of stone or calcite and then rolled over the soft clay. This cylinder seal would have a hole bored through the centre so that it could be threaded with a cord for a 'necklace' for safety. When Tamar, disguised as a prostitute, demanded payment for her liaison with Judah, she was accepting his ID to ensure against future repayment.

In some cases, it also protected an elaborate hair style and even carried mystic symbolism. The young Pharaoh Tutankhamun was buried with eight headrests and the one illustrated here is ivory and depicts the god Shu supporting the king's head.

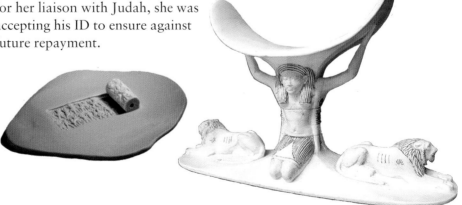

1. See *Evidence for the Bible* pp. 53,69,86,87 for many examples of this. See also here pages 41–43 for more seals.

# More light on the detail

**B**eauty
'They made the bronze basin and its bronze stand from the mirrors of the women who served at the entrance to the Tent of Meeting' (Exodus 38:8).

Before glass, mirrors were highly polished brass, like this one illustrated from Egypt. The bronze mirrors that the Israelite women donated for the basin of ceremonial washing at the tabernacle, probably came from among the items given by the Egyptians as Israel escaped slavery (Exodus 12:36).

**'Jezebel ... painted her eyes, arranged her hair and looked out of a window'** (2 Kings 9:30).

Egyptian men and women both used cosmetics, deodorants and perfumes (including eye-shadow, rouge and lipstick) together with lavish jewelry. God drew attention to this shameless obsession in Jerusalem (Isaiah 3:16–23). This Egyptian lady is dated around AD 60–70. Doubtless Joseph confronted Potiphar's wife like this (Genesis 39:6–7).

A beautiful woman with '**a neck like the tower of David... like an ivory tower**' (Song of Songs 4:4 and 7:4) was a serious compliment. A long, slender neck was considered graceful. An Egyptian love poem refers to 'lovely of eyes when she glances ... *Long of neck*, white of breast.' [2] Such a neck would be adorned with jewellery. The statue of the Mari fertility goddess illustrates the decorated neck, and Nefertiti, the Egyptian beauty and queen of Amenhotep IV (Akhenaten), is depicted with a long slender neck (opposite page).

The extravagant 'metaphorical comparisons' in the love poems of Song of Songs are not descriptive but evocative of what is considered best and beautiful. See especially 4:1–7 and 7:1–9. There is a connection, a bond, between the metaphor and the reality, but it is not direct. The metaphor suggests a concept; so, 'Your teeth are like a flock of sheep just shorn, coming up from the washing. Each has its twin; not one of them is alone' (4:2), refers partly to whiteness but chiefly to everything perfect and in place: 'a peaceful, fruitful world, resplendent with the blessings of nature... ewes, white and clean, bear twins and never miscarry.' Similarly from Egypt: 'Her hair is true lapis lazuli, her arm surpasses gold' are expressions of the 'girl's loveliness and preciousness.' [3]

2. An Egyptian love poem, Song of Seven, 31, stanza I.
3. Michael V. Fox 'Love, Passion, and Perception in Israelite and Egyptian love poetry' (The *Journal of Biblical Literature* 1983 pp. 225–228). A helpful article on understanding the imagery of the Song of Songs.

## Birthing

'When you help the Hebrew women in childbirth and observe them on the delivery stool, if it is a boy, kill him; but if it is a girl, let her live' (Exodus 1:16).

The 'birthing stool' has been known across the world from ancient times; the earliest is found in the 'birthing house' in Luxor c.1450 BC which is close to the time of Moses. The illustration (far right) is from the temple of Kom Ombo in Upper Egypt; the temple was built in the 2nd century BC, much later than Moses. The value of a woman giving birth in a more upright position and also taking advantage of gravity, has experienced a resurgence in recent years.

## Barrenness

'When Rachel saw that she was not bearing Jacob any children… she said to Jacob, "Give me children, or I'll die!"' (*Genesis 30:1*)

This cry from Rachel led a 3rd century AD Jewish teacher to claim, 'Any person who does not have children is considered like a dead person… Four are considered as if they were dead: A pauper, a leper, a blind person, and one who has no children.' [4] To be without children was regarded as being less than a complete human; and it was considered a sign of divine displeasure. In Luke 1:25 Elizabeth described her barrenness as a 'disgrace'; the same word is used for an 'insult' in Matthew 27:44. Compare 1 Samuel 1:5–7. Among prayers and curses in the ancient world, fertility and infertility are some of the most frequent. A 'closed womb' was God's judgment on Abimelech's household (Genesis 20:18).

In Proverbs 30:16 the barren womb is compared to the grave and dry ground that are never satisfied. However, Isaiah 54:1 looks to the future when the barren woman can rejoice in the glory of the redeemed.

## Beards

'When Joseph had shaved and changed his clothes, he came before Pharaoh' (Genesis 41:14).

As a matter of religious purity, cleanliness, and avoiding lice, the Egyptians were unusual in the ancient world for shaving off all bodily hair and replacing it with elaborate false wigs and beards. For the poor, a pumice stone was used to rub off stubble! Royalty and the elite could afford a bronze razor, like the one here from 14th century Egypt. The Royal palace was a temple and to approach Pharaoh one had to be ritually pure. Compare Numbers 8:6–7 for the Israelite priests. [5]

4. Joshua ben Levi, *Nedarim* 64b.
5. See Lisbeth S Fried, 'Why did Joseph shave?' (*Biblical Archaeology Review* July/August 2007).

# Development of the Chariot

**Chariots are often mentioned in the Old Testament and we can compare the rise and fall of their use in the Ancient Near East with their appearances in the biblical text**

The earliest chariots were heavy wagons built by the Sumerians (around 2500 BC). A fine image of one appears on the royal mosaic known as the 'Standard of Ur'. It shows an armoured wagon, with a shield at the front, and a holder for spears. With four solid wheels and drawn by donkeys, they had poor maneuverability and therefore limited use in battle.

By 1700 BC chariots had developed into a more effective weapon of war with the use of spoked wheels and the domestication of horses. A ceremonial example of a lightweight, fast moving Egyptian chariot was found in the tomb of Tutankhamun. Joseph could have ridden in an earlier version of such a chariot when they were first introduced to Egypt (Genesis 41:43).

The Egyptians and Canaanites both deployed chariots against the Israelites. Pharaoh sent out his 600 'best chariots' along with the rest of his chariot force (Exodus 14:7), and Jabin, King of Hazor, deployed 900 'iron chariots' under Sisera's command against the Israelites (Judges 4:3). The Israelites were militarily at a disadvantage in these conflicts, but the natural environment is used against the chariots. The wheels of Pharaoh's chariots grounded in the seabed and the chariots were washed

**Above**
*A chariot from the tomb of Tutankhamun c.1300 BC*

**Right**
*A scene from the Standard of Ur c. 2600 BC*

away (Exodus 14:25); Sisera's chariots were lured into mountainous territory where they were unstable and abandoned (Judges 4:15).

The Philistines dominated the coastal plain with their two-man chariots (1 Samuel 13:5) and the Bible refers to the advantage chariots give when fighting 'on the plains' (1 Kings 20:25).

During Solomon's monarchy there was a large investment in developing a chariot army (1 Kings 10:26), including imported chariots from Egypt (2 Chronicles 1:17). The Kurkh Stela of the Assyrians from 853 BC refers to King Ahab of Israel having 2000 chariots.[1] An example of an Israelite chariot is seen on the Lachish relief where it is among the Assyrian plunder.[2]

1. See *Evidence for the Bible* pp. 50–51.
2. David Ussishkin, *The Conquest of Lachish by Sennacherib*, (Tel Aviv: Tel Aviv University, 1982).

# Decline of the Chariot

**Chariots are referred to in the New Testament but their function as weapons of war had already been in decline and they are simply a means of transport for the wealthy**

The numbers of Israelite chariots towards the close of the Old Testament had shrunk dramatically to a mere ten (2 Kings 13:7). The Israelites had been defeated and their military capacity declined. Chariots were being replaced by the use of cavalry. Wagons were no match for riders on horseback able to use the composite bow. The last known historical reference to a chariot battle was between Alexander and the Persians at the Battle of Gaugamela in 331 BC.

In 55 BC Julius Caesar noted that the Celts of Britain still used chariots in combat even though they had fallen into disuse in Gaul.[3] For warfare, the Romans proved that chariots could not defeat disciplined foot soldiers and well-trained cavalry. The Romans retained them for sport. At Caesarea Maritima, near to the palace of Pontius Pilate, archaeologists found a hippodrome (Latin for 'horse-course') that Herod had built for the dangerous sport of chariot racing. See here page 173.

The chariot in which the Ethiopian eunuch was travelling (Acts 8:28) was probably a single axle *carpentum* with a covered roof. It was a status symbol to ride in one, used by officials and even the emperor. As such, it would have been fitting for the treasurer of the queen of the Ethiopians; it would not have travelled at much speed and therefore it was easy for Philip to catch up with on foot (Acts 8:30).

**Above**
*Lachish Relief Panel showing an Israelite chariot being removed by the Assyrian army c.700 BC*

**Below**
*A Carpentum on a coin of Livia, wife of Augustus, c. AD 22, of the style probably used by the Ethiopian Eunuch*

3. Julius Caesar, *Gallic Wars*, IV.33.

# David and Goliath

**Recent excavations at Khirbet Qeiyafa are bringing not only the period of King Saul to light but details of narratives like David's confrontation with Goliath[1]**

**Left**
*The foundations of Khirbet Qeiyafa's western Gate, one of the city's two gateways*

Khirbet Qeiyafa is located a day's walk from Jerusalem at the Elah Valley. Excavations from 2007 to 2013 have shown an intense period of settlement during a relatively brief period during the time of the early Israelite monarchy. [2]

The Elah Valley is the strategic place where David confronted Goliath when Saul was at war with the Philistines. In the aftermath of the battle the Biblical text describes the dead as 'strewn along the Shaaraim road to Gath and Ekron.' (1 Samuel 17:52). The reference to 'Shaarim' had been obscure until discoveries at Khirbet Qeiyafa. [3]

Khirbet Qeiyafa is a relatively small site with two levels of occupation. One is from the period after the close of the Old Testament. But beneath those later remains, archaeologists found a single but impressive period of occupation from around 1020–980 BC. Carbon dating, pottery remains, and associated artefacts made this a secure date. During the time of Saul and David this was an occupied, fortified settlement.

There is a substantial 'casemate' wall, non-Philistine pottery (including 693 impressed jar handles) and, very importantly, an absence of any pig bones. Pork was popular among the Philistines and Canaanites, and its absence is an indicator that people of Judah lived here.

One of the major discoveries at Khirbet Qeiyafa are two massive gateways. Gates are the weakest points in fortified walls and so these are unusual and unique for the time. One gate opens to the west and one to the south. An explanation for the two gateways is because of its strategic position for the Israelites. One gate gave access to the road to Jerusalem the other controls the road from Philistine territory. This unusual feature also helps us understand the reference to the 'Shaaraim road' referred to in the narrative of Goliath (1 Samuel 17:52); the Hebrew word probably means 'Two Gates'. Archaeologist Yosef Garfinkel has suggested that Khirbet Qeiyafa was the Shaaraim of the Biblical narrative.

---

1. See pp.78–79 for a likely identification of Goliath's city of Gath.
2. *Debating Khirbet Qeiyafa: A Fortified City in Judah from the time of King David*, Yosef Garfinkel, Igor Kreimerman, and Peter Zilberg, Israel Exploration Society: The Hebrew University of Jerusalem, 2016.
3. See also *Evidence for the Bible* pp. 40–41.

# The Rise of the Monarchy

**Artefacts from Khirbet Qeiyafa may provide a direct connection to the early development of the monarchy, the Hebrew script, and Solomon's Temple**

One of the most significant finds from Khirbet Qeiyafa is possibly the earliest Hebrew text ever discovered. On a broken piece of pottery (ostracon) are five lines of writing. [4] Although its meaning is still unclear, it appears to include the Hebrew words 'judge', 'king', and 'widow'. Some scholars are more cautious, pointing out that while containing Semitic names, it is not clear that it is a Hebrew text at all. The writing is poor and some illegible. Alan Millard concludes that it only establishes 'that someone was writing a document of several lines with pen and ink in Israel at a time from which no other examples had been known.' [5]

Since its discovery, a further inscription has been discovered at Khirbet Qeiyafa in 2012. Incised on a pottery storage jar is the name 'Eshbaal son of Beda'. This is also the name of a son of Saul (1 Chronicles 8:33) showing it is an appropriate name for the period.

In keeping with these texts and associated remains, the site is now identified as part of the Kingdom of Judah and demonstrates some kind of central town planning at the time of Saul and David.

One further recent find is shedding more light on the period of Israel's united monarchy. In 2011 broken fragments of a model

temple were found in a building that had some religious function. When carefully reassembled they were found to be a 35cm high stone box structure. A façade was carved on one side of the box to resemble a doorway with recessed frames, roof beams and painted red. Two small holes had been drilled into the box to allow an opening door to be fitted to it. There are a number of remarkable ways in which this model is suggestive of King

Solomon's building programme. The temple's 'narrow windows with recessed frames' (1 Kings 6:4) fits well with the model. Solomon's palace was built with the wooden planks arranged in groups of three (1 Kings 7:3). Garfinkel notes, 'The stone model temple from Khirbet Qeiyafa and the biblical description of Solomon's palace are the earliest examples known to us of an organization of roof beams in groups of three.' [6]

**Left**
*The Stone Temple model found at Khirbet Qeiyafa c 10th Century BC*

4. See *Evidence for the Bible* p. 41 for a picture of this.
5. Alan Millard, 'Is the Bible Fake News?', *Perspectives* 68, Spring 2020, pp. 36–37.
6. Yosef Garfinkel and Madeleine Mumcuoglu, *Solomon's Temple and Palace*, Biblical Archaeology Society, 2016, p. 96.

# Inscriptions of Hebrew kings

**The ancient kings of Israel and Judah have sometimes been dismissed as figures of later fiction. However, archaeology has increasingly identified evidence for the historical existence of these rulers**

Over 50 different personalities from the Old Testament alone have been confirmed from ancient sources outside of the Bible.[1] Among those are some of the leaders of ancient Israel. This is a remarkable number given how fragmentary are our records of the ancient world and how many of these examples come from enemies of the ancient Hebrews. The following Kings of Israel have their names included on contemporary inscriptions from the Ancient Near East.

## Kings of Israel in the north

- **Omri** c.885–874 BC (1 Kings 16:16), is mentioned on the Moabite Stone.[2] Having moved the capital of the northern kingdom of Israel to Samaria his dynasty is acknowledged in a number of other sources outside the Bible.

- **Ahab** c.874–853 BC (1 Kings 16:28), is given attention on the limestone Kurkh monolith of Shalmaneser III of Assyria. This standing stone, bearing the image of the Assyrian King, describes his victories in battle, including his defeat of a coalition of kings of which he names the Israelite King Ahab as one.[3]

- **Jehu**, c.841–814 BC (1 Kings 19:16), is not only named on the Black Obelisk of Shalmaneser but it has an image of him or his representative appearing before the Assyrian King.[4] Jehu is also mentioned in Assyrian annals and on the Kurba'il Statue of Shalmaneser III.[5]

- **Jehoash**, c.798–782 BC (2 Kings 13:9), appears on the Tell al-Rimah inscription of Adad-Nirari III.[6]

- **Menahem**, c.752–742 BC (2 Kings 15:14), **Pekah**, c.740–732 BC (2 Kings 15:25) and **Hoshea** c.732–733 BC (2 Kings 15:30) are all mentioned on a stela of Tiglath-Pileser of Assyria.

**Left**
*The Kurba'il Statue of Shalmaneser III records his victory over Hazael, the King of Damascus, along with King Jehu's tribute from Israel*

**Above**
*The Stela of Adad-nirari III from Tell al-Rimah refers to Jehoash 'the Samarian' who paid tribute to Assyria. Samaria was the capital of Israel*

1. Lawrence Mykytiuk, 'Archaeology Confirms 50 Real People in the Bible', *Biblical Archaeology Review*, March/April 2014. In *BAR* May/June he added three more.
2. See *Evidence for the Bible* p. 36.
3. T. C. Mitchell, *The Bible in the British Museum*, pp. 49–50 and *Evidence for the Bible* p. 51.
4. See *Evidence for the Bible* p. 52.
5. Mordechai Cogan, *The Raging Torrent: Historical Inscriptions from Assyria and Babylonia Relating to Ancient Israel*. (Carta Jerusalem 2016). 2nd ed.p. 28.
6. *The Raging Torrent*, pp 39–41.

# Kings of Judah in the south

**Later kings of Judah are mentioned directly in contemporary inscriptions by enemy nations but there are even possible references to earlier kings in the archaeological record**

**D**avid 1010–971 BC. Any inscriptions from the period of the united monarchy are rare. However, the dynasty of King David is directly referred to in 800 BC on the Tel Dan inscription and probably on the Moabite Stone.[7]

An Egyptian reference to King David is possibly found on a temple wall at Karnak from the tenth century BC. A military campaign by Pharaoh Shishak (1 Kings 14:25) may refer to King David's territory as the 'heights of David'.[8]

**Solomon** 970–930 BC. *So far* there is no clear extra-biblical reference to King Solomon, but there are few extra-biblical sources from this period to draw upon. In the words of one scholar of the period, Egyptian records are limited, Babylon was 'in eclipse', and Assyria 'equally silent'.[9]

- **Ahaz** c.732–716 BC (2 Kings 15:38), appears in a list of kings paying tribute to Assyria.[10] The Bible gives his abbreviated name while the Assyrian inscription gives his full name 'Jehoahaz' which means 'Yahweh has held'.

- **Hezekiah** c.716–687 BC (2 Kings 16:20), is mentioned numerous times in Assyrian sources including the Taylor Prism which describes him trapped 'like a caged bird' during King Sennacherib's siege of Jerusalem c.701 BC.[11]

- **Manasseh** c.687–642 BC (2 Kings 20:21), is acknowledged by two Assyrian Kings, Ashurbanipal and Esarhaddon, as having paid them tribute.[12]

- **Jehoiachin** c.597 BC (2 Kings 24:6), is referred to four times in contemporary Babylonian sources including a tablet describing the rations permitted to him during the exile.[13]

**Above**
*The Tel Dan Inscription that refers to 'the House of David' in Aramaic, less than two hundred years after his death*

**Below**
*Tiglath Pileser III of Assyria stands over King Hanunu of Gaza. The inscriptions above list his defeated enemies. It is from inscriptions like this that we read the names of some of the Hebrew kings. From the Central Palace at Nimrud*

75

7. *Evidence for the Bible* pp. 36–37
8. Kenneth A. Kitchen, *On the Reliability of the Old Testament*, p. 93.
9. Alan Millard, 'Texts and Archaeology: Weighing the Evidence. The Case for King Solomon', *Palestine Exploration Quarterly* (January-June 1991) pp. 19–27.
10. *The Raging Torrent*, pp. 58–59.
11. *Evidence for the Bible* p. 75.
12. R. Campbell Thompson, *The Prisms of Esarhaddon and Ashurbanipal* (London: Trustees of the British Museum, 1931), p. 25.
13. *The Raging Torrent*, p. 209. See also *Evidence for the Bible* p. 82 for a picture of this ration list.

# Key stones

**The Temple of Solomon was built with great stones cut and 'dressed' at the quarry; Christians are described as living stones bult into a holy temple**

**Left**
The dressed cornerstone is seen here on the Temple Mount in Jerusalem

**Right**
*Illustrations of the cornerstone, keystone (from Nimrud) and capstone. The capstone is called a Pyramidion when used to complete a Pyramid*

Dressing the stone refers to preparing and shaping each block for its specific location. It is known as an *ashlar*. This takes great skill and care and every stone for the Temple of Solomon was uniquely prepared at the quarry (1 Kings 6:7). Christians are prepared by God the Holy Spirit to fit into Jesus' spiritual building—his church (1 Peter 2:5).

Two main stones are referred to in the Bible. The **Cornerstone** (Greek: *akrogonaios*) is literally the chief stone lying at an angle to the two walls that it binds together. It is vital for the strength and security of the whole structure. In Ephesians 2:20, Paul uses the cornerstone (*akrogonaios*) as a vivid picture of

Christ who, as Paul's context makes clear (vs 14–22), binds both Jew and Gentile together in one firm building, the church. This perfect stone was placed on one corner of the building and all measurements and levels were related back to it. In the same way, all beliefs and practices must be related back to and taken from Christ (1 Peter 2:6).

The **Capstone and Keystone** (Greek: *kephale gōnias* literally the head or chief stone at an angle). It is the stone that completes a wall or an arch, binding it together. The Hebrew and Greek use the same word for both. Today some building sites conclude with a 'topping out' ceremony, and this is reflected in Zechariah 4:7 when the capstone is laid; it signified that the building was ready for occupation. A prophetic image of the Lord

Jesus, who makes his people presentable, and he is their security.

In Romans 9:33 Paul combines both Isaiah 8:14 and 28:16 to show Christ as the stone (Greek: *lithos*) of stumbling for many and the rock (Greek: *petra*) over which men fall, but the one who is utterly trustworthy for those who believe.

### Praising stones [1]

As Jesus and the crowd were descending the Mount of Olives, directly in front of them would have been the beautiful Second Temple rebuilt by Herod. The Temple was the place of praise, worship and devotion to God. Jesus answered the accusation of the Pharisees that if the crowds fell silent even the stones would cry out (Luke 19:40). As he died on the cross, we read that great rocks (*petra*) cracked apart (Matthew 27:51).

1. Note that Standing Stones and Boundary Stones are described in *Evidence for the Bible* pp. 30–31.

# Peter and the Rock

**When Jesus gave both Peter and his testimony of faith a new name, it is not surprising this influenced his preaching and writing**

'Peter' was not a Jewish name and it does not appear as a personal name at all until the Christian era. Jesus gave his disciple Simon the nickname *kepha* (cephas) in Aramaic, which means a rock, and this translates as *petros* in Greek (John 1:42).[2]

In addition to the Greek word *lithos* (the general word for a stone, large or small), two significant words are used to distinguish between a large rock or boulder (*petros*) and a solid rock mass (*petra*, see the rock cut tomb of Matthew 27:60 and the split rocks of Matthew 27:51). The clear distinction Jesus made in Matthew 16:18 is intended. Peter is given the nickname *petros*, a strong boulder, but his testimony of Jesus as the Messiah is the *petra*, bedrock of the Gospel.[3]

That Peter appreciated this distinction is clear from his preaching and writing. Before the Sanhedrin (Acts 4:11) and in his first letter, Peter quoted Psalm 118:22 referring to Jesus as the rejected capstone (*kephale gōnias*).

In 1 Peter 2:4–8 Jesus is the 'living stone' (*lithos zōnta* v 4) and so are his people (v 5); they are built into a spiritual house (the church).

Jesus is the stone laid in Zion as the cornerstone (*akrogonaios* v 6), chosen and precious. This is clearly a reference to Isaiah 28:16 where the precious cornerstone is 'a sure foundation'. This stone (*lithos*) that the builders (ie the unbelieving Jews) rejected, has become the capstone (*kephale gōnias* v.7). And 'a stone (*lithos*) that causes men to stumble and a rock (*petra* v 8)) that makes them fall'.

Peter would have remembered that Jesus applied the capstone (*kephale gōnias*) of Psalm 118:22 to himself in his parable of the tenant farmers (Matthew 21:42).

**Above**
*A reconstructed tomb at Nazareth Village in Israel. It provides a good image of how graves were cut into the rock (petra) and a rolling stone (petros) guarded the entrance*

---

2. The single reference to a Peter in Jewish inscriptions comes from the 5th century when a Papario, son of Olympius the Jew converted to Christianity and adopted the name Petros: *The Book of Acts in its First century Setting* (The Paternoster Press, Carlisle 1995). Vol 4 p. 104.
3..This was understood by most of the early church Fathers during the first few centuries, including Augustine in his *Retractations* 1:21. He wrote, '"Thou art *Petrus*, and on this *petra* I will build my church", must be understood of him whom Peter confessed as Son of the living God.'

# Gath and the Philistines

## Archaeology has recently revealed much more of the culture and presence of the Philistines in the land of Israel

There is some uncertainty over their origins, although it is clear that the Philistines were seafaring people from Crete (Amos 9:7), Cyprus, and other islands of the Aegean.[1] A great deal is now understood about the Philistines as they came to occupy the Mediterranean coastline of Israel. The cities of Ashkelon, Ashdod and Ekron all referred to in the Old Testament have been located.

More recently, excavations at Tell es-Safi have identified the site as biblical Gath, the hometown of Goliath. An extensive city has been found, with Philistine cultural remains, such as pottery, appropriate burial customs and the use of metal, dating to the time of King David. Remains from this time have revealed exceptionally large fortifications built with huge stones.

Archaeologists have found massive trenches that demonstrate a costly siege took place during the 9th century BC. This may be the remains of the Aramean siege of Gath described in 2 Kings 12:17. The city had been even larger in an earlier period, and the Bible notes that the Philistines had brought advanced knowledge of metallurgy to the land in the time of Saul (1 Samuel 13:19–21). Excavations have also found a temple and a two horned altar of the Philistines.

In 2005 archaeologists discovered an inscription dating around the mid-10th century BC, when the Bible claims David fought against Goliath. On a broken pottery shard two names have been scratched using the Semitic alphabet but in the Philistine language. Both names are similar to 'Goliath'. Aren Maeir, the director of the excavations, does not claim that the inscription refers to the Goliath of the biblical narrative, but points out that it does demonstrate that at the time there were people there named Goliath and that the account reflects the cultural reality of the period.[2]

**Above**
*Inscribed 7cm long shard of pottery from Tel es-Safi (Gath), bearing Semitic letters AWLT and WLT, which may represent two Philistine words similar to the original name of Goliath*

**Top and opposite**
*On-going excavations at Tel es-Safi revealing massive monumental building works*

1. *Evidence for the Bible* p. 35.
2. 'Gath Inscription Evidences Philistine Assimilation'. *Biblical Archaeology Review*, March-April 2006, p. 16.

# 'Tell it not in Gath'

Ziklag is a significant location for Biblical history because David used it as a base for sixteen months when he took refuge from King Saul (1 Samuel 27:1–7)

In 1993 an article in the *Biblical Archaeology Review* stated 'Thus far, modern scholarship's search for Ziklag has been unsuccessful.'[3] However, in 2015 Yosef Garfinkel began excavations at Khirbet a-Ra'i and now believes that he has found enough evidence to suggest this could be identified with biblical Ziklag.

The excavations are at a site 43 miles south west of Jerusalem. Beneath a 10th century BC rural settlement with evidence of Jewish presence, were the remains of a Philistine town occupied from 12th to 11th centuries BC. Archaeologists have found a structure with 1.5-meter-wide walls, along with stone and metal tools similar to finds from the known Philistine cities of Ashdod, Ashkelon, Ekron and Gath.

The transition from Philistine culture to a Jewish settlement in the 10th century BC would fit the period described in the Bible. Khirbet a-Ra'i even has a destruction layer of fire that dates to c.1000 BC and that could be evidence for the Amalekite raid on Ziklag (1 Samuel 30:1).

It was at Ziklag that David heard of the death of King Saul and offered the lament: 'Tell it not in Gath, proclaim it not in the streets of Ashkelon' (2 Samuel 1:20). David did not want the Philistines to gloat over the death of Saul.

A key problem in the identification of Ziklag is that critics suggest it should be further south than Khirbet a-Ra'i. It appears in a list of cities that are near the Negev (Joshua 15:21–32). However, given what we read in the Bible we would expect it to be nearer to Gath than the Negev and so the site remains a strong possibility.

3. 'Where is David's Ziklag?' Volkmar Fritz, *Biblical Archaeology Review* 19:3, May/June 1993.

# Jonah sitting in the East

## Jonah and a fishy event!

Jonah disobeyed God when refusing to go to Nineveh (modern Iraq). Instead, he travelled in the opposite direction and took a ship to Tarshish (possibly Benidorm in modern Spain). After being thrown overboard and swallowed by a great fish, he was then spewed up on the Mediterranean coast to the west of Nineveh. Reluctantly, he eventually arrived at the great city of the Assyrians. A city whose kings had a gruesome reputation for cruelty. Ashurnasirpal II (883–859 BC) boasted:

'I built a pillar over against the city gate, and I flayed all the chief men who had revolted, and I covered the pillar with their skins. Some I walled up within the pillar, some I impaled upon the pillar on stakes, and others I bound round the pillar; and I cut off the limbs of the officers who had rebelled. From some I cut off their hands and from others I cut off their noses, their ears, and their fingers, of many I put out their eyes. Their young men and maidens I burned in the fire. The rest of them I consumed with thirst in the desert of the Euphrates.' [1]

This was a century before Jonah's time, but nothing had changed. See the image below.

If Jonah had his way, this vile people did not deserve forgiveness. After announcing his message (Jonah 3:4), disgusted he voluntarily expelled himself from the city. From a vantage point he turned to look at the great city waiting (and wanting) to see the Judgement of God fall. Jonah deliberately sat 'east of the city' (4:5) so when he looked back to the west, the sun would not obscure his view of the destruction that must surely follow; having been through the entire city, he knew how large it was and how great the inferno would be. Compare Genesis 19:24,25 and the obliteration of Sodom.

But God had a better plan for the city. For others who wanted to enact judgement instead of mercy, see Luke 9:51–55.

**Top**

*A Phoenician merchant ship carved on the face of a sarcophagus. 2nd century AD. It would not be dissimilar to the one Jonah boarded*

**Left**

*Shalmaneser III, the son of Ashurnasirpal II, boasted that he 'smashed all his enemies and showed no mercy in battle… built pillars of skulls… and dyed the mountains with their blood'.[2] This is the bronze band at the bottom of the massive Balawat gates guarding his palace*

1. Daniel David Luckenbill. *Ancient records of Assyria and Babylonia – Part 1.* (Histories & Mysteries of Man Ltd 1989. p. 145.
2. Pritchard, *Ancient Near Eastern Texts* (Princeton University Press 1967). p. 277.

# A prophet of another colour

**Jonah's maritime experience would doubtless have impressed the inhabitants of Nineveh!**

**Left**
Apkallu *from Nineveh and Nimrud (Nimroud)*

**Right**
*A fish-god from Nimrud*

The people of Nineveh worshipped fish-garbed images called *Apkallu* (in Akkadian). They were depicted as human-looking figures with some dressed in the skin of a fish, appearing as if they had been swallowed by a fish; others were bird-headed or human-headed. These were placed either side of doorways in Assyrian temples and palaces as guardians against evil spirits. Plaques were placed in houses and were believed to ward off evil.[3]

*Apkallu* means 'wise' or 'sage' and they are associated with human wisdom. The *Apkallu* were a group of seven sages, messengers and mediating figures, entrusted by a creator god Enki, to bring the civilizing arts to humanity following a catastrophic flood. A number of *Apkallu* are said to have committed various transgressions which angered the gods; those negative deeds, along with the roles of others as wise councilors, has led some scholars to equate them with the Nephilim of Genesis 6:4.

*Apkallu* are one of the more prominent supernatural creatures that appear in the art of Ashurnasirpal II. They have also been found on reliefs from the reign of Sennacherib (704–681 BC).

When Jonah arrived in Nineveh did the people, seeing and hearing him, think of their fish-garbed figures and what they stood for? It was very likely that the prophet, having been swallowed and then regurgitated by an enormous fish, resembled their own images. Some think the gastric juices of the great fish may have coloured Jonah's skin orange or very white, giving him a striking appearance. Did God use this association to trigger their conscience so that they responded immediately (Jonah 3:4–9)?

**Above**
*A drawing of an* Apkallu *(fish-god) made by Austen Henry Layard in situ from the ruins of Nimroud and published in* A second series of the monuments of Nineveh *(London 1853)*

3. Jeremy Black and Anthony Green, *Gods, demons and symbols of Ancient Mesopotamia.* (The British Museum Press 1992). p. 83.

# Manasseh in Babylon

**'The army commanders of the king of Assyria, who took Manasseh prisoner, put a hook in his nose, bound him with bronze shackles and took him to Babylon'**

This verse in 2 Chronicles 33:11 was long seen as a simple error in the Bible. The reference to Manasseh's captivity in Babylon was once commonly regarded as a mistake on the part of the chronicler; most scholars thought that the chronicler really meant that he'd been held captive in Nineveh. Why would the king of Assyria (Esarhaddon or Ashurbanipal) take Manasseh, the king of Judah, as a prisoner to Babylon in 642 BC when Babylon had been totally destroyed by the Assyrian king Sennacherib fifty years earlier? The capital of Assyria was Nineveh, and in his inscriptions, Sennacherib claims that following a series of revolts against Assyrian rule, the city of Babylon was entirely destroyed by the Assyrian army in 689 BC.

However, it is now known from letters and documents found at Nineveh, that Esarhaddon rebuilt Babylon and returned to Babylon the cult statue of Marduk the patron god that his father Sennacherib had removed to Nineveh. Esarhaddon was a superstitious, almost neurotic man, suffering from a recurring and incurable illness. Was he afraid of divine retribution that caused him to start to rebuild Babylon? Or was rebuilding Babylon his way of substantiating his claim to be king over Assyria *and* Babylon. He even made one of his sons future king in Babylon.[1]

Another challenge by critics is the uncomfortable fact that Manasseh, although a vigorous supporter of pagan Canaanite religion, enjoyed a long reign of fifty-five years, longer than any other king of Israel or Judah (2 Kings 21:1). It is therefore assumed that his repentance (recorded in 2 Chronicles 33:12–13) was fictitious. This is a typical critical assumption without the slightest evidence.

The reference to Manasseh taken into exile with 'a hook in his nose' was a humiliating way for defeated kings to be treated. Literally led like a pig or a bull. Amos 4:2 refers to the same.

**Above left**
*A small monument (21.5cm) recording Esarhaddon's restoration of Babylon. Dated c. 670 BC and discovered in Babylon*

**Above right**
*King Esarhaddon of Assyria who rebuilt Babylon after his father had destroyed it in 689 BC. On this stela he leads the defeated son of Pharaoh Taharqa by a nose ring. Manasseh also suffered this humiliation (2 Chronicles 33:11).*

82

1. Piotr Bienkowski and Alan Millard, *Dictionary of the Ancient Near East* (British Museum Press 2000). p. 108.

# Who was Manasseh?

'The word "History" describes the science of recording events and making sense of them in a coherent narrative.' [2] The reign of Manasseh is written as history for us to learn from

His father was King Hezekiah of Judah and his mother, Hephzibah (2 Kings 21:1). Manasseh grew up in a time of religious revival as Hezekiah reinstated the true worship of God across the land (2 Kings 18:4–6). Sadly, as is often the case, succeeding generations chose to follow a different pathway when they came into positions of responsibility.

Manasseh had become king at the age of twelve, and although he was on the throne from 687–642 BC, it is likely that Hezekiah's near fatal illness (Isaiah 38:1) meant that he was crown prince with his father for five years, hence the fifty-five years of 2 Kings 21:1.

Upon Hezekiah's death he lost his father's example and guidance and Manasseh apparently lacked or ignored any wise counsellor.[3]

Tragically Manasseh, in both spiritual and royal leadership, was the exact opposite of his father. He reverted to the cruel pagan cults that had plagued Canaan before the conquest of the Promised Land (Exodus 23:23–24).[4] This included human sacrifice, offering his own sons through fire in the Valley of Hinnom in Jerusalem, and encouraging false religion throughout the rest of Judah. His reign was an extended example of spiritual and moral backsliding,

made popular by royal example (2 Kings 21:2–16). However, he was largely a peaceful ruler with his eyes always on the mighty Assyrian Empire ruled by Esarhaddon.[5]

Finally, from exile Manasseh's cry of repentance was heard and, as an example of God's grace, he was restored to Jerusalem, where he began to reverse all his vile policies; on his death he was buried in his palace (2 Chronicles 33:12–20). Sadly, his godless example was perpetuated by his son, Amon. It was left to his grandson, Josiah, to continue the reforms.

**Left**
*Some ruins of Ancient Babylon*

2. Chris Sinkinson, *Time travel to the Old Testament* (Inter-Varsity Press 2013). p. 22.

3. Alan Millard, *Bible study commentary 1 Kings to 2 Chronicles* (Scripture Union/CLC 1985). p. 123.

4. See here 'The conquest of Canaan' on p. 44

5. Gwendolyn Leick, *Who's who in the Ancient Near East* (Routledge 1999). p. 100.

# Siege Warfare

**Ancient Near East cities were built 'on their hills' which gave them some protection from invading armies. Locked up tight, they functioned like fortresses, and would require enemies to mount a siege against them**

**Left**
*A reproduction of an Egyptian wall relief of The Siege of Dapur by Ramesses II*

**Below**
*From Ashurnasirpal II, showing an Assyrian siege tower being brought up to the wall where defenders have used a chain to disable the battering ram. Torches are thrown from the battlements but the Assyrians pipe water to put out the fire. To the left soldiers are digging under the walls to undermine the defences*

The Bible frequently refers to cities under siege. The Israelites besieged Jericho whose gates 'were securely barred' (Joshua 6:1); King David led the Israelites in the siege of Rabbah (2 Samuel 11:1), and Ben-Hadad of Syria besieged Samaria (2 Kings 6:24). Lachish fell to the Assyrians after a siege, and Hezekiah prepared for a follow-on siege of Jerusalem; although this never happened (Isaiah 37:33), Assyria extracted a hefty payment from King Hezekiah (2 Kings 18:14).[1]

Kings had their successful sieges illustrated on palace and temple walls and these record many historical details regarding siege warfare. The siege of a town called Dapur c.1269 BC by Ramesses II, is recorded on a wall relief in Thebes. It shows an assault on the fortified town using ladders while those climbing them are supported by archers below.

Assyrian wall reliefs also show the use of ladders, but the soldiers were trained to climb without using their hands so they were free to use their bows. Joel refers to this Assyrian skill when he describes their armies as like a swarm of locusts who 'scale walls like soldiers' (Joel 2:7).[2] Assyrian reliefs also record the building of siege ramps and large siege engines equipped with battering rams, archers and the ability to put out fires caused by the defenders. These were probably built on location from local timber. Ezekiel could describe the use of siege engines from personal experience (Ezekiel 26:8–9).

1. *Evidence for the Bible*. pp. 65–75.
2. Israel Eph'al, *The City Besieged: Siege and its Manifestations in the Ancient Near East*, (Hebrew University Magness Press, 2013). pp. 72–73.

# Life Under Siege

**With the city and surrounding inhabitants secure inside a well-fortified city, a siege could become a long and miserable captivity for the besieged**

Spring was the season for warfare (2 Samuel 11:1). It was the dry season with crops growing in the fields, fruit on the trees and good weather for maneuvering and encamping.

For those in a besieged city, supplies of water and food needed to be protected and the gates barred. At the time of an Assyrian invasion, by 701 BC, the water source from the Gihon spring for Jerusalem was fortified and King Hezekiah had built a tunnel to bring the water into the city (2 Kings 20:20).[3] Similar secret water tunnels from the ancient world can still be seen at Hazor, Megiddo, Gezer and Gibeon.

Grain was stockpiled, but when that ran out starvation followed. Ben-Hadad's siege of Samaria lasted so long that the scarcity of food led to people paying exorbitant prices even for a donkey's head (2 Kings 6:25). In such extreme hunger the citizens turned to cannibalism (2 Kings 6:28–29). Little wonder Jeremiah thought it better to die by the sword than experience such a siege (Lamentations 4:9). For those who had the resources, the threat of inevitable destruction turned them to indulgence before they died (Isaiah 22:12–13). However, with sufficient resources a city could hold out for a long time: the Roman siege of Jerusalem in AD 70 lasted almost half a year, and that of Masada in AD 73/74 perhaps even longer.

The invading army would attempt a settlement, accompanied by demoralizing threats whether verbal (2 Kings 18; 2 Chronicles 32:18) or physical, with captives impaled and the local environment destroyed, including its fruit trees and orchards.[4] God's law proscribed such activity for the Israelites (Deuteronomy 20:19–20).

Jerusalem was besieged a number of times during the Biblical period. Sometimes this was unsuccessful, as in the time of the Assyrian king Sennacherib in 701 BC. But Jerusalem was successfully conquered by Pharaoh Shishak in 925 BC (1 Kings 14:25–26), twice by the Babylonians in 597 and 587 BC (2 Kings 24–25), and three times by the Romans under Pompey (63 BC), Herod the Great (37 BC) and Titus (AD 70 see here page 118).

**Above and below left**
*The footprint of the Roman camps that surrounded Masada are still clearly visible today as is the massive Roman siege ramp that allowed them to breach the walls of Masada*

**Below right**
*During the much earlier siege of Lachish, the Assyrian siege engines are shown using their siege ramps*

3. See the details in *Evidence for the Bible*, pp. 66–67.

4. Israel Eph'al, *The City Besieged: Siege and its Manifestations in the Ancient Near East*, (Hebrew University Magness Press 2013). p. 69.

# Julius Caesar, Octavian and Philippi

**The settlement of Philippi as a Roman military colony was a direct result of the assassination of Julius Caesar in March 44 BC [1]**

Crossing the Rubicon River in January 49 BC to face-off Pompey, Caesar precipitated the Roman civil war—any Roman general crossing this border into Italy with his legion was seen as a traitor. Caesar's eventual victory over Pompey ended years of factions and chaos in the democratic Senate. Caesar was a brilliant, visionary and unyielding leader; he re-organised Rome into a strong and efficient government. His adopted son and heir, Octavian, eventually became the Caesar Augustus of Luke 2:1. He ruled over an extensive, powerful and well-ordered empire which, with its *pax Romana* (peace of Rome), efficient road and travel communications and rule of law for its citizens, prepared in advance, and for the advance, of the Christian message.

## The battles of Philippi

Following Caesar's assassination in March 44 BC a violent civil war erupted between the army of Brutus and Longinus defending the old order of the Roman Republic, against the new order established by Julius Caesar and now led by Octavian, Mark Anthony and Lepidus. Two decisive battles, in which 36 legions clashed (the largest number in Roman military history), settled the future of Roman government for the next five hundred years. They were fought outside a village in Macedonia

whose future was changed for ever. Mark Anthony and then Octavian both settled their veterans in Philippi and it became a Roman military colony renowned for its nearby gold mines, good harbour—and, during Paul's visit in AD 49 (Acts 16), the first Christian church established in Europe.

Since the Roman military were everywhere in Paul's travels, it is only natural that military imagery and vocabulary appears frequently in his letters. For example: 1 Corinthians 9:7 enlistment; 1 Thessalonians 5:8 and Ephesians 6:11–17 armour and weapons; 1 Thessalonians 4:16–17 the battle trumpet; Colossians 2:15, 2 Corinthians 2:14–16 the stripped enemy and triumphal procession.

Roman troops were garrisoned in Philippi and possibly many in the church were connected with the military. Hence the special greetings from those in 'Caesar's household' in Rome (4:22) from where Paul wrote his letter.

**Above**
*A coin minted in 48 BC celebrating Caesar's victories in Gaul. On the reverse is a Gallic shield*

**Below**
*Discovered in Arles France, some scholars think this is the most lifelike portrait of Julius Caesar*

---

1. See *Evidence for the Bible* pp. 116, 158–159.

# Paul and his military metaphors for Philippi

**Paul would have known the military history of Philippi and he appears to have used this to colour his letter to the church there [2]**

By the time of Paul's letter to the church in Philippi around AD 62, the descendants of the veterans would be proud of their family history: 'Upholding the fame of the ancestors increased the honour of the family presently living.' (101)

The pre-battle, morale-boosting speech of a Roman general included the objective of the war, the confidence of victory, and the rewards for courage and obedience. He provided examples of these and Paul may reflect this in Philippians. Out of the one hundred and four verses, half describe the exemplary behaviour of Christians or Christ, including, as a general would, himself (158). Philippians 1:21 is what every legionary believed in the service of Caesar or his general, and 3:20 reflects his prize of Roman citizenship.

Paul uses words and phrases found in early literature relating to the military, for example: 'conduct yourselves worthy…contending as one man… without being frightened' (1:27), echo the soldier's maxim: 'Better to die honourably while boldly facing the enemy instead of saving oneself through cowardly and disgraceful flight' (164).

Epaphroditus is a 'fellow-soldier' (2:25) and the phrase 'fellow-worker' (here and 4:3) is a phrase frequently used of 'deeds of

war'. 'Contended at my side' (4:3) refers to the close and disciplined formation of the legions. 2:29 reflects the honours rewarded to a brave combatant, and 2:9–11 the victory procession. The metaphors in 3:12–13 are possibly not athletic but military: pressing on, straining, and the soldier's prize.

Paul and Silas knew the rigours of gospel active service (4:12,15), the value of payment and supplies (4:18), and the confidence of ultimate victory (3:20–21) Unlike Brutus and Longinus who lost everything, Paul wrote: 'For me to live is Christ and to die is gain' (Philippians 1:21).

**Above**
*The battlefield, seen from the Acropolis of Philippi*

**Below**
*Paul would have known the theatre at Philippi built during the reign of Philip II in the 4th century BC, after whom the town was named*

---

2. This page is indebted to the doctoral thesis of Dierk Mueller 'Military Images in Paul's letter to the Philippians', (The University of Pretoria, S.A. 2013), which challenges many interpretations of the phrases and metaphors in Philippians. Page numbers in brackets here refer to this thesis.

# Once in royal David's city

## The significance of Bethlehem lay not in its size or wealth but in its importance for a royal line

Bethlehem's earlier name was Ephrathah, meaning fruitful, and here Jacob buried Rachel (Genesis 35:19; 48:7). Joseph and Mary travelled from Nazareth in Galilee to Bethlehem in Judea, a journey of some 150km (93mi). As to the birthplace of Jesus there is no confusion with another Bethlehem, near Nazareth (Joshua 19:15), because the Gospel writers emphasise its location in Judea (Matthew 2:1; Luke 2:4).

Bethlehem means 'House of Bread' and reflects its importance for agriculture. The events of the book of Ruth centre on this town and its surrounding fields when Naomi returned with her Moabite daughter-in-law after their bereavement.

David, the son of Jesse, was born in Bethlehem and he tended his father's sheep in the area. Later Samuel anointed him here to be Israel's future king (1 Samuel 16). During his time as a fugitive, David longed to drink water from a Bethlehem well (2 Samuel 23:15). Despite these accounts, Bethlehem was never a prominent town, nor did it have a large population.

In 2012 the Israeli Antiquities Authority announced that a bulla[1] had been found in the City of David excavations (in Jerusalem) bearing the earliest extra-biblical reference to the name Bethlehem.[2] Dating to

**Left**
*A star marks the traditional site of the nativity in Bethlehem*

**Below**
*Beneath the floor of the Church of the Nativity are Byzantine mosaics dating to the fourth century*

**Bottom**
*The 2,700 year old 'Bethlehem' bulla found at excavations in Jerusalem*

the time of Hezekiah (c.700 BC), it would have sealed a tax payment probably in the form of agricultural produce.

The prophet Micah referred to 'Bethlehem Ephrathah' as a small town with a great significance because of its royal connections (Micah 5:2 cf John 7:42).

One of the earliest churches was built at Bethlehem during the time of Constantine over a cave associated with the birth of Jesus. Whether it was the exact spot, as marked by a star today, it is certainly one of a number of caves that had been inhabited as part of domestic dwellings at the time of Jesus. A nearby cave was occupied by Jerome (c. AD 342–420) when he was translating the Bible into Latin, and these traditions add to the likelihood that this was the correct place.

1. See here pages 42-43, 66 for seals and bullae.
2. ""Bethlehem" from IAA Dig Found by Archaeologist IAA Arrested', *Biblical Archaeology Review*, September/October 2012 38:5, 12.

# Who were the Magi?

**The identity of the Magi remains a mystery; however, there are credible suggestions that confirm their place in history**

Bethlehem was visited by wise men from the east searching for a child born to be king (Matthew 2:1–12). There is no evidence that they were kings or were three in number; the names Melchior, Caspar and Balthasar are later traditions.

'Magi' is derived from an Old Persian word meaning 'magicians' or wise men.[3] Many Greek and Roman writers refer to Magi at the court of the Parthian Kingdom.[4] Xenophon of Athens, writing in the 4th Century BC, describes King Cyrus of Persia creating a 'college of the Magi' (*Cyropaedia* 8.1.23) who would act as royal advisors.

Josephus refers to Magi in the Babylonian court of Nebuchadnezzar (*Jewish Antiquities* 10.195–203), just as we read in Daniel 5:11. Perhaps a knowledge of Daniel's prophecies remained among these schools of wise men?

A 3rd century AD text, the *Revelation of the Magi*, describes them as from Shir, a land of silk, which one scholar identifies as China.[5] There is some evidence of Chinese silk reaching Rome as early as 259–210 BC, but given the enormous distance, goods and ideas were probably traded through intermediaries.

A more likely identity for the Magi were the Nabateans. Their capital was the famous city of Petra which was about 117km (110mi) from Bethlehem. They traded regularly across the desert, invented the camel saddle, created a network of wells and understood the stars to enable them to navigate. At the time of Jesus, they controlled the trade in Frankincense and Myrrh and therefore possibly had access to King Herod in their trading with Judea.

Whoever they were, after their visit, Herod unleashed his fury on the young boys of Bethlehem and district (Matthew 2:16). We have no reference to this outside of the Bible, but there are similar murderous decrees of Herod recorded by Josephus.[6]

**Right**
*The 'Treasury' of Petra, actually a mausoleum, is carved from the rock itself and part of an extensive city that had once belonged to the Edomites as described in Jeremiah 49:16–18*

**Below**
*The incredible city of Petra carved into the rock; a possible home-base for the journey of the Magi*

3. See here page 19 for Persian Loanwords.
4. An extensive account is provided by George van Kooten, 'Matthew, the Parthians, and the Magi: A Contextualization of Matthew's Gospel in Roman-Parthian Relations of the First Centuries BCE and CE', in *The Star of Bethlehem and the Magi*, edited by Peter Barthel and George van Kooten (Brill Boston, Leiden, 2015).
5. Brent Landau, *The Revelation of the Magi: The Lost Tale of the Wise Men's Journey to Bethlehem*, (Harper Collins, 2010).
6. R. T. France, 'Herod and the Children of Bethlehem', *Novum Testamentum*, Vol XXI, 1979, 1–23. See also here on Herod page 164–166

# Synagogues of Jesus

**Not many years ago there was little evidence for synagogues in the region of Galilee from the time of Jesus. Some thought the gospel accounts were anachronistic in referring to them at all**

**Top**
*The white limestone synagogue at Capernaum is built on much older black basalt foundations of an earlier synagogue. See also* Evidence for the Bible *p. 135*

**Above**
*A recently excavated synagogue of Magdala with a stone block carved with imagery from the temple. Jesus probably taught here (Matthew 4:23)*

The word 'synagogue' is a Greek word that means a gathering of people. It came to mean a specific place of assembly for worship and it was here that Scripture was taught (Matthew 4:23).

On a ridge overlooking the Sea of Galilee are the remains of a small Jewish town called Gamla that was destroyed by the Romans in AD 67. The remains of a synagogue were found here which was built between AD 23 and 41. It was a rectangular building lined with tiered benches.

The first century town of Capernaum, with its black basalt stone has been excavated and revealed a house that had been converted into a church that many believe to have been the home of Simon Peter.[1]

However, a beautiful white limestone synagogue was built centuries after the time of Jesus, but it is built on earlier foundations of a black basalt synagogue. Jesus taught here (Mark 1:21) and the gospels tell us a Roman centurion helped to finance it (Luke 7:5).

In 2009 another synagogue was discovered at Magdala on the north west shore of the Sea of Galilee. It was an important fishing town at the time of Jesus. The synagogue dates from c.50 BC and includes frescoes, mosaics, benches and a stone block carved with a menorah candelabrum. It is thought that the menorah had been carved by someone who had actually seen the original menorah in the temple of Jerusalem.

After the destruction of the Jerusalem temple in AD 70, Jewish religious practice centred on the synagogue. In the centuries that followed synagogues were built wherever Jews were dispersed. There is now clear evidence that already the synagogue was important to the Jews of Galilee from the time of Jesus.

1. *Evidence for the Bible*, p. 135.

# Weddings in the Bible

**The modern wedding service owes much to ancient traditions found in the Bible, from the giving of rings to the role of a bridegroom**

A marriage is a contract between a man and a woman that forms a new family (Genesis 2:24). Marriages were commonly arranged by parents, however, consent was sought from the partners (Genesis 24:8).

Although some Israelites practiced polygamy in the Old Testament, the Bible often draws attention to the problems this created (1 Samuel 1:2–3; 1 Kings 11). It was expected that a brother would marry a brother's widow to ensure his family line continued (Ruth 4:5).

Agreement of a marriage contract included public witnesses and the exchange of gifts (Genesis 24:51–53). This would develop into the wedding service that we know today.

At the time of Jesus, an engagement would be a binding contract to marry and included the groom making a payment to secure his bride's commitment. There are many details in the gospels that refer to first century wedding practices.

- The engagement would often last a year, but could be longer and would require a divorce settlement to break it (Matthew 1:19).

- Weddings took place in the evening and included a torchlit procession (Matthew 25:1).

**Left**
*Large Stone Water Jars from a first century Jewish house in Jerusalem of the type that would have been used in Cana*

- It was expected for everyone, including guests, to dress appropriately for the occasion (Matthew 22:11–12).

- A friend of the bridegroom, the forerunner of a best man, would help the groom prepare (John 3:29).

- The wedding banquet could last seven days. It would be a matter of honour to provide enough food and wine for the guests throughout the celebration.

The wedding recorded at Cana in John 2 fits with what we know of the region. Large stone jars were used for Jewish ritual purification as, unlike clay jars, they were considered less likely to become impure. There are two possible sites for the wedding, Kafr Cana and Khirbet Cana, both in lower Galilee.

Stone jars of the appropriate size were found at Khirbet Cana.

**Above**
*A Jewish marriage certificate, c.449 BC from Elaphantine in Egypt*

They were manufactured at great expense from stone using a Roman lathe. Until recently it was thought that they were only made near Jerusalem, but archaeologists have recently found a first century factory that manufactured stoneware one mile from Kafr Cana in Galilee.

# The language Jesus spoke

**There were at least three languages commonly spoken in Judah at the time of Jesus. So, which did Jesus use?**

Most people would be at least bilingual. Apart from local dialects and accents (Matthew 26:73), **Aramaic** was the common language of much of the Ancient Near East and the official language of Assyria, Babylonia, and the Persian Empire. Parts of Ezra and Daniel were written in Aramaic. It remained significant even after the conquest of Alexander the Great and was the most widely used language across the whole of Judea.

However, after the extensive conquests of Alexander in the 4th century BC, **Greek** had become the everyday language for trade; clearly the disciples of Jesus were familiar with this, which is why the Gospels and Epistles were written in Greek.

Capernaum was on a trade route and the centre of a thriving fishing industry where Greek would be in daily use. It was here that Jesus made his base (Mark 2:1). Ten cities founded after the Roman conquest in 63 BC were known as the Decapolis (meaning 'ten cities'); apart from Beth Shean they were across the River Jordan and were largely Greek in culture. Here, Jesus would have preached in Greek (Mark 5:20; 7:31).

However, since the time of the Roman occupation of Judea, the language of law and the military was **Latin**. For this reason, the sign above the cross on Golgotha 'was written in Aramaic, Latin and Greek' (John 19:20).

Where does **Hebrew** fit in? By the time of Jesus Hebrew was chiefly confined to religious worship. The Scriptures, written on scrolls, were all in Hebrew. Most of the Dead Sea Scrolls are in Hebrew.[1] The exact origin of Hebrew is uncertain and, like Aramaic and all languages, it has changed over the millennia. Today, only scholars can understand Mediaeval or Anglo-Saxon English.

If Hebrew was the language of Canaan, some see Genesis 31:47 as a significant marker. When Jacob parted from Laban he named the memorial stones *Galled*, which is a Hebrew word meaning 'witness heap'. Laban called it *Jegar Sahadutha*, which is the equivalent in Aramaic. Does this indicate that Hebrew was the language of the patriarchs as distinct from Aramaic?

**Right**
*A chart showing the few phrases in the Gospels that retain the original Aramaic; they are the actual words (Ipsissima verba) of Jesus. In addition, there are Aramaic names such as: Golgotha, Bethsaida, Bethesda and Martha*

## Aramaic Phrases in the New Testament

| Reference | Meaning | Greek | Aramaic | Pronunciation |
|---|---|---|---|---|
| Mark 5:41 | "Girl, arise!" | ταλιθὰ κούμ | טליתה קומי | taliṭáh qúm |
| Mark 7:34 | "Be opened." | ἐφφαθά | איתפתח ← אפתח | 'a(t)fatáh |
| Mark 14:36; Romans 8:15; Galatians 4:6 | "Father/my father" | ἀββᾶ | אבה | 'abbáh |
| Matthew 5:22 | "Idiot" | ρακά | רקה / ריקה | raqáh |
| John 20:16 | "My teacher/master" | ραββουνί | רבוני | rabbúni |
| Matthew 27:46 | "My God, my God, why have you left me?" | ἠλὶ ἠλὶ λεμὰ σαβαχθανί | אלי אלי למה שבקתני | 'alí 'alí lamáhševáqtani |
| Mark 15:34 | "My God, my God, why have you left me?" | ἐλοΐ ἐλοΐ λιμὰ σαβαχθανί | אלהי אלהי למה שבקתני | 'alahí 'alahí lamáh ševáqtani |
| Matthew 27:6; Mark 7:11 | "Offering/sacrifice" | κορβάν | קורבן | qorbán |
| Mark 3:17 | "Sons of Thunder" | βοανηργές | בני־רעם ← בני־רעם | bané-ra'ám |
| John 1:42, etc. | "Rock" | κηφᾶς | כיפה | kéfah |

1. See *Evidence for the Bible* p. 112.

# Who spoke what?

## There are clues in the Gospels and Acts to the languages spoken in Jesus' day

It is not likely that Pilate understood either Aramaic or Hebrew and, unless he was using an interpreter, he would have addressed the Jewish leaders in Greek. Years later in Jerusalem, Paul spoke to the crowd in Aramaic (Acts 20:40; 22:2). Evidently the Roman commander did not understand Aramaic and had no idea why Paul's long speech so upset the people (22:24). As a well-educated Jew and Roman citizen Paul was at least trilingual.

We know little of Jesus' education, except that most Jewish boys were taught to read and write. However, the Jewish historian Josephus refers to Jesus as 'a wise man' and in his mind that phrase linked him with well-educated Jews.[2] Significantly, in AD 69 when the Roman army surrounded the city of Jerusalem, Josephus informs us that he himself pleaded with the Jews 'in the Hebrew language' (probably to identify himself with them) to surrender in order to spare the temple.[3] Therefore, Hebrew was still spoken at this time.

Soon after the resurrection of Jesus, the Hebrew Scriptures were translated into Aramaic. It was known as the *Targum* (a word meaning 'interpretation') and was more of a paraphrase. Aramaic continued to be the common language across Israel until the Islamic conquest in the 7th century

when it was replaced by Arabic. Aramaic is spoken only by small minorities today.

In the 20th century, Hebrew was reestablished as the official language of the State of Israel. However, even this evolved from the Aramaic and therefore is not the same as the Hebrew Jesus knew.

**Summary**: By the time of Jesus, Hebrew had become a symbolic language of Jewishness. Aramaic was the normal everyday language, Greek the language of international trade, and Latin the language of law and the army of occupation. Doubtless, Jesus was able to converse in all four languages wherever appropriate. However, since few among the crowds would be knowledgeable of Hebrew, Jesus generally taught in Aramaic, and in the Decapolis most likely in Greek. He would have little need to use Latin.

93

2. Josephus *Antiquities* XVIII 3.2.
3. Josephus *Wars* Book 6:2:1.

# Calendars

## There is no evidence that the main Christian festivals—Christmas, Easter, Pentecost—were celebrated by the churches in the first century

**C**hristmas. Various dates had been suggested for the Nativity, from January to May. Hippolytus, a leader in Rome (martyred in AD 235), concluded 25 December in his commentary on Daniel. This date appears as a festival of the sun-god Mithras in the *Philocalian Calendar* of AD 336.[1] A bishop of Rome in AD 354 officially adopted the date as the nativity of Christ. According to Clement of Alexandria (AD 153–216) the Eastern churches placed Jesus' birth on 6 January because they were using (and still do) the Julian Calendar for their festivals.[2] In AD 386 Chrysostom indicated that Christmas was a new festival at Antioch. Augustine (died 430) was aware of both dates.

**Easter** was celebrated early in the life of the churches. From the 2nd century the word *Pascha* was used in both Greek and Latin as the equivalent for the Hebrew and Aramaic 'Passover'.[3] Many older Greek and Latin writers identified *Pascha* with the Greek *paskein*, 'to suffer'; Augustine rejected this, preferring to see it as a passing over from death to life. For the first three centuries the death and resurrection were probably celebrated on the same day.[4] However, few of the early church leaders referred to *Pascha* as a regular celebration. In AD 325 the Council of Nicaea confirmed Sunday as the day to celebrate the *Pascha*.

A celebration on **Palm Sunday** in Jerusalem to commence Easter week is first mentioned (though not by name) in the *Pilgrimage of Sylvia* c.AD 379:[5]

**Pentecost** (Greek 'fiftieth') is referred to in Acts 2:1; 20:16; 1 Corinthians 16:8. It is the fiftieth day after Easter. Various church leaders used the word to refer to the day the Holy Spirit was given (Irenaeus) and also the whole Easter period (Origen). Tertullian uses the word in both senses. As a Christian festival it can be found as early as Irenaeus in the mid second century. The **Ascension** is not noted as a festival until the mid-4th century. The *Pilgrimage of Sylvia* refers to a 'station' (remembrance) on the Mount of Olives 'in that place whence the Lord ascended into heaven.'

### MENSIS DECEMBER
habet dies XXXI.

| | | | | |
|---|---|---|---|---|
| 1 | D F G | KAL · DECEMB | SARMATICI · CM · XXIIII | |
| 2 | G H | IIII · NON | INITIVM · MVNERIS | |
| 3 | A A | III | SENATVS · LEGITIMVS | |
| 4 | E B B | PRIDIE | MVNVS · ARCA | DIES · AEGYPTIACVS |
| 5 | C C | NON | MVNVS · ARCA | |
| 6 | F D D | VIII · IDVS | MVNVS · ARCA | |
| 7 | E E | VII | | |
| 8 | F F | VI | MVNVS KANDIDA | |
| 9 | G G G | V | | |
| 10 | A H | IIII | | |
| 11 | B A | III | SEPTIMONTIA | |
| 12 | H C B | PRIDIE | LVDI · LANCIONICI | |
| 13 | D C | IDIB | LVDI | SENATVS · LEGITIMVS |
| 14 | E D | XIX · KAL · IAN | LVDI | DIES · AEGYPTIACVS |
| 15 | I F E | XVIII | N · DIVI VERI · CM XXIIII | |
| 16 | G F | XVII | LVDI | |
| 17 | A G | XVI | LVDI | SATVRNALIA |
| 18 | K B H | XV | LANCIONICI CM · XXIIII | SOL · CAPRICORNO |
| 19 | C A | XIIII | MVNVS ARCA | |
| 20 | D B | XIII | MVNVS · KANDIDA | |
| 21 | A E C | XII | MVNVS ARCA | |
| 22 | F D | XI | | |
| 23 | G E | X | MVNVS · ARCA | |
| 24 | B A F | VIIII | MVNVS · CONSVMMAT | |
| 25 | B G | VIII | N · INVICTI · CM · XXX | |
| 26 | C H | VII | | |
| 27 | C D A | VI | | |
| 28 | E B | V | | |
| 29 | F C | IIII | | |
| 30 | D G D | III | N · DIVI TITI · CM · XXIIII | |
| 31 | A E | PRIDIE | MAGISTRATI · IVRANT | |

This illustration shows the month of December as it is found in the Philocalian Calendar. Note that the 25th of December is the *Natalis Invicti* (the Birthday of the Invincible Sun).

**Above**
*Philocalus was a Christian who reproduced a pagan calendar. This page shows the 'Nativity of the Invincible [sun-god]' at 25 December*

1. Philocalus was a Christian who reproduced a pagan calendar in AD 336. Only a later copy remains today.
2. The *Julian* calendar, from the time of Julius Caesar in 46 BC, began the year on 25 March. In 1582, all Europe switched to the more accurate *Gregorian* calendar (after Pope Gregory XIII), and the new year now began in January. There is a difference of eleven days between the *Julian* and *Gregorian* Calendar (ie 26 December to 5 January). Britain did not adopt the *Gregorian* Calendar until 1752.
3. See *Evidence for the Bible* pp. 205–207 for a discussion on the precise date of the crucifixion. See here page 60 for the Jewish festivals.
4. Hastings, *Dictionary of Christ and the Gospels*. p. 256.
5. Who St Silvia was is unknown for certain. She was clearly an important person who pilgrimaged widely in the 4th century. Her 'diary' was discovered in 1883 and is an interesting historical travelogue of the Holy Land.

# Clocks

## Before mechanical clocks, for most people timing could only be approximate at best

**S**undials provided timing on a clear day, and the **water clock** could divide the hours accurately at night—if calibrated by a sundial.[6] For the Romans, the day began at sunrise, although this could vary by as much as six hours according to the season.

The Jews began each day at sunset (and still do); therefore the Sabbath began on Friday evening. However, they adopted the Roman real day commencing at sunrise, approximately six am. The 'third hour' of Mark 15:25 would be nine in the morning, the 'sixth hour' of John 4:6 and Matthew 27:45 would be midday, and 'about the tenth hour' (John 1:39) around four pm—although John may have intended simply 'late afternoon'.

There is an apparent discrepancy between John 19:14 where Jesus is handed over by Pilate for crucifixion 'about the sixth hour', and Mark 15:25 where he is crucified in the 'third hour' (which agrees with Matthew 27:45). However, since John nowhere else in the crucifixion account mentions the hour of the day, his '*about* the sixth hour' is intended to note that all this happened around midday ie approaching the sixth hour. Mark, on the other hand, is more specific referring to the third, sixth and ninth hours (Mark 15:25,33,34).

**Above**
*A Roman Sundial discovered at Interamna Lirenas (Italy). It was given to the town by the Plebeion Tribune, Marcus Novius Tubula, at his own expense mid 1st century BC*

**Below**
*An Egyptian water clock from the Temple of Amen-Re at Karnak (Egypt) from the time of Amenhotep III (1391–1353 BC). The alabaster bowl had twelve columns and eleven fake holes to cover the hours of the night. Water slowly drained out of a small hole in the bottom and the time could be read by the water level inside aligned with the nearest fake hole*

When Acts 10:30 reads 'three days ago' (NIV) or 'four days ago' (ESV), the Greek word 'four' is preceded by a small preposition that carries the idea of 'before'. This can be understood as four days or part of three days.

The Romans divided each day into two parts of twelve hours (John 11:9) and their night into four military watches of three hours each. The 'third watch' of Luke 12:38 would be from midnight to three am. Jesus came to his disciples on the Galilee between three and six am (Mark 6:48).

For the Jews, part of a day or night was considered as the whole day or night, therefore from Friday midday to Sunday early morning would be 'three days and three nights' (Matthew 12:40). Paul's 'a night and a day in the open sea' (2 Corinthians 11:25) need only have been part of each.

The earth's reliable rotation around the sun was part of God's creation for timekeeping (Genesis 1:14).

95

---

6. See *Evidence for the Bible* p. 15 for details of early water clocks by the Egyptians and Babylonians.

# Gone Fishing

**Fishing was an important industry throughout the Fertile Crescent. Whether the open seas or inland lakes and rivers all who lived in this region benefitted from the abundance of fish**

Archaeology has found the remains of nets, fishing hooks and anchor stones from throughout the biblical period. Fish were caught using different types of nets along with spears and hooks.[1] Isaiah described line-fishing in the Nile with hooks (Isaiah 19:8), Job was asked whether he could pull in leviathan with a fishhook (Job 41:1), and Amos referred to the Assyrians taking their Israelite prisoners of war away with fishhooks (Amos 4:2).[2] Ezekiel prophesied a time when the Dead Sea (which is devoid of life) would teem with fish (Ezekiel 47:9–10).

In the New Testament time, fishing was a major industry around the Sea of Galilee. A previously unknown harbour from the first century was discovered by archaeologists in 1970 at Kursi, the biblical site of the Gerasenes (Mark 5:1–20).[3] A 500 feet (154m) stone breakwater was found beneath the surface providing a shelter for the fishing boats against, 'the vicious storms that could quickly arise on the lake.'[4]

Many discoveries have been made around the Galilee associated with the vibrant fishing industry. Bethsaida has been identified from the large range of fishing equipment found in excavations.[5] Recent discoveries at Migdal have revealed markets and tanks used for salting fish.[6] In 1986 a well preserved first century fishing boat was discovered similar to that Jesus and his disciples would have used.[7]

Many of the apostles were associated with the fishing trade and depended upon it for their livelihoods. In his Gospel John, who was in a family fishing business (Matthew 4:21–22), carefully recorded the one hundred and fifty-three fish caught during a miraculous catch (John 21:11). As a businessman who traded in fish it should not surprise us he recorded the precise number caught, no doubt he would have also known the value they would fetch at market.

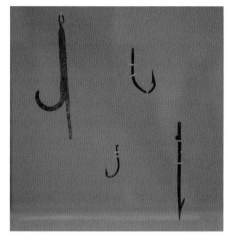

**Above**
*Bronze fish hooks and harpoon heads from Deir el-Bahri, Egypt*

**Below**
*This fishing scene from Tunisia c.300 AD shows the abundance of fish in the Mediterranean*

1. Tyler R. Yoder, *Fishers of Fish and Fishers of Men: Fishing Imagery in the Hebrew Bible and Ancient Near East.* (Eisenbrauns, Winona Lake 2016).
2. See *Evidence for the Bible* p. 77 for an example of this.
3. Mendel Nun, *Ancient Anchorages and Harbours Around the Sea of Galilee,* (Kibbutz Ein Gev, Israel: Kinnereth Sailing Co., 1988).
4. James K. Hoffmeier, *The Archaeology of the Bible,* (Oxford: Lion, 2008).
5. See here Bethsaida on page 103.
6. See here Towns of Galilee page 102.
7. See *Evidence for the Bible,* p. 131.

# Ancient Games

**Life was not only work (Ecclesiastes 3:1–8). Both adults and children found time for games. Archaeology has brought back to light the games that people once played**

A sign of God's blessing is that children will be able to play games in safety (Isaiah 11:8; Zechariah 8:5). Throwing a ball is used as an image of God bringing judgement but assumes that ball games were common (Isaiah 22:18). An Egyptian wall relief from c. 2345 BC illustrates children playing a game that has been compared with 'cops and robbers.' A boy acts as a leader, wearing a mask and holding a baton while his friends chase other children who are pretending to be prisoners trying to escape through a hole in the wall.

Sports were important opportunities to compete and show strength outside of combat including gymnastics, fencing, boxing, wrestling and archery. Paul was familiar with athletics and often used the image of running a race as a metaphor for the Christian life (1 Corinthians 9:25–27; Philippians 3:13–14; 2 Timothy 2:5).

Board games were common in the ancient world, many taking the form of a 'move and capture' style of game. Fragments of the boards and pieces have been found throughout the Fertile Crescent. A game associated with 'hounds and jackals', represented by pegs on a board, has been found from Egypt to Assyria. A copy of the beautiful 'Royal Game' of Ur which was found in a tomb from the region where Abram came from, was also found in the tomb of Tutankhamun in Egypt. Evidence of board games have been found in excavations at Samaria, Gezer and Megiddo.

**Above**
*On a limestone tomb inscription from Giza, Children are playing a 'cops and robbers' game, 5th Dynasty Egypt*

The use of dice or lots was common and could be called upon for important decisions (Jonah 1:7; Nahum 3:10; Joshua 18:6; Acts 1:26). A lot might be a broken piece of pottery pulled out at random. The biblical writers always knew that God's providence guided even what we might consider mere chance (Proverbs 16:33). The earliest dice were the knucklebones of sheep that gave four different positions when rolled. It may have been these that were used by the Roman soldiers when they 'cast lots' for the garments of Jesus (John 19:24).

**Below left**
*'Mehen', the 'snake' game from Egypt, involved racing marbles around the board representing a coiled snake, Abydos 1st Dynasty Egypt*

**Below centre**
*The Royal Game of Ur was another chase game popular across the Ancient Near East. It is considered one of the oldest known games and Abraham was no doubt familiar with it*

**Below right**
*The Game of Hounds and Jackals, using pegs in a board, was played throughout the Middle East and examples are found in Canaan, though this one is from an Egyptian tomb c. 2000 BC*

# Shekels and Talents

Coins arrive late in Old Testament history; at first, transactions relied on weights and measures

**Left**
*This Egyptian wall painting from the tomb of Nebahum and Ipuky (c.1350–1300 BC) shows metals being weighed and the ring shaped objects may be early forms of coin*

**Below**
*A mina lion weight from Assyria and sleeping duck weight from Mesopotamia c.1000 BC*

The Hebrew word 'shekel' means 'weighing' because originally it was a measure of weight. An early example of its use was when Abraham bought a burial plot for Sarah from Ephron, the Hittite: Abraham 'weighed out for him… four hundred shekels of silver, according to the weight current among the merchants.' (Genesis 23:16). Joseph was sold for twenty shekels of silver to the Midianite merchants (Genesis 37:28).

The best estimate is that a shekel was around 10 grams in weight. The weight itself was probably based on a number of grains of barley which would have provided a rough, common measure for the Fertile Crescent. But this allowed some flexibility that could be taken advantage of by the unscrupulous (Proverbs 20:23; Amos 8:5–6). Therefore, God's Law demanded standardised weights and measures to prevent cheating (Leviticus 19:35–36). In order to ensure proper weights were used, witnesses could be called upon for a transaction (Jeremiah 32:9–10).

Coins developed from fragments of metal probably assembled as rings.[1] This would have been easier to transport, such as the 'pouch of silver' hidden in the sacks of Joseph's brothers (Genesis 42:35). A talent was a disc of metal, usually gold or silver, weighing about 35 kilograms (about 3000 shekels!). Talents of gold would have been very valuable and heavy. The Israelites use 29 talents of gold in the building of the Tabernacle (Exodus 28:2). David's crown was one talent in weight (2 Samuel 12:30).

The first coins mentioned in the Old Testament are 'darics' in Ezra 8:27.[2] The Persians and the Greeks develop the use of coins so that by the time of the New Testament they are in common use for business transactions. A reference to 'darics' at the time of King David (1 Chronicles 29:7) is an example of 'prolepsis'—an author using a term commonly known at time of writing to describe something from an earlier age.

---

1. John Dayton, 'Money in the Near East Before Coinage', Berytus: Archaeological Studies Vol XXIII, American University of Beirut, Lebanon, 1974, pp. 41–52.
2. See here pp. 18–19 for Persian loanwords.

# Coins and Currency

**The different coins that are mentioned in the New Testament carry important information and also enable archaeologists to date when a site was occupied**

Jesus often told parables that related to coins. Matthew was a tax-collector and his Gospel makes the most frequent reference to coins.[3] The images on coins would be offensive to the Jews who refused to worship emperor or king as divine.

**The Prutah.** The most common and smallest unit of currency. A prutah could buy two sparrows (Matthew 10:29). A lepton was worth half a prutah, and was the smallest coin of all; a poor widow brought two leptons as an offering—the 'widow's mites' (Mark 12:41–44). [4]

**The Silver Denarius** at the time of Jesus bore an image of Tiberius and Jesus used this to challenge his hearers over their attitudes to tax and worship (Luke 20:24). The good Samaritan used two denarii to cover the costs of the injured Jew (Luke 10:35). A vineyard worker was paid a daily wage of one denarius and a scribe could earn 12 denarii in a week.

**The Tyrian Shekel** had a high proportion of silver content (14.2 grams) and was desirable as an investment. The money changers in Jerusalem converted other coinage into the Tyrian shekel for paying the temple tax, and this led to profiteering (John 2:13–16).

**Judea Capta Coin.** At the end of the First Jewish Revolt in AD 70, when the Temple was destroyed, Rome issued a coin to commemorate their victory with the inscription 'Judea Conquered' in Latin. This coin was issued in gold, silver and bronze for over 25 years. It often shows a male and female in mourning after their defeat by the Romans.

**Bar Kochba Revolt Coin.** After the time of Jesus there were a number of Jewish rebellions against the Roman authorities. The third Jewish revolt, AD 132–136, had some measure of success and coins were issued from Jerusalem to commemorate this. One includes a simple image of the Temple in Jerusalem which had been destroyed by the Romans decades earlier. It represents the Holy of Holies and Ark of the Covenant.

**Above**
*Judea Capta coin commemorating Emperor Vespasian crushing the first Jewish Revolt AD 68–70*

**Below**
*Bar Kockba Revolt coin with simple representation of the Temple in Jerusalem*

3. Peter J. Williams, *Can we Trust the Gospels?*, Crossway Books: Wheaton, 2018.
4. See also for coins *Evidence for the Bible* p. 125.

# Burying the dead

**Many of the most sensational archaeological discoveries have been made at ancient tombs. In Egypt, the lavish burials of their Royal and high officials has provided archaeologists with a wealth of artefacts and information**

The care with which a body was interred reflected a general attitude in the Ancient Near East to the physical body. (See here page 28–29). Cremation—common in Hindu, Greek and Roman cultures—was generally not practiced. It was definitely avoided by the Israelites.

Abraham purchased a cave at Machpelah from the Hittites that could be used as a burial site for his family (Genesis 23). The large Herodian structure built at Hebron commemorates the location of the tombs of Abraham, Sarah, Isaac and Rebekah. There is evidence that it is a site of ancient burials. While archaeological investigation has been forbidden, Old Testament period pottery has been recovered from the caves beneath the shrine.[1]

Egyptian mummification dried out the body and, in an arid climate, the human remains could survive indefinitely. Elaborate tombs were the preserve of the wealthy. Joseph ensured his father Jacob was embalmed, and the Bible notes that the process took forty days (Genesis 50:1–3). Joseph himself was also embalmed and his body placed in a coffin (Genesis 50:26). This allowed his bones to be carried back to Canaan by the Israelites centuries later (Exodus 13:19).

The importance of preserving the bones of the deceased included placing them in a family tomb (2 Samuel 19:37) and is reflected in the expression 'he was gathered to his people' when an Israelite was buried (Genesis 25:8; Numbers 20:24; Judges 2:10).

The care with which bones were interred in a tomb and a person laid to rest with their ancestors, is demonstrated by the large number of Iron Age (1200 BC on) tombs throughout the Holy Land. Many tombs have been used over multiple generations. The accumulation of bones would have been a constant reminder that the Israelites trusted in a God who could restore dry bones to life (Ezekiel 37:1–13).

**Above**
*The Tomb of the Patriarchs, Hebron, marks the site of the Cave of Machpela. While the main structure was built at the time of King Herod there is evidence of much earlier burials*

**Below**
*Inside the Tomb of the Patriarchs in Hebron, cenotaphs mark the burials of Abraham, Sarah, Isaac and Rebekah*

1.  David Ben-Shlomo, 'Iron Age Pottery from the Cave of the Patriarchs at Hebron', *Israel Exploration Journal* 70/1:49–63, 2020

# Bone Boxes at the time of Jesus

**Throughout Biblical history wealthy Jewish families interred their dead in rock-cut tombs but in the first century a new style of burial was practiced**

The body was first laid on a bench in a rock cut tomb. When the soft elements had decayed, the bones were placed in a chalk or limestone bone box (an ossuary) which was stored in a niche (plural *kokhim*) in the cave wall.[2] Ossuaries were first used during the reign of King Herod (around 20 BC) and ceased with the destruction of the Temple in AD 70. They were plain or decorated, sometimes with the name of the deceased. Wealthy Jews had probably modified the custom from the Roman tradition of using burial urns.

The burial of Jesus fits with what we know from the period. When the body of Jesus was taken down from the cross, Jewish law required immediate burial. Without a family tomb, the body of Jesus would have been laid in a simple trench grave common among the poor. Instead, Joseph of Arimathea had the body wrapped in linen and placed in his own family tomb (Matthew 27:57–60). The suggestion that a victim of crucifixion would not be given a proper burial is contradicted by the discovery of the remains of a crucified man in an ossuary from the first century.[3]

The stone secured the grave but permitted access for those who would tend the body as it decomposed over the next year before an ossuary was required. The soldiers who guarded the tomb of Jesus (Matthew 27:62–66) would have allowed access for the anointing that the women intended to carry out. Archaeologist Jodi Magness concludes, 'The gospel accounts describing Jesus' removal from the cross and burial accord well with archaeological evidence and with Jewish law.'[4]

Many bone boxes from the time of Jesus have survived and include common names also found in the gospels. Excavations in 1980 at a tomb in Talpiot, Jerusalem, found ossuaries with some names that also belonged to the family of Jesus, including those of Joseph and Mary. But no scholar accepted the sensational claim that this was the family tomb of Jesus. These were common first century names and Jesus, being from Galilee, would have required a borrowed tomb for a burial in Jerusalem.

**Above**
*A large collection of first century ossuaries on the Mount of Olives, Jerusalem*

**Below**
*The remains of a rock cut tomb on Mt Scopus, Jerusalem, from the time of Jesus with the bench for laying out the body and niches for placing the ossuaries*

2. See *Evidence for the Bible*, pp. 142–143.
3. See *Evidence for the Bible*, p. 138.
4. Jodi Magness, 'Ossuaries and the Burials of Jesus and James', *Journal of Biblical Literature*, 124/1 (2005), p. 149.

# Towns in Galilee

**The Gospel writers provide evidence that they had first-hand knowledge of the towns and villages at the time of Jesus**

**Left**
*Beneath the modern Church of the Annunciation in Nazareth lies evidence of habitation from the time of Jesus. Rock cut caves, later used for burials, had been part of domestic homes*

**N**azareth (Matthew 2:23) had been dismissed as having no substantial occupation at the time of Jesus. However, archaeological excavation in 2009 revealed a first century house and cisterns; it is now evident that the town had a population of up to one thousand, substantially more than previously thought.[1] Ken Dark observes, 'The settlement clearly did exist in the early first century, contrary to some recent ill-informed speculations, and was an agricultural community with a population following a strict interpretation of Second Temple Judaism.'[2] Nazareth was probably settled by Jewish farmers and labourers who helped in the construction of Sepphoris, a town some 6 km from Nazareth, while maintaining their own distinctive laws and a strict observance of Jewish religion. Its relative poverty and simplicity gave it a poor reputation (John 1:46). After the time of Jesus Nazareth became a site for burial, and caves were reused as tombs.

**Capernaum** was the base for Jesus after he left Nazareth (Matthew 4:13). Excavations at Capernaum reveal a thriving first century fishing town with evidence of wealth from tax collected on local trade. Foundations for a home where Jesus may have lived and the synagogue where he preached have all been identified.[3]

**Tiberius** was the most important town in the Galilee at the time of Jesus. No mention is made of the town itself in the gospels as Jesus generally avoided such Roman cities. However, John notes that the Sea of Galilee is also known by this name (John 6:1).

Other important towns in the gospels have been identified at **Chorazin** and **Bethsaida**.

The site of **Migdal** has been excavated since 2007 and revealed a first century hub for Jewish worship, the fishing industry, including the production of salted fish. The name Mary Magdalene (Matthew 27:56) may indicate that Mary was originally from the town of Migdal.[4]

While gospel writers with local knowledge call **Galilee** a 'sea', which it would have been for the fishermen who lived there, Luke calls it 'the lake' which reflects his Mediterranean background and awareness of its relative small size.

Peter Williams concludes a historical study with the comment, 'The four Gospels demonstrate familiarity with the geography of the places they write about.'[5]

1. Ken Dark, 'Has the Childhood Home of Jesus been found?', *Biblical Archaeology Review*, March/April 2015.
2. Ken Dark, *Roman-Period and Byzantine Nazareth and Its Hinterland*, (London: Routledge, 2020).
3. *Evidence for the Bible*, pp. 134–135
4. An unclear reference to Magadan in Matthew 15:39 was certainly to a town in this general area and may now be identified as Migdal.
5. Peter Williams, *Can We Trust the Gospels?* (Crossway Books, Carol Stream, IL) p. 55.

# The Lost Town of Bethsaida

**For centuries pilgrims visited Galilee to see important locations associated with the ministry of Jesus. But the location of one very important town in the gospels had been lost to history**

Bethsaida was the hometown of at least three apostles: Philip, Peter and Andrew (John 1:44). It features in all four Gospels and is associated with the feeding of the five thousand and healing of a blind man. After Jerusalem and Capernaum, it is the third most mentioned town in the Gospels.

The location of Bethsaida disappears in the historical record and early accounts of pilgrims are unclear regarding which site in the Galilee they had visited. As a fishing village, Bethsaida needed access to the sea and no viable location had been found on the north east shoreline of Galilee.

In 1988 archaeologist Rami Arav began exploratory work on the north east shore of Galilee and demonstrated that two thousand years ago the lake had stretched further north. The new geological insight made what is today a landlocked Tel (ruin mound) 2km inland, a possible contender.

Since then, thirty years of excavations have revealed a town that fits the description of Bethsaida.

- A coin sequence showing occupation throughout the 1st century.
- Many oil lamps from the time of Herod in the 1st century.
- A low percentage of pig bones, and the remains of limestone vessels that fit with Jewish religious observance.
- Evidence of a Roman development of the site in AD 30 which would have expanded a modest fishing village into a more important Roman town shortly after the time of Jesus.
- A large number of hooks, anchor stones, lead weights and other artefacts associated with a fishing industry.

Another site, closer to the modern shoreline, El-Araj, has also been considered a possible site for Bethsaida.[6] But the remains are mostly from the later Byzantine period (from Constantine in the 4th century), and the finds are more limited. Some consider that it may represent an outpost of Bethsaida as the shoreline gradually changed.

**Above**
*From et-Tell (Bethsaida?), looking towards the Sea of Galilee. The green grass beyond is where the Jordan River and Galilee shoreline have silted up and shifted*

**Below**
*Fishing implements from et-Tell, including hook, weights and net repair kit*

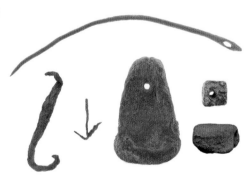

6. See 'Searching for Bethsaida: the Case for El-Araj', R. Steven Notley and Mordechai Aviam and 'Searching for Bethsaida: the Case for Et-Tell', Rami Arav, *Biblical Archaeology Review*, Spring 2020 46:2.

# A Ring of Pontius Pilate

**The ministry of Jesus took place during the time when Pontius Pilate was governor of Judea (Luke 3:1). Archaeology continues to find remains that testify to his period in government**

A stone inscription records the name of Pontius Pilate from the time of Jesus. The 1961 discovery of the Pilate inscription at Caesarea was of a stone that had originally been part of a public building dedicated to emperor Tiberius. It was in secondary use as recycled stone in another building.[1]

In 1969 archaeologists were excavating at the Herodium, near Bethlehem. This was a royal palace built by Herod the Great that had been converted into a residence by Pontius Pilate. They unearthed a dull, tarnished signet ring of copper alloy which was unidentified and stored for fifty years.

More recently, the ring was subjected to imaging photography which combines multiple photographs to bring out fine details otherwise lost to corrosion and weathering. What would have been impossible in 1968 has now revealed a name and an image of a bowl.

The name of Pilate appears on the ring and runs in the reverse direction indicating it was a signet ring designed to be stamped into wax. Being of cheap metal it probably belonged to an administrator in Pilate's household or a local regional servant working for Pilate.

Pilate's name was uncommon at the time and the Greek form in which the name has been inscribed on the ring is unusual. It may be a transliteration into Greek of the Latin meaning 'for Pilate'. When stamped into wax it was probably used 'by someone working for Pilate, who may have collected goods for the governor on behalf of Rome in the region south of Jerusalem and sent those goods to Pilate.'[2] Pilate is one of at least twenty-three New Testament figures whose existence has been confirmed by archaeology from outside of the Bible.

**Above**
*A signet ring inscribed with the name of Pilate*

**Below**
*The site of Herodium with the remains from Herod's palace and Pilate's headquarters*

1. *Evidence for the Bible*, p. 146
2. Robert Cargill, 'Was Pontius Pilate's Ring Discovered at Herodium?', *Biblical Archaeology Review* Feb 2020.

# Roman Judea

**At the time of Jesus, the region in which he ministered was under Roman control. The Gospels include many details that reflect an accurate knowledge of the politics of Rome [3]**

In 63 BC Rome created the province of Syria. The territory was later divided, becoming the Roman province of Judea. Following the death of the first Roman governor, Antipater, the Roman Senate designated his son Herod as 'King of the Jews' and he took control of Judea (Judah).

Herod embarked on major building projects across the province, most significantly the substantial rebuilding of the Temple. John's Gospel includes an accurate reference to when this project had begun, forty-six years earlier (John 2:20). Herod was king at the time of the birth of Jesus. His fear of a rival claimant to the throne and his order to murder the children of Bethlehem fits what we know of his character from the Jewish historian Josephus.

After Herod's death his Kingdom was divided into regions and shared among his sons. While Herod Antipas ruled the Galilee, Judea was given to Archelaus who was so unpopular with the people that in AD 6 the province came under direct Roman control.

- Josephus tells us that Quirinius would not become governor of Syria until AD 5–6, but Quirinius had a senior military role in the region as early as 6 BC and this explains his role in an earlier census at the time of Christ's birth.[4]

**Above**

*A silver denarius, tribute penny, from the time of Tiberius and bearing his image*

105

- The Gospels identify the birth of Christ as at the time of Caesar Augustus (Luke 2:1) who reigned from 27 BC to AD 14.

- During the ministry of Jesus, the Emperor was Tiberius, and Luke correctly identifies him along with the regional rulers (Luke 3:1).

- The Roman occupation permitted a Roman soldier to compel a civilian to carry their supplies within the limit of one Roman mile.[5] Jesus creates a new idiom with his command that we go the 'second mile'. (Matthew 5:41).

- Jews avoided making images of people, but the Roman tax system required them to handle the denarius that bore the image of the Caesar. Jesus asked for such a coin in order to draw attention how much more we owe to God (Matthew 22:19).

In the trial of Jesus, the roles of the Jewish High Priest, Herod the King and Roman governor Pilate all accurately reflect their distinct areas of jurisdiction at the time.

Their concern with unrest during the Passover festival explains why all three officials were in Jerusalem at the same time.

3. See also here pp.154–158 for 'Rome in Israel' and 164–166 for Herod.
4. See *Evidence for the Bible*, pp. 203–204 for details of Quirinius and the Census.
5. For an example from the time of Augustus see G. H. R. Horsley, *New Documents Illustrating Early Christianity*, (The Ancient History Documentary Research Centre, Macquarie University, 1981), pp.42–43.

# Soldiers of the Empire

**Five centurions and a tribune are referred to in the Gospels and Acts. What do we know about the military occupation of Judah in the first century?**

**Left**
*From left to right: a legionary, spearman and centurion. Note the centurion's distinguishing mark: his sword worn on his left side and his transverse plume*

*Cohors II Italica ciuium Romanorum* was stationed in Syria by AD 69.

Julius was a centurion from the 'Imperial Regiment' (Acts 27:1 in AD 60). The *Legio X Fretensis* (10th Legion) an Auxiliary royal unit serving under King Agrippa II was stationed in Syria, which included Judah. [2]

Centurions were the backbone of the Roman army. In every legion there were approximately seventy centurions, each with around eighty men under his command. He may have less if he was on headquarters staff. He was loyal and proven in battle. Centurions often suffered the major casualties. During Caesar's attack on Georgia in 52 BC, one centurion was killed for every fifteen soldiers. On retirement after twenty years' service, the centurion received a small pension and citizenship, if he was an auxiliary. His pay and share in spoils were much higher than a legionary's (hence Luke 7:4–5; Acts 10:2).

Roman troops entered Palestine under General Pompey in 63 BC and in 31 BC Caesar Augustus renamed it **Judea** (Judah). In AD 6 Judea became a Roman Province—the occasion for a census undertaken by Publius Sulpicius Quirinius, the Governor (Legate) of Syria (Acts 5:37). [1]

Rome maintained control over its empire through **legionaries**—mainly infantry and under the orders of the Emperor, **auxiliaries**—generally local volunteers, and the local **royal units**—under the control of the regional king; Herod therefore had his own military (Matthew 26:47). In Acts 23:23, Luke accurately describes the three divisions of Roman forces: the heavy infantry, cavalry and lightly armed spearmen.

Cornelius was a centurion from a 'cohort of the Italian Regiment' (Acts 10:1 in AD 41). A cohort was approximately 600 men, a tenth part of a legion. It is known that the

1. See *Evidence for the Bible* pp. 203–204.
2. 'Military Forces in Judaea 6–130 CE'. Zeichmann Emmanuel College at the University of Toronto, Canada. *Currents in Biblical Research* 2018, Vol. 17(1) pp. 86–120. Also: 'The Roman Army in Judea under the Procurators' M.P Speidel (Ancient Society 1982/83) pp. 233–240.

# Caesarea and 'the dagger men'

**Judah simmered with discontent throughout the life of Jesus, and soon after the close of Acts Jerusalem was the catalyst for a disastrous rebellion**

The Roman garrison was stationed at the provincial capital Caesarea Maritima, 112 km (70 mi) from Jerusalem on the coast.³ Caesarea was a pagan city rebuilt by Herod the Great between 22 and 9 BC. From Caesarea detachments would be sent out for garrison duty in hot spots like Jerusalem and frontier towns like Capernaum. Be careful not to confuse Caesarea Maritma (Acts 8:40) with Caesarea Philippi (Matthew 16:13).

The centurion whose servant Jesus healed (Luke 7) was on duty protecting the hated tax collectors in Capernaum, the strategic fishing town on the north coast of Galilee. Julius, who took Paul to Rome (Acts 27) was one of the cohort of officer-couriers for communications. The unnamed centurion at the cross was in charge of the squad of four men (a *quaternion*) assigned to the execution (John 19:23). He allowed a drink to be offered to Jesus from their own *posca*, a sour vinegar (v.29); the only drink allowed legionaries on duty. It is likely Pilate's troops were auxiliaries recruited from the local, non-Jewish, population — this would make them largely Syrians or even Samaritans!

Throughout the life of Jesus and the apostles, the Zealots, and a splinter group known as the *Sicarii* (dagger men), were urban terrorists who would murder collaborators with Rome; note therefore the last two names in Matthew 10:4! Rome was constantly confronting rebellion: see John 18:40, Acts 5:36–37 and 21:38 referring to three occasions.

The 'more than forty men' ready to ambush Paul and his escort (Acts 23:12–15) were almost certainly *Sicarri* (see here page 151). Claudius Lysias, the Tribune, was the highest-ranking officer in Jerusalem with a cohort of around 760 infantry and 240 cavalry under his command. He took no chances and sent a strong force by night to escort Paul beyond the point of danger (v 31–32). Antipatris was approximately halfway at 64km. A route march for a Roman legionary could cover 36km in five hours with 31kg of kit and weapons! ⁴

Conflict culminated in AD 70 by possibly the most brutal siege in history. Within the city, war between the Zealot factions, massacre of civilians, and terrible starvation, decimated the population. The city and temple were utterly destroyed

**Above**
*A Tribune. His red cloak and sash indicate his rank*

(Matthew 24:2) by General Titus and the Temple treasures were displayed in a victory celebration on the Titus arch in Rome.⁵

107

3. See *Evidence for the Bible* pp. 120–123
4. *Conquest, The Roman invasion of Britain*, John Peddie (Sutton Publishing 2005). *Caesar*, Michael Grant (Weidenfeld & Nicholson Ltd 1974).
5. See *Evidence for the Bible* pp. 180–181.

# Saul of Tarsus and the philosophers

**From birth, 'Saul' was his Jewish (Hebrew) name and 'Paul' his Latin name as a Roman citizen. When he set out to preach to the Gentile world, he chose the latter (Acts 13:9 cf. 1 Corinthians 9:20–21)**

The university at Tarsus was widely acclaimed, and many agreed with Strabo, the Greek historian and philosopher (63 BC–AD24), that Tarsus surpassed 'Athens, Alexandria, or any other place that can be named where there have been schools and lectures of philosophers.' However, it is unlikely that Paul was educated at the university since he came from a staunchly Jewish family whose father was a Benjamite Pharisee (Philippians 3:5–6) and unlikely to expose him to the Greek culture there. The only education Paul refers to was under the renowned Gamaliel in Jerusalem (Acts 5:34–40; 22:3; 23:6). However, Paul's brilliant mind was clearly aware of the philosophy around him and this enabled him to challenge the false views of his day throughout his mission and letters.

He also quotes from the Athenian writer Menander in 1 Corinthians 15:33 and Acts 17:28, and the Cretan prophet and poet Epimenides (Titus 1:12). At Athens, the city of Plato and Aristotle, Paul debated with Epicurean and Stoic philosophers and probably Cynics also (Acts 17:18). Luke reflects Paul's dismissal of worldly philosophy: 'All the Athenians and the foreigners who lived there spent their time doing nothing but talking about and listening to the latest ideas' (Acts 17:21).

**Above**
*Plato (centre left) and Aristotle surrounded by philosophers, a detail from the School of Athens fresco by Raphael (1508–11)*

Paul later warned against 'Hollow and deceptive philosophy' (Colossians 2:8).

Tarsus was a city of many religions, especially the worship of Mithras, a Roman mystery religion based on Zoroastriansim and popular among the soldiers. But Tarsus was much more. It supported Julius Caesar in his battle with Pompey and as a reward was given tax-free status as the self-governing capital of the Roman province of Cilicia. Jews were allowed to worship freely. It was a proud and loyal Roman city (reflected in Romans 12:1–7?) and at one point renamed itself 'Juliopolis' in honour of Caesar. It was a lucrative trading port, and acknowledged as 'No mean city' (*asamos* 'unimportant, obscure' Acts 21:39). At some point Paul's immediate or past family must have been significant in the city since his Roman citizenship was not purchased (Acts 22:27–28).

# 'Hollow and deceptive philosophy'

**In Athens, Paul began 'preaching the good news about Jesus and the resurrection' but soon found himself debating with the disciples of the great philosophers**

The response to the gospel in Athens was not great: 'A few men became followers of Paul and believed'—including only one member of the philosophical circle (Acts 17:34). Perhaps for this reason, when Paul moved on to Corinth from Athens he 'resolved to know nothing … except Jesus Christ and him crucified' (1 Corinthians 2:2). By no means all across Paul's mission field worshipped the gods.

**Cynics.** Antisthenes (445–365 BC) preached a negative philosophy. God is unknown and unknowable and therefore worship is pointless. Good meant abstinence from pleasure and indifference to pain. It was self-centred, not seeking any social good but inner truth and knowledge.

**Epicureans.** Epicurus (341–270 BC) taught that since suffering and evil are universal, there can be no good God and the gods are almost irrelevant. The only ultimates in the universe are atoms (things) and emptiness. There is no judgement or afterlife, so death need not be feared. The elimination of fear and desire would leave people free to pursue the human goal of physical and mental pleasure.

**Stoics.** Tarsus was a centre for Stoicism and one of its most important teachers was the philosopher Athenodorus (74 BC–AD 7) who tutored Octavian (Augustus). Paul would be familiar with his philosophy, and was certainly familiar with his disciple Seneca, whose writings were hugely popular.

**Lucius Annaeus Seneca** was a politician, satirist, playwright, Stoic philosopher and the brother of Gallio (Acts 18:12). Seneca was tutor and later adviser to the Emperor Nero who, suspecting him of complicity in an assassination plot, ordered him to take his own life in AD 65. Paul and Seneca were therefore contemporaries and died within a year of each other in the same city and under the same emperor.[1]

Seneca believed in four great powers in the universe: Fate, Nature, Fortune and God. The first three were synonymous with God. Stoicism was materialistic and pantheistic. Everything is material and everything is God. Therefore, God is not spirit. Seneca's high ethical standards emphasised the importance of freedom, which is possibly why his brother wanted nothing to do with religious squabbles (Acts 18 14–15). This reflected Rome's acceptance of all religions providing they were peaceful and tolerant. The Christians were persecuted because they were exclusive (only one way) and evangelistic (all must believe).

**Left**
*The original plaster sculpture of Nero and Seneca by Eduardo Barrón (1904). Barrón never completed it in bronze or marble*

1. For a discussion of Seneca's view of God, see Robert James Koehn 'Seneca's concept of a Supreme Being in his Philosophical Essays and Letters' (MA for Loyola University, Chicago 1947. Paper 641).

# 'Slaves of Christ'

## In the time of Jesus and the apostles one in five in the Roman Empire were slaves. In Rome it was as high as one in three

Therefore at least one fifth of all Christians were probably slaves.[1]

Slavery was entered through birth, poverty, war or criminality. The work of slaves ranged from the cruel galleys and quarries to domestic duties and high executive responsibilities. Able and trusted slaves could live well and eventually gain their freedom; some even owned 'under slaves'. Marcus Antonius Pallas, on his freedom, became the financial secretary of Emperor Claudius.

The price of slaves ranged from 500 to 2000 denarii depending on the slave's education and skill. A denarius was a labourer's daily pay. Slave ownership reflected wealth and status. 'Caesar's household' (Philippians 4:22) consisted of around 20,000 slaves and freedmen.

The slave owner held the absolute right over the slave and his labour. He could buy, sell and treat his slave as he pleased. Property was described as vocal (slaves), semi-vocal (animals), and dumb (tools). The slave had no access to the law or justice, could not own property or serve in public office or the army. He could not legally marry, only cohabit. A child born to a slave was the property of the mother's owner, regardless of the father.

Many slaveowners were brutal, and flogging was routine. Tacitus, the Roman historian, described crucifixion as 'a punishment belonging to slaves.' In AD 61 a slave murdered a city prefect and all 400 of the household slaves were executed. The punishment for a runaway slave could range from death to branding on the forehead with the letters FVG (short for 'runaway'). The offence of harbouring a runaway may not have extended to the provinces, so Paul may not have been legally obliged to return Onesimus to Philemon. The loss of an expensive slave, the cost of a 'slave catcher', and the danger of copycat would have been a concern to Philemon.

There were benevolent slaveowners. The Stoic philosopher Seneca encouraged slave owners to gain respect and love from the slave — compare Paul in Colossians 4:1 and Philemon 16. A slave could purchase his freedom (redemption) or be set free by his master (manumission). Generally, a slave served his master between ten and twenty years before freedom; even then he was expected to retain loyalty and service to his previous owner. See page 205 for an image of a freedman and his wife.[2]

**Left**
*A Roman slave collar from the 4th century AD. The inscription reads: 'I have run away. If you bring me back to my master Zoninus you will receive a solidus [gold coin].'*

**Right**
*A first century slave chain discovered at a Roman camp outside Canterbury in Kent*

---

1. See also *Evidence for the Bible* page 133

2. ' For a full presentation of this subject see Murray J Harris, *Slave of Christ — a New Testament metaphor for total devotion to Christ* (Apollos, IVP 1999, Leicester).

# Abolition?

## The frequent New Testament references to 'households' (e.g. Acts 16:15 and 1 Corinthians 1:11 literally 'those of Chloe') almost certainly included the domestic slaves

The noun 'slave' (*doulos*) occurs over 120 times and is *incorrectly* rendered 'servant' by many translations. Slavery provides the background to much of Paul's teaching, for example 1 Corinthians 7:20–24. The phrases, 'not your own… bought with a price' (1 Corinthians 6:19, 20) would be immediately understood. Similarly, with Jesus in Luke 17:10 where *doulos* is used.

People can be slaves of sin (John 8:34), depravity (2 Peter 2:19), passions and pleasures (Titus 3:3), false gods (Galatians 4:8), drink (Titus 2:3) the fear of death (Hebrews 2:15), the law (Galatians 5:1). Even creation is in slavery to decay (Romans 8:21).

Paul wrote openly against 'slave-traders' (the word used in 1 Timothy 1:10); that was radical, because the entire economy depended upon the slave/owner relationship. The idea of total abolition would have been seen by both slaves and free as a social quirk; to encourage a slave revolt would have been futile — they all failed, including Spartacus.

Acknowledging the *status quo* does not mean that Jesus and the apostles endorsed it.

The thrust of the New Testament is not first for Christians to change society, but for Christ to

**Above**
*A marble relief of Roman slaves roped to the neck. From Smyrna (Turkey) c. 200 AD*

change people. Only when people and relationships are changed will society change. In 18th century England, spiritual revival changed sufficient people to bring an end to the slave trade.

In Ephesians 6:5–9 Christian slaves and masters are reminded of their equality as slaves of Christ in the eyes of the God with whom there is no favouritism—something unknown in the first century. Masters are instructed to be just and fair (Colossians 4:1). Romans 12:16 'be willing to associate with people of low position' refers to

giving equal honour to both slave and free. In 1 Corinthians 7:21 Paul encourages manumission where possible. Paul's wise advice in Titus 2:9–10 would help a slave towards freedom!

Paul's letter to Philemon is a model of a transformed relationship between slave-owner and slave. Paul, a well-educated Roman citizen, is pleading the cause of a converted thief and runaway slave, urging that he be reinstated and considered a 'dear brother in the Lord' (v.16). That was radically subversive in the eyes of Rome!

# The gods have come down—at Lystra

**Two ancient legends lay behind the events in Lystra and Athens, and doubtless Paul was familiar with both**

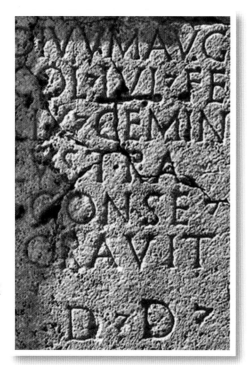

**Above**
*There has been little archaeology at Lystra. Its location was identified by a 2nd century inscription discovered in 1855 by J. R. S. Sterrett*

**Right**
*A coin of Lystra between 27 BC and AD 14. The obverse shows the head of Augustus. The reverse, a priest ploughing with a yoke of oxen to establish the boundary of a Roman city*

Lystra was a remote Roman colony and a military staging post on the via Sebaste (known as the 'Imperial' road). The population was diverse: retired solders, educated and wealthy Greeks and Jews (which was Timothy's background Acts 16:1), and the local largely uneducated Lycaonians of the Anatolian tribe. It was these 'locals' who immediately assumed Paul and Barnabas were the gods returned. Since the apostles did not understand the Lycaonian tongue (Acts 14:11), they could not immediately understand the response until it was well under way (v 13). The healing of a lame man led to Barnabas being honoured as Zeus—the 'father' of all gods, and Paul as Hermes—the messenger of the gods. A fable by Ovid, the Roman poet during the reign of Caesar Augustus, told the following story:[1]

**Jupiter and Mercury** (the Roman equivalents of the Greek Zeus and Hermes), disguised themselves as travelers and called at 'a thousand houses [in Phrygia], seeking a place to rest.' But every home was denied them. Only two old and poor peasants, Baucis and her husband Philemon, offered hospitality. They provided hot water for the visitors to wash, and arranged a bed for the night. They prepared a meal of bacon, vegetables, eggs and cheese and finished with figs, dates, nuts, plums, apples and grapes. Incredulously the old couple watched the wine and the fruit replenish spontaneously.

Realising that they were entertaining gods, they prepared to sacrifice the goose that guarded their home. At this, Jupiter and Mercury warned them that for its lack of hospitality the city would be punished. Baucis and Philemon were escorted to the top of the mountain where they watched the entire city destroyed and their poor home transformed into a beautiful temple. The couple served as priests in the temple until they died together and were transformed into a lime and an oak tree. The story concludes: 'Let those who cared about the gods, be gods themselves, and those who worship gods be worshipped, too.'[2]

Afraid that history might repeat itself, the native Lystrians assumed the gods had returned. Soon after, Paul was stoned, dragged outside the city and left for dead!

1. See also *Evidence for the Bible* p. 157
2. Ovid, *Metamorphoses* Book 8: 620–720. Trans. by Ian Johnston, (Vancouver Island University).

# The unknown god—at Athens

**Athens was a city known for hundreds of idols and altars. It was said: 'As well haul rock to a quarry as bring another god to our city'**

A legend lay behind the altar to the 'unknown god' in Acts 17:23. Six centuries before Paul entered the city, Athens endured a terrible plague that decimated the population. Offerings had been made to the many gods represented in the city but to no avail. Finally, the City Council on Mars Hill was encouraged by an oracle from the priestess at Delphi to send for Epimenides, a prophet and poet at Knossos on the island of Crete. Reluctantly, because Crete was despised by the Athenians, Epimenides was brought to Athens. He ordered a flock of sheep to be assembled at the Areopagus (a word meaning 'high hill' ) in Athens and wherever one of the sheep lay down to rest an altar to the god of that place was to be erected. The plague stopped, but Epimenides did not reveal the name of the god and would accept no reward, requesting only that there should be a treaty of peace between Athens and Knossos.[3]

Unnamed altars grew up all over the city and at least one was inscribed with the words *agnosto theo* (to the unknown God). [4]

In the mid second century AD Pausanias, a Greek traveller and geographer recorded, 'The Athenians have … altars of the gods named Unknown…'[5]

Early in the third century a Greek writer, Philostratus, wrote, 'It is a much greater proof of wisdom and sobriety to speak well of the gods, especially at Athens, where altars are set up in honour even of unknown gods.'[6]

Evidently Paul was aware of the work of Epimenides because he quotes this 'prophet' in Titus 1:12, 'Even one of their own prophets has said, "Cretans are always liars, evil brutes, lazy gluttons."' Incidentally, this is known as 'the liars' paradox'—since Epimenides was himself a Cretan he too must be a liar and therefore the statement is false…!

Paul's sermon (Acts 17:22–31) is a perfect example of step-by-step logic and cross-cultural communication. Rather than dismiss or ridicule the multiplicity of gods in Athens he began with their own visual aid and allowed the logic to follow. In v.28 Paul quoted from two Greek philosopher poets: Epimenides[7] and Aratus[8].

**Above**
*A stone discovered in 1820 in the Palatine Hill, Rome reads: 'Whether to a god or goddess'. Early 2nd century*

3. See also *Evidence for the Bible* p. 163
4. Diogenes Laërtius *The Lives of Eminent Philosophers* (Book 1 'The life of Epimenides' III). Diogenes was a third century A.D. writer of Greek philosophers. His work therefore post-dates Paul but it authenticates Luke's account.
5. In *Description of Greece*. 1:1.4. Translated by WHS Jones.
6. Philostratus, *The life of Apollonius of Tyana*. 6:3
7. In *Cretica* of Zeus: 'in thee we live and move and have our being.'
8. In *Phaenomena* 1–5 'For we are indeed his offspring.'

# Journey to Rome

**Paul's journey to Rome provides some of the clearest evidence that Luke, who wrote the Acts of the Apostles, was an eyewitness of the dramatic events**

In 1848 James Smith published *The Voyage and Shipwreck of St Paul*[1] and it is recognised as a perfect vindication of Luke's accuracy as a historian. Smith sailed for sixty years and as a Fellow of the Royal Society and a member of many scientific societies, he was an able scholar of geology, archaeology and conversant with Greek, Latin and many European languages; he was a recognized authority on ships of the ancient world.

Luke's gospel (Acts 1:1) must have been written well before the close of Acts in AD 61/62 when Paul arrived in Rome, the point at which Luke completed his account. If Acts 16:10 is where Luke joined Paul at Troas, it would be around AD 49. He was possibly an experienced sea passenger with Paul and shared with him those three earlier shipwrecks (2 Corinthians 11:25).

Smith analysed, in minute detail, Luke's account of the entire journey in Acts 27–28. From his own knowledge of those waters, his experience as a sailor, and the records of ancient shipwrecks, naval logs, and others who had travelled the same route, Smith concluded that although Luke was thoroughly acquainted with nautical language, he writes not as a professional

seaman but an accurate observer. What follows are a few of Smith's many details.

The word Luke used for the wind in v 14 was *Eurakulon*, the sailors' term for the 'east north-east wind'; a compound of Greek *euros*, 'east wind' and Latin *aquilo* 'northeast wind'.[2] With that wind direction, an experienced sailor can reconstruct the ship's course and speed from Clauda to the north of Malta. Tacking eight points to the north—as close to the wind

**Left**

*A copy of a drawing of a ship of Paul's day showing its rudders and a hawser towing from the stern passing through the rudder-port. (A drawing by James Smith taken from 'Antichita di Ercolano')* [4]

**Below**

*An African corn ship, from the reverse of a coin of the Emperor Commodus, gives a good idea of the type of ship Paul and Luke were on and the relative size and position of the two principal sails. (Drawn from a coin in the Museum at Avignon, by James Smith)* [5]

Euraquilo as was safe—would carry them 476 miles in a little over thirteen days.[3] On the 'fourteenth night' (v.27) they had arrived a few miles from Malta. The sailors could see nothing, but they 'sensed (suspected) they were approaching land'. They must have heard the breakers on shore.

114

1. The full title is: *The Voyage and Shipwreck of St Paul with dissertations on the life and writings of St Luke and the ships and navigation of the ancients.* (Longman Green and Co 1848). The 1880 edition is used here.
2. Above pp. 159–161
3. Smith supports this conclusion with his detailed calculations and a similar experience recorded by Admiral Sir Charles Penrose. p. 27.
4. Above p. 207.
5. Above p. 201–202.

# The Shipwreck

**There can be no doubt that Luke's account of Paul's journey to Rome and the final shipwreck was not a made-up story but a careful record of an eyewitness**

The phrase 'undergirding' (or frapping) a ship with ropes or chains (v.17) was not uncommon especially for an older vessel. It meant passing four or five turns of a large cable-laid rope round the hull to support her in a fierce storm.

The phrase 'lowered the sea anchor' is better understood as lowering the top gear of the ship. To steady the vessel, everything above deck (spas, sales, rigging etc) would be brought down; the sailors' jargon was sending down the 'top hamper'.[6]

vs 18,38 Luke used the technical term for lightening the ship (*ekouphizon*).

v.28 Similarly, he used the correct nautical term for taking soundings (*bolisantes*)

v.29 It was common for ships at this time to be anchored from the stern. This was the correct action to prevent the ship swinging around broadside and being smashed helplessly onto the rocks.

v.30 At this point, it would be no advantage in lowering anchors from the bow, except as a pretext for escape. Did Luke understand the ploy and inform Paul?

v.37 The careful note of 276 on board is not excessive. This was almost certainly a vessel supplying corn from Egypt ('the breadbasket of Rome') to Italy, and some

were sufficiently large to hold 600 passengers.[7]

v.40 Ships in Paul's day were steered by two large paddles at the stern, hence Luke's plural.

v.41 The reference to a sand-bar (*dithalassus*) is literally a sandbank formed where two opposing currents flow together. The *Authorised Version* accurately translates 'where two seas meet'. In what is known as St Paul's Bay, Selmoon Island (a long, rocky ridge) separates the bay from the sea with a channel and mudbank that produce strong currents. It was here the ship inevitably 'stuck fast'.[8]

Smith illustrated the final shipwreck with almost identical experiences, though in different

**Above**
*The state of Paul's ship on the 15th day with 'the glowing of morning sun'. It reflects Acts 27:40 as the crew 'cut loose the anchors' — and untied the rudders. Selmoon Island is in the background. (Drawn by the marine artist and naval officer 'Mr Henry Smartley of St Heliers' under the direction of James Smith)*[10]

waters, of two early 19th century ships *Terror* and *Bridgwater*.[9]

28:13 from Rhegium to Puteoli is approximately 182 miles due north by sea. With the following South wind, that Luke is careful to note, a single masted vessel could cover that distance in twenty-six hours — 'the following day'.

6. Above pp. 108–111
7. According to the Jewish historian Josephus above p. 187.
8. Above pp. 143–146.
9. As above.
10. As above p. 140.

# Paul — a prisoner

## Almost one third of the Acts of the Apostles concerns Paul as a prisoner

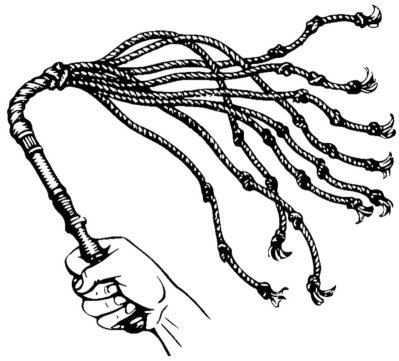

**Left**
*A Roman* flagellum—*leather straps were knotted and fitted with bone or lead*

For Rome, imprisonment was not intended for punishment but to confine the accused before trial; every city had its lockup. However, during the time of Tiberius this was changing, and he was known to leave some prisoners alone, in the dark, chained and with little food and with no hope of release. One contemporary described a state prison: 'Neglect, darkness, and stench make it hideous and fearsome to behold.' Prisoners spent most of their time in total darkness. Many would prefer execution to incarceration. Women prisoners shared the same cells with men. [1]

Beating before and after trial ranged from a severe scourging to a light corrective beating; whichever Paul and Silas received at Philippi (Acts 16), their flesh would be torn and blood would flow. They were then thrown into the 'inner cell' (Acts 16:24), reserved only for the most serious criminals and intended to demoralise and humiliate. The stocks that clamped their feet were known to cause great pain in any movement; it was a form of torture normally reserved for the lowest in society. It was customary for a jailer to cram all his prisoners into the 'inner cell 'at night for security. Their backs raw and bleeding, their feet painfully fastened in stocks, the total darkness of their cell, their gnawing hunger and thirst, and the constant rattle of chains when anyone moved — the response of Paul and Silas was to sing psalms!

During his final imprisonment in Rome, while awaiting trial before the Emperor Nero, Paul refers to being 'chained like a criminal' (2 Timothy 2:9) which implies a much harsher incarceration. Heavy iron chains, ten pounds or more, soon opened sores on a sweaty skin.

In Philippi, as Paul and Silas were stripped naked and severely beaten, the crowd would jeer at the humiliation and torture (Acts 16:22–23). Paul was no stranger to this treatment (2 Corinthians 11:23–25) and his back would have been a mass of scars. In Jerusalem (Acts 22:24–25), Paul was stripped and prepared for a flogging with a Roman *mastix* (Latin *flagellum*). Many were permanently crippled or died after this.

---

1. For a full discussion of this subject: *The book of Acts in its first century setting*, volume 3 'Paul in Roman custody' Brian Rapske, (The Paternoster Press, Carlisle. 1994).

# Paul — a Roman citizen

## Roman citizenship could be obtained by birth, freedom from slavery (manumission), completion of military service, reward or payment

Paul's citizenship is referred to on two occasions: in Philippi (Acts 16:37) and in Jerusalem (22:25, 27). It is also the basis of his appeal to the Emperor (25:10–11). Roman citizenship and the Jewish faith were neither unusual nor incompatible.

Paul was born a citizen (Acts 22:28) and this was registered at the public record office in Tarsus. The current emperor, Claudius, executed any who tried to 'invent' their citizenship. A traveller could carry a *testatio*, (like a birth certificate copy), or a *diploma*, (like a passport). Without this, or the presence of reliable witnesses, the public records of the birth town would have to be searched.

Among the many privileges of Roman citizenship was the right to a fair trial and, ultimately, an appeal to the Emperor (Acts 25:11). No Roman citizen could be beaten before trial or crucified if guilty.

At Philippi, Paul and Silas did not declare their citizenship before the beating; probably because Paul constantly encouraged Jew and Gentile converts to stand firm in persecution (e.g. 1 Thessalonians 3:4), and he did not want to avoid what he anticipated the young Christians would endure.

When Paul was arrested in Jerusalem (Acts 21), he delayed revealing his Roman citizenship because he wanted to use his identity as a Jew to address the crowds. The tribune, Claudius Lysias, was unknowingly about to flay an untried Roman citizen of higher status than himself—custom dictated that Paul's citizenship by birth placed him in a higher status than the tribune's by purchase.

In Caesarea, Paul was given some freedom and allowed visits from his friends to provide for him (24:23). In Roman custody the higher the status of the prisoner, the higher the rank of the officer guarding him — hence a centurion. However, he was still manacled to a Roman soldier. In Rome, for two years Paul was held in 'light custody' and given the freedom of living in his own rented accommodation and at his own expense (28:30). The reference to him manacled to a mere soldier indicates that Paul is no longer seen as a significant prisoner.

**Right**
*A Diploma granting citizenship to an Isaurian soldier named Lualis in the time of Emperor Claudius. Isauria was an area in the south of modern Turkey*

117

# The Temple and the Colosseum

**Herod's magnificent Temple in Jerusalem took forty-six years and '10,000 of the most skillful workmen' to complete, but its glory was short-lived**

Solomon's Temple (966 BC) had been destroyed by the Babylonians in 586 BC. When the Jews were freed from exile in 539 BC, a new temple was built. In 20 BC Herod the Great began to remodel it. His was a magnificent structure set high in the centre of Jerusalem.

Josephus, the contemporary Jewish historian, vividly describes its lavish detail.[1] The pillars were of one entire block of white marble and the roof of cedar was beautifully polished. Nine gates were covered with gold and silver. Separating the Holy of Holies was a 'Babylonian curtain embroidered with blue and fine linen, and scarlet and purple and of a contexture that was truly wonderful.' Josephus wrote that the plates of gold 'dazzled the eye' and outwardly the Temple lacked nothing to surprise the mind and eye. Approaching the city from a distance, the Temple was 'like a mountain covered with snow.'

### The glory departed

In AD 66 the bubbling bitterness of the Jews because of the misrule of the Romans burst into a cauldron of hate. Led by Simon bar Giora, the Roman garrison was destroyed and a relief column ambushed. The Roman general Vespasian arrived,

and the terrifying five-month siege of Jerusalem began.[2] Following the suicide of Nero in AD 68, three emperors were successively murdered within a year and Vespasian, leaving his son Titus in charge of the siege, rushed back to Rome to claim the throne.

Within the city, deadly factions slaughtered many, and all who considered surrender were mercilessly killed. The Romans battled brutally to take the city and losses were heavy on both sides. For miles around, the land became a desert as every tree was used for the siege. Titus built a wall around the city and slowly, horribly, the inhabitants starved: 'The upper rooms were full of women and children that were dying by famine;

**Above**
*A model of the Temple as it appeared in AD 66, created by Israeli archaeologist Michael Avi-Yonah in 1966 and now in the Israel Museum*

and the lanes of the city were full of dead bodies'. Josephus was present, though not in the city, throughout the siege and his gruesome detail is possibly the most horrific recorded siege in history. Compare Matthew 24:21 with Josephus *The Wars of the Jews* Book v.6 to vi.10.

Jesus had given a clear warning of the suffering and devastation of the impending siege (Matthew 24:2,15–21). However, there is no reference in the New Testament to its fulfilment—evidence that the Gospels were complete before AD 70.

1. Josephus' description: *The Antiquities of the Jews* Book XV ch 11.2–6 and *The Wars of the Jews*, Book V ch.5. See also John 2:20.
2. The population of Jerusalem at this time is uncertain; a figure of 100,000 is possible, bearing in mind it was Passover with thousands of pilgrims plus fugitives from the Roman devastation of Judea. See *The Book of Acts in its first century setting* (Paternoster Press, Carlisle 1995), vol.4 pp. 237–265 for a careful discussion of Jerusalem's population numbers.

# What price the Colosseum?

**Finally, against the orders of Titus, the Temple itself was looted and set on fire and the revengeful legionaries began a general massacre without regard to age, sex or rank**

The new emperor Vespasian planned his *Amphitheatrum* to win the support of the citizens of Rome.[3] At the centre of the city, Nero had built his own *Domus Aurea*, or Golden House, after the great fire of AD 64 conveniently cleared the ground for him. This would now be the site of popular entertainment.

At 190m by 155m (620ft by 513ft) it was the largest amphitheatre in the Roman world. Its imposing three tiers of eighty arches, supported by Doric, Ionic and Corinthian columns, were constructed largely of stone, marble, and concrete bricks. The Colosseum was built in just ten years and, on his father's death, it was Vespasian's son, Titus who opened it in AD 80 with one hundred days of 'games' including a mock sea battle, the slaughter of slaves, criminals, gladiators and 9,000 wild animals.

It is uncertain whether Christian's were ever martyred in the Colosseum, although it is likely because of the brutal nature of the 'games' that entertained the 50,000 and more spectators crammed into the tiered rows. The male population of Rome at this time was possibly around 300,000.

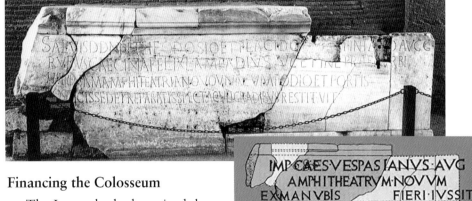

## Financing the Colosseum

The Jews who had survived the siege of Jerusalem were sent to the mines, the arena for sport, or sold as slaves.[4] Many were sent to Rome and doubtless were slave labour for the Colosseum groundworks, in addition to the professional Roman builders, engineers, artists, painters and decorators for the specialized work.

In 1995 Prof Géza Alföldy discovered, under a 5th century inscription in the Colosseum, an earlier bronze inscription from the time of Vespasian (c.AD 79–80). This claimed that the Amphitheater was financed by 'the spoils of war', a reference to the Temple treasures, some of which are displayed on the nearby Arch of Titus. Josephus lists many of the valuable and sacred temple treasures that the priests finally gave to the Romans in exchange for their lives. Much more was simply looted.[5]

**Above**
*The 5th century inscription underneath* which was the reference to the spoils of war financing the Colosseum

119

**Inset**
*The first century 'hidden' inscription*

**Below**
*A Sestertius of Titus celebrating the inauguration of the Colosseum in AD 80*

---

3. Later known as the *Flavian Amphitheatre* and much later *The Colosseum*. See *Evidence for the Bible* p. 178–180.
4. Josephus, perhaps extravagantly, records over a million deaths and 97,000 prisoners.
5. Josephus *Wars* Book VI 8.3.

# Jerusalem: The Walled City

**For anyone visiting the old city of Jerusalem with its maze of narrow alleys and bustling markets, the great city walls inevitably capture the imagination**

The walls as we see them today were built at the time of the Muslim leader Suleiman the Magnificent in the 16th century. But some of their features go back to biblical times.

The enormous Temple Mount platform was constructed at the time of King Herod the Great. It served to create a larger enclosed area for his magnificent new Temple. Many features of the Temple Mount were functioning at the time of Jesus, including the gateways on its southern wall which served as access to the Temple.

- King Hezekiah built a great wall running to the west of the city, some of which is still visible today (2 Chronicles 32:5). See here page 4.

- Nehemiah helped to rebuild the walls along similar lines to those of Solomon and some of these have been identified by archaeologists (Nehemiah 12:31).

- The modern-day Jaffa Gate is where Herod once had a palace; it marks the western limit of the city at the time of Jesus. Part of those Herodian fortifications are still visible today.

- A lame man was healed by the apostles at the 'Beautiful Gate' (Acts 3:10) which is unmentioned outside the New Testament. Given that the lame were not allowed onto the Temple Mount,

it is most likely one of the gates at the southern end that gave access to the Temple. The 'Double Gate' fits the description because inside it has beautifully carved ceilings.[1]

- Thousands of years of rebuilding work have retained the significance of the fortifications for this small city so that today a visitor may still say with the Psalmist: 'Our feet are standing in your gates, Jerusalem … built like a city that is closely compacted together.' (Psalm 122:2–3).

**Above**
*The Impressive walls of Jerusalem were rebuilt at the time of Sulieman (1494–1566 AD) but many follow the foundations of walls that date back to the biblical periods of Jerusalem*

**Left**
*Steps leading up to what remains of the right hand 'Double Gate' to the south of the Temple Mount. A later period building has blocked our view of the rest of the gate but this is possibly the 'Beautiful Gate' of Acts 3*

**Bottom left**
*Inside the 'Double Gate' beneath the Temple Mount Platform, where traces of Herodian style remain*

1. Leen Ritmeyer, *The Quest*, Carta: Jerusalem, 2006.

# Excavating Jerusalem

**Jerusalem offers many problems for archaeology, not least are the political tensions that continue over the ownership of the land**

Religious sensitives surrounding the Temple Mount have prohibited archaeological investigation. However, excavations to the south of the Temple Mount have provided a clear understanding of the Israelite presence from the time of David to Jesus.

The South West Corner of the Temple Mount has been excavated since 1968. A street from the time of Jesus and various gateways leading onto the Temple Mount have been uncovered. The many Jewish ritual baths found here explain how so many baptisms could have taken place on the day of Pentecost (Acts 2:41).

Excavation at the spur of the mountain to the south of the Temple Mount has revealed the earliest period of Jerusalem. Known as the Ophel (meaning 'hill' or 'fortress') it provides clear evidence for early Canaanite occupation and the development of a city from the First Temple period (Solomon). Underground excavations of fortifications and a water system have revealed a road from the New Testament time leading up to the Temple (see here page 123).

Since 2007 excavation at the Givati Parking Lot to the west of the Ophel has revealed even more of the history of Jerusalem, through the Muslim and Roman occupation back to the time of Old Testament Israel. Currently, from the largest excavation in Jerusalem, large buildings and tiny artefacts have come to light from the First Temple period. A clay seal impression (bulla) of Nathan Melech, servant of King Josiah (2 Kings 23:11) was found here in 2019.

121

**Top right**
*The excavations of the Givati Parking Lot are extending our understanding of the City of David*

**Above**
*A clay seal stamped with the name Nathan Melech, from the Givati Parking Lot excavations*

**Right**
*Though explored by Charles Warren in the 19th century, excavations since 1968 have exposed the road and shops from the time of Jesus at the south west corner of the Temple Mount*

# Living Waters—Pool of Siloam

**A city needs a source of water that, at a time of siege, must be accessible and protected from the enemy. In 701 BC, King Hezekiah diverted water from the Gihon spring into a pool within the city**

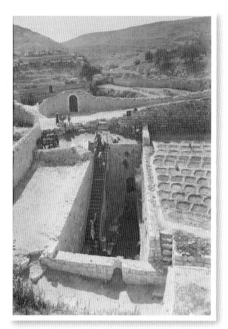

The water entered the city by an underground tunnel (2 Kings 20:20; 2 Chronicles 32:2–4), and a recent discovery has revealed the pool as it was at the time of Jesus. This may be the 'Pool of Siloam' repaired after the time of the exile (Nehemiah 3:15). [1]

Jesus sent the man born blind to the 'Pool of Siloam' to be healed (John 9:1–7). According to Jewish traditions (the Talmud and Josephus) the pool was the starting point for an ascent from the lowest point of Jerusalem to the Temple and so may have served as a place of ritual washing.

By the Byzantine period (4th century on) this pool had been lost and forgotten and around AD 450 a smaller pool had been built where the water emerged from Hezekiah's tunnel. For centuries this was thought to be the Pool of Siloam that we read about in the Bible.

However, in 2004 work on a drainage pipe accidentally discovered ancient steps. Excavation revealed that the steps were the edge of an enormous pool from the time of Jesus. Much of the pool remains beneath the earth, but it is estimated to be 70m long and up to 60m wide—twice an Olympic swimming pool! The steps and depth were designed so that it could be used for ritual washing, which may explain why Jesus sent the blind man here.

The pool was lost to history because it was part of the destruction by the Romans when they demolished the Temple in AD 70. Evidence from the water channel revealed that Jewish rebels had hidden here when the Romans conquered the city. After it was buried in the debris, the inhabitants forgot the location of the original pool and built a smaller replacement.

The fact that John makes reference to the original pool, and expects his readers to know where it is, indicates that he must have written before its destruction in AD 70.

**Far left**
*The Byzantine Pool of Siloam as it was in 1900 and* **below** *as it is today*

**Above**
*One section of the newly discovered but much earlier Pool of Siloam from the time of Christ*

1. See *Evidence for the Bible*, pp. 66–67, 128.

# A Pilgrim's Road?

**According to Josephus, up to two million Jews would visit the Temple during the major festivals, and the Pool of Siloam was possibly the site for ritual washing**

After six years of excavation, in 2017 archaeologists re-opened the road that was in use in the time of Jesus that led from the Pool of Siloam to the Temple. The two thousand year-old street is 8m wide and 600m long. It was built around AD 30 under the government of Pontius Pilate—over 100 coins found under the pavement confirmed the date.[2] In the destruction of AD 70 the road was buried which is why the pavement has been so perfectly preserved. The stepped paving stones would have been the main route leading from the pool to the area of the Temple.

Archaeologists excavating the site dubbed it 'The Pilgrimage Road'. The connection between the pool and Temple certainly illustrates the sense of 'going up' to worship at the Temple described in the Psalms of Ascents (Psalm 120–134). The road has evidence of shops, a drainage channel, a podium and many smaller artefacts including an etching of the menorah. More is yet to be revealed at this site.

Some criticism has focused on the method of archaeology here, which has been considered out of date and risky. Instead of digging down through the layers (strata) of the site, archaeologists are digging a horizontal tunnel underground. Some object that it is motivated by political or tourist concerns rather than true archaeology. However, given the residential neighbourhood above ground, there is no other way to excavate, and engineers on site have an elaborate system to stabilize the tunnel, as can be seen in the photograph.

The road gives a much clearer sense of how worshippers visited Jerusalem and the Temple at the time of Jesus. In the drainage channel that flowed down from the Temple a tiny golden bell was retrieved of the sort that would have been worn by a priest (Exodus 28:33–35). Whether it belonged to the High Priest or not, it helps to confirm that the stepped road served as a ritual pathway leading from the waters of cleansing directly to the Temple itself.

**Top**
*The wide processional pavement leading up to the Temple*

**Above**
*A tiny golden bell found in the drainage channel beneath the street and dating to the time of Christ*

2. Nashon Szanton, Moran Hagbi, Joe Uziel & Donald T. Ariel, 'Pontius Pilate in Jerusalem: The Monumental Street from the Siloam Pool to the Temple Mount', *Journal of the Institute of Archaeology of Tel Aviv University*, 46:2 2019. pp. 147–166.

# Learning from Landfill—Oxyrhynchus

**An ancient rubbish dump has become a valuable source of documents from New Testament times**

The town of Oxyrhynchus in Upper Egypt, west of the Nile, became a regional capital from the time of Alexander the Great. After the time of Christ it was an important centre for early Christianity in Egypt. Though the modern town has not been excavated, ancient mounds on its outskirts have, since 1896. Two English scholars, Bernard Grenfell and Arthur Hunt, first excavated the dumps in Victorian times and found a vast collection of fragmentary papyri documents. The dry climate was ideal for preserving manuscripts, and this particular location was not subject to the annual flooding of the Nile. Many of these manuscripts were sent to the Ashmolean Museum at Oxford University where they continue to be catalogued.[1]

New Testament texts were found, along with other Christian literature, private letters and classical works like those of Homer and Plato. Our understanding of the Bible as originally written has been extended by many finds such as:

- Fragments of Matthew, Mark, Luke and John all dating no later than the 3rd century.

- A manuscript of Mark 1 (P137), controversially suggested from the 1st century but now known to be c. AD 150–250. This makes it one of the earliest copies of Mark in existence.

- Many of the New Testament letters including very early fragments of Romans (P27) and Hebrews (P13) dating to AD 250.

- A fragment of Thomas, a non-canonical gospel, dating from around AD 200 was the first manuscript to be identified.

- Many sections of the Greek Old Testament (the *Septuagint*) including Genesis and Psalms.

The earliest New Testament papyri from Oxyrhynchus date from the middle of the 2nd century, only decades after it was completed. Excavations continue at Oxyrhynchus and more manuscripts continue to emerge. One clear lesson from this landfill is that the copying tradition of ancient books was very reliable. These texts help inform our reconstruction of what was originally written and help to explain how variations emerged.

**Left**
*A papyrus fragment of Romans (P27) from Oxyrhynchus dating to early third century*

**Above**
*The early excavations at Oxyrhynchus c.1903 which yielded half a million papyri*

---

1. For example, see Peter M. Head, 'Some Recently Published NT Papyri from Oxyhynchus: An Overview and Preliminary Assessment', *Tyndale Bulletin* 51.1 (Tyndale House: Cambridge, 2000). pp. 1–16. Oxford University has a website which continually publishes discoveries from the site which can be browsed at www.papyrology.ox.ac.uk.

# From Scroll to Codex

**Old Testament texts were written on a continuous scroll. During the 1st century AD the development of the codex (book) coincided with the spread of the New Testament**

There are around 5300 Greek New Testament manuscripts, from postage stamp size to whole books. From these we can reconstruct the New Testament as originally written. The survival of so many ancient fragments owes much to the climate of Egypt where papyrus could survive, and to the development of the codex or book format.

Binding pages together means that both sides of the parchment or papyrus can be used and more text can be held than on a scroll. This new invention was very popular with Christians. Discoveries at Oxyrhynchus show that for Christians the 'codex was the favoured format by a large margin.'[2]

- The earliest papyrus fragment of a New Testament book is P52, held at the John Rylands Library in Manchester (UK). One side contains John 18:31–33 and the other John 18:37–38. Based on the handwriting it is dated to the early 2nd century.

- The Chester Beatty Biblical Papyri are a collection of early Greek codices dating to AD 250. Bought between 1930 and 1934, they originated in Egypt and include most of the books of the New Testament. A single codex (P45) binds together the four Gospels and the book of Acts. Another manuscript (P46) contains the letters of Paul.

**Left**
*A page from* Codex Sinaiticus *containing Matthew 6:4–32 on display at the British Library*

**Below**
*St. Catherine's monastery in the dry Sinai desert has the perfect conditions to preserve ancient books*

- *Codex Vaticanus* contains a complete Greek Old Testament and most of the New Testament. Dating to the 4th century it is named after its current home in the Vatican.

- *Codex Sinaiticus*, from St Catherine's Monastery in Egypt, is the earliest complete New Testament, and was copied sometime between AD 325 and 360. It uses animal skin rather than papyrus.

The invention of the codex was an enormous leap forward in technology, allowing for the easy transmission of large volumes of text. Its continued value is proven by our modern cheap paperbacks,

and the fact that even digital readers resemble the format of the codex.

Christians clearly had an influential role in the development and spread of books!

125

2. Brent Nongbri, *God's Library: The Archaeology of the Earliest Christian Manuscripts*, (Yale University, 2018). p.439. For more on these papyri see Brian Edwards, *Nothing but the Truth* pp. 437–452.

# City Life in the Bible

**Cities in the Bible are quite different from cities as we know them in the modern world. This explains their significance in the conquest and their role in social life**

A 'tel' is the Hebrew word for an artificial hill that is the result of many centuries of occupation. As one city was destroyed or abandoned another was built on top of its ruins creating a hill like a tabletop.

The tel of Megiddo (Judges 1:27) is formed from twenty-six distinct city ruins, one on top of another. Tel es-Sultan is the site of biblical Jericho (Joshua 2:1), one of the oldest cities in the world. Some of those levels relate to biblical history. One of the reasons a tel could survive for so long is that these were cities with massive walls, ramparts and fortified gates.

We have the remains of many Old Testament cities in Canaan and know a great deal about them. Hazor is the largest of them at around 200 acres, while Old Testament Jerusalem was never larger than 40 acres with a population no more than 4000.[1] As a fortification, a city was not the place where most people lived. Those who farmed the land lived in simple homes near their fields. Little would survive of these villages in the archaeological record.

In the conquest under Joshua, God directed the Israelites to destroy cities like Jericho, Ai and Hazor because they represented a significant military threat. The weakest point in a city's defences would be the gate and so these

**Above and inset**
*An aerial view of the tel of Megiddo with the remains of the massive gateway*

**Below**
*An extensive plaza at the city gate of Dan provided an area for commerce and socialising*

became highly developed both for security but also as a place of meeting, worship, law giving and storage.[2] The Bible describes the city gate being used for judgement (Deuteronomy 21:18–21), marriage matters (Ruth 4:1–11), news (1 Samuel 4:18) and audiences with the king (2 Samuel 18:1–5). King Solomon invested in developing the city gates and walls at Gezer, Hazor and Megiddo (1 Kings 9:15). Evidence has been found at each of these cities for elaborate defensive building work which may be associated with Solomon.

1. See Hershel Shanks 'Ancient Jerusalem: The Village, The Town, the City' (*Biblical Archaeological Review* May/June 2016). It significantly increased in population by the 1st century AD, see footnote here on page 118.
2. See also the strong city gate at Khirbet Qeiyafa in *Evidence for the Bible* p. 40 and here pages 72–73.

# The lost city of Geshur

**The biblical text assists archaeologists in trying to identify ancient cities they have found. Geshur is one such example**

Apart from a possible reference in the Amarna tablets in Egypt,[3] we only know of the Geshurites from the Bible. They are placed somewhere north-east of Israel from the shore of the sea of Galilee to the Golan heights (Joshua 13:13; 2 Samuel 15:8). Geshur was their capital and the word means 'Stronghold' or 'Fortress'. King David was on friendly terms with the Geshurites; he married the king's daughter Talmai (2 Samuel 3:3); his son from this marriage, Absalom, spent three years in exile here (2 Samuel 13:38). Geshur flourished during the time of King David but lost its independence soon after and was subsumed by other nations to the north.[4]

In recent years archaeologists have found a major city in this region near Galilee at et-Tell, with impressive fortifications and dating to the period of David. It had its own independent culture and was a large city reflecting a wealth generated from the area of the Golan heights. The formidable city gate shows evidence of being destroyed in 734 BC which would coincide with the campaigns of the Assyrian king, Tiglath-Pileser III (Pul in 2 Kings 15:19). The gate from this period demonstrates the significance of the city at the end of its time of independence.

However, a recently discovered city gate from the earlier 10th century, with associated remains, demonstrates that the city and the Geshurite culture was prospering at the time of King David. The archaeological record fits well with the Biblical references to the rise and fall of the Geshurite people. The destruction of the city gate from the time of David would fit with the period when we know Pharaoh Shishak was involved in a military campaign in the area c.925 BC (1 Kings 14:25).

---

3. See *Evidence for the Bible* p. 29 for the Amarna letters.
4. K. Lawson Younger Jnr., *The Political History of the Arameans*, (SBL Press, 2016). pp. 204–213.

# Josephus: Eyewitness to the First Century

**Anyone interested in the background to the New Testament will come across Titus Flavius Josephus (AD 37–100). Who was he and can his record of the first century be trusted?**

**Left**
*A first century Roman sculpture that is considered to represent Josephus*

Born into a priestly family, Josephus would have been an orthodox Jew in Palestine during the period of Roman occupation. During the first Jewish-Roman war (AD 66–73) he was a commander of the Jewish forces in Galilee fighting against the Romans. In AD 67 he was besieged by the Romans at Jotapata in Lower Galilee. Preferring death to enslavement he and his men planned to commit mass suicide. They drew lots to kill each other in turn. However, the remaining two decided to surrender. One of them was Yosef ben Matityahu (Josephus) who became a useful Jewish interpreter for the Roman general Vespasian.

When Vespasian became Emperor of Rome in AD 70, Josephus was granted freedom, but he remained as an advisor to Vespasian's son, Titus. He was present at the destruction of the temple in Jerusalem and was also able to record the siege and fall of Masada.[1] Gaining Roman citizenship, he changed his name to Titus Flavius Josephus in honour of his patrons.

In Rome, Josephus wrote a detailed account of Palestine in the first century. This included:

- The life of Herod the Great. From the record of Josephus,[2] archaeologist Ehud Netzer was able to locate and excavate the tomb of Herod in 2007.

- Many of the dates that we use for the chronology of the New Testament rely on Josephus such as the date for the death of Herod the Great in 4 BC.

- Key political figures in the New Testament are mentioned by Josephus including Claudius (Acts 11:28; 18:2), Felix (Acts 24:25) and Festus (Acts 24:27), all in correct chronological sequence.

- A reference to a census under Quirinius,[3] along with a number of people we meet in the Gospels: John the Baptist, Pontius Pilate, James and Jesus.

- Josephus confirmed that at the time of Jesus the Jews were using the same books that we have in our Old Testament, though organised differently.

Understandably, Jewish tradition dismissed him as a collaborator with the Romans and his works were not preserved by them. Though his writings are self-promoting and sometimes confused in their account of history, he is recognized as a generally reliable eyewitness to his times.

**Below**
*The site of Herod's tomb at Herodium (12km south of Jerusalem), and his sarcophagus discovered there with the help of Josephus' Antiquities*

---

1. See also here p. 118 and *Evidence for the Bible* p. 181.
2. *Antiquities* 17:197–199.
3. See also here p. 149 and *Evidence for the Bible* pp. 203–204

128

# The Testimony of Josephus

**Josephus provides us with one of the first references to Jesus outside the New Testament. However, the authenticity of some of the references are subject to debate**

Josephus provides background to John the Baptist, including the tone of his preaching, his following, his popularity with crowds and his execution by Herod.[4] He includes some details that the Gospels do not provide, such as where John's execution took place, at Machaerus, a palace of Herod.

There are two references to Jesus in Josephus' *The Antiquities of the Jews*. The most well known, *The Testimonium Flavianum*, records:

*"Now there was about this time Jesus, a wise man ... a doer of wonderful works – a teacher of such men as receive the truth with pleasure. He drew over to him both many of the Jews, and many of the Gentiles. He was [the] Christ; and when Pilate ... condemned him to the cross, those that loved him at the first did not forsake him, for he appeared to them alive again the third day, as the divine prophets had foretold ... and the tribe of Christians, so named from him, are not extinct at this day."[5]*

Many consider this was originally a simple reference to Jesus executed under Pilate, but the final form was elaborated by a Christian editor. However, no versions of Josephus exist without it.[6] Even a skeptical scholar like Bart Ehrman affirms, 'It is far more

likely that the core of the passage actually goes back to Josephus himself.'[7]

There is a second reference to Jesus in the works of Josephus 'the authenticity of which has been almost universally acknowledged.'[8] Josephus mentions Jesus in connection to the martyrdom of James.

*"Albinus ... assembled the Sanhedrin of judges, and brought before them the brother of Jesus, who was called Christ, whose name was James..."*

There is good reason to trust Josephus as a useful witness to the world of the first century, and his reference to Jesus and the people of the Gospels affirms their historicity.

**Top**
*The remains of Jotapata, where Josephus made his last stand while still a General of the Jewish forces in Galilee*

**Above**
*Machaerus, in modern day Jordan, where John the Baptist was executed by Herod*

4. Whiston's Josephus, *Antiquities* 18:116–119. See also Steve Mason, *Josephus and the New Testament,* (Hendrickson: Peabody, MA, 1992). p. 153.
5. *Antiquities 18.63–64.*
6. For a defence of its authenticity see Brian Edwards, *Nothing but the Truth*, (Day One Publications, Leominster, 2020). pp. 77–81.
7. Bart Ehrman, *Did Jesus Exist?* (HarperOne: New York, 2012). p. 64.
8. Louis H. Feldman and Gohei Hata (editors), *Josephus, Judaism and* Christianity (Wayne State University Press: Detroit, 1987). p. 56. See *Antiquities 20.9.*

# Antioch in Syria

## Syrian Antioch was an unlikely setting for the birth of the first Gentile church

Twenty miles from the Mediterranean coast and situated in a broad fertile plain, the city of Antioch in Syria[1] took advantage of the navigable Orontes river to create a thriving seaport at Seleucia (Acts 13:4); this, together with caravan routes from Arabia and Mesopotamia opened up trade from the Orient. It was a city of wealth and luxury with two miles of marble-paved streets. When occupied by the Romans in 65 BC, Antioch became capital of the province of Syria with a Roman legate in residence and, according to the Jewish historian Josephus, was 'Third city in the habitable [Roman] world.. both in magnitude and other marks of prosperity'[2] — behind only Rome and Alexandria.

Its affluence and art led to its decadent reputation. The historian Edward Gibbon wrote, 'Fashion was the only law, pleasure the only pursuit, and the splendour of dress and furniture was the only distinction of the citizens of Antioch.' The pleasure garden at Daphne, five miles away, 'With its sanctuary of Apollo, its groves of laurel and cypress, its sparkling plantains, its colonnades and halls and bars, has come down through history with an evil name.'[3] The Roman poet Juvenal (born AD 55), jibed that Antioch allowed its delinquency to travel to Rome:

'The Orontes flowed into the Tiber flooding Rome with the superstition and immorality of the East.' Mommsen, the 19th century German classical scholar and historian commented that the reason there are so few memorial stones or inscriptions from ancient Antioch is because 'this people valued only the day'; they had no concern for the future. The existing mosaics from Daphne bear witness to the city's pagan decadence.

The population was made up largely from the local Syrians, many Greek immigrants, and a strong Jewish settlement in Antioch enjoying all the privileges of Rome; many of these had been encouraged to settle at Antioch in the time of Antiochus Epiphanes in the second century BC, although others were possibly descended from Jews exiled in the time of Nebuchadnezzar of Babylon in 586 BC. The population steadily grew and by the fourth century the Christian leader, Chrysostom, estimated it around two hundred thousand of whom half, he suggested, were Christians! The remains of forty churches have been discovered dating from the fourth century.

---

1. Do not confuse this with Pisidian Antioch (Acts 13:14).
2. Josephus *Wars* III.2.4.
3. Hastings, *Dictionary of the Apostolic Church*.

# The birthplace of the Gentile church

**The community of Christians at Antioch unknowingly modelled an example of church life for Christian communities across the empire**

After the martyrdom of Stephen and the rising persecution, significantly led by Saul of Tarsus, many Jerusalem Christians were scattered across the empire (Acts 8:1–4). At Antioch, young converts from Cyprus and Cyrene 'began to speak to Greeks also' (Acts 11:19–21).

### First, Antioch was the first Gentile/Jewish congregation

Many Greeks had joined the Jewish faith as proselytes, presumably because of their disgust at the decadence around them—'Nicolas from Antioch, a convert to Judaism' was one of the seven deacons (Acts 6:5). It was largely from this Greek community that the young Christians were drawn. Luke 2:32 was accomplished.

### Second, Antioch was the first congregation to be called 'Christian'

The word 'Christian' (literally 'belonging to Christ' 11:26) was likely used as a disparaging nickname by the local population when they first distinguished the Christian message from Judaism. Mommsen comments on Antioch: 'Their only talent was mastery of ridicule'— whether of actors, rulers, and even the emperor. Christians accepted it as appropriate and far better than the 'foreign superstition' dismissively used by the Romans. Peter was certainly happy to employ it (1 Peter 4:16).

### Third, Antioch was the first congregation to collect for overseas aid

It must have been something unheard-of in Antioch when the Christian community began collecting famine relief for their brothers and sisters in Judaea whom they had never met (11:27–30).

### Fourth, Antioch was the first congregation to organise for world evangelism

The church at Antioch established the first planned overseas mission during a time of prayer (13:1–3). This became the 'home base' for Paul and Barnabas and they naturally returned there at the end of their first gospel outreach (14:26–28). From here they were commissioned for their second journey (15:36,40).

### Fifth, Antioch was the first church to call for an international Christian conference

What resulted from the council at Jerusalem has been referred to as the 'charter of spiritual freedom', but it was requested by the church in Antioch (15:1–4).

### Sixth, Antioch was the first congregation to establish a legacy of Bible teaching

'Paul and Barnabas remained in Antioch, where they and many others taught and preached the word of the Lord' (15:35). Antioch became a known centre for Bible teaching through men like Ignatius (?50–115), Lucian (240–312), Chrysostom (347–407) and Theodore (350–428). Between AD 252 and 380 ten Christian councils were held at Antioch.

**Left**
*A Roman road leading out of Antioch*

# Beyond the Acts

The abrupt ending of the Acts of the Apostles may signify Luke's intention to add a third book to record the spread of the Gospel. Before the close of Acts the Christian church was rapidly expanding

From Judea in Acts 2 to east Africa in Acts 8 Jewish proselytes returned as Christians to lands that would become modern day Israel, Jordan, Greece, Italy, Turkey, Iran, Iraq, Syria, Libya, Egypt, Saudi Arabia and Ethiopia—covering three continents (Acts 2:8–11).[1]

Paul was not exaggerating when he wrote, 'All over the world [the Roman world at least] this gospel is bearing fruit and growing' (Colossians.1:6). Already the Gospel had penetrated the staff of the emperor (Philippians 4:22) and others in positions of prominence, for example Acts 10:1; 13:7,12; 16:14; 17:4,12; Romans 16:23.

Leaving aside the legends of Joseph of Arimathea and King Arthur, in the 6th century the British monk Gildas claimed that the Gospel came to Britain '... as we know, in the last years of Tiberius Caesar'. Tiberius died in AD 37, only a few years after the Resurrection. When the Roman General Plautius invaded Britain in AD 43, he was accompanied by his wife Pomponia; the Roman historian, Tacitus, informs us that by AD 57, the year in which Paul arrived in Macedonia (Acts 20) and wrote to the Christians in Rome, Pomponia was 'charged with being tainted with that foreign superstition.'[2] Only Christianity was dismissed by Rome as a 'foreign superstition'. Was she a Christian when in Britain?

Writing around AD 200, the African bishop, Tertullian, wrote of the rapid expansion of the Gospel. He listed many nations including:

*'...all the limits of the Spains, and the diverse nations of the Gauls* [the Roman name for an area which included parts of France, Luxembourg, Belgium, Switzerland, Italy, the Netherlands, and Germany], *and the haunts of the Britons— inaccessible to the Romans, but subjugated to Christ... and of many remote nations, and of provinces and islands many, to us unknown, and which we can scarce enumerate... in all these places dwells the "people" of the Name of Christ.'*[3]

Even if Tertullian slightly exaggerated, the Christian message was rapidly expanding beyond the Empire. By AD 314 the churches in Britain were sufficiently strong to send three bishops, a presbyter and a deacon to the Council of Arles in southern France, called by the Emperor Constantine.

**Above**
*A 4th century silver spoon from West Row (near Mildenhall) in Suffolk engraved with the early Christian symbols of Chi-rho and alpha and omega* [4]

**Below**
*Evidence of Christianity in England early in the 4th century: part of a mosaic of Christ from a Roman villa in Hinton St Mary, Dorset with the Chi-rho symbol*

132

1. F F Bruce helpfully identifies many of the places in Acts 2 in *The Acts of the Apostles* (Tyndale Press 1962).
2. See *Evidence for the Bible* p. 149 and a fuller account of her life, *The Tyndale Society Journal* no.37 Autumn 2009. pp. 32–39.
3. Tertullian, *Answers to the Jews* VII.4. (Translated by S.Thelwall).
4. For early Christian symbols see *Evidence for the Bible* p. 191.

# Christians in Pompeii?

**In 1862, archaeologist Giuseppe Fiorelli, discovered a graffiti written in Latin on the wall of a building in Pompeii that revealed the presence of Christians in the town**

| | |
|---|---|
| | VINA |
| | MARIA |
| | ADIA · A·V |
| | BOVIG SAVDI CHRISTIANOS |
| | SEVOSO ONIS |

*The first line-drawing of the Christianos graffiti made in 1862 by the Italian scholar Giulio Minervini and published in 1864 by Giovanni de Rossi, together with its likely transcription.*

Unfortunately, it was written in charcoal and soon faded when exposed to the light. However, two other scholars saw it, and each made almost identical drawings of the words. The text has been discussed in detail.[5] Some scholars translate lines 4 and 5 as: 'Bovio is listening to the Christians, cruel haters.' Most agree that someone called Bovio is possibly mocked for listening to the Christians. No one questions the word *Christianos*. Suggestions that the building was a Christian centre are speculative.

In 2016 Bruce W Longenecker published his thoroughly detailed research on Christianity in Pompeii.[6] He credibly suggests the above charcoal graffiti should be understood as: 'Listening to the Christians is good for the neighbourhood' followed by an incomplete derogatory response—

typical of graffiti 'conversations' in Pompeii. Longenecker also discusses in detail the carefully crafted cross in raised plaster on a wall in a bakery discovered in 1813, a graffiti which included the Latin *Vivit* (he lives) where the final *it* had been combined into a cross, a cross on a stamp ring belonging to someone called 'Meges', and nineteen crosses inscribed into town paving stones, which may have identified homes or businesses of 'Jesus-followers'.

There is no reason why there may not have been Christians in Pompeii. When Paul arrived at Puteoli as a prisoner on his way to Rome in AD 60/61 he was allowed to stay with 'some brothers' for the week (Acts 28:13–14). Puteoli (modern Pozzuoli) was less than 50k (30mi) from Pompeii and was Italy's leading port city; Cicero referred to

it as 'Little Rome'. Regular trade between the two is evident from a quantity of Puteoli pottery found in Pompeii, as well as the numerous graffiti in Pompeii left by travelling merchants from Puteoli. Whether Bovio was a tradesman or resident is impossible to know. When some suggest, as one scholar has, that Christians at Pompeii before AD 79 'is a bit of a fantasy',[7] they forget that two decades earlier there was a thriving Christian community a day's journey down the road at Puteoli!

133

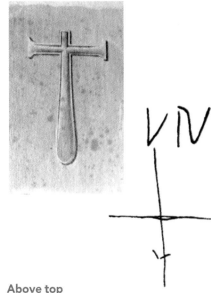

**Above top**
*The drawing by François Mazois of the cross in the Pompeii bakery of the Insula Arriana Polliana when he discovered it in 1813*

**Above**
*The vivit (he lives) inscription*

5. Thomas A. Wayment and Matthew J. Grey, 'Jesus Followers in Pompeii: The *Christianos* Graffito and "Hotel of the Christians" Reconsidered' (Brigham Young University *JJMJS* No. 2 (2015). pp. 102—146.

6. Bruce W Longenecker, *The Crosses of Pompeii—Jesus devotion in a Vesuvian Town* (Fortress Press, Minn.2016).

7. Mary Beard, quoted by Longenecker p. 59.

# From flame to fame

**The message that Christ alone was the way of salvation and that everyone must believe, brought Christians into conflict with the state**

From Tiberius in AD 37 to the death of Constantine in AD 337 there were almost sixty Roman emperors of whom more than half were murdered or committed suicide. This violence of the leadership was reflected in the treatment of those who challenged Rome. At first Christians were seen as a sect of Judaism, however their significant increase posed a threat to stability. Early in the third century, the Christian leader **Tertullian** explained in a tract *To the Nations:*

*'Every day you groan over the proliferating number of Christians. You fret that the state is overrun by Christians… You mourn the fact that every sex, every age, and every social class is crossing over from you to us. Nor does it occur to you that something good might lie hidden here. You avoid straight thinking and you shun an open mind.'*

For three hundred years persecution from Rome was severe but sporadic, and times of peace allowed the church to expand. The reign of **Marcus Aurelius** (AD 161–180) provided two decades of relative peace and he instructed that Christians should not be punished for their religion, but only if they break the law.[1] Here are some of the persecuting emperors:

**Caligula** (AD 37–41) deified himself and declared it treason not to worship him.

**Claudius** (AD 41–54) expelled all Jews from Rome because of quarrels over 'Chrestus' (Acts 18:2).

**Nero** (AD 54–68) blamed Christians for the great fire of Rome in AD 64 and many in Rome suffered; probably including Paul and Peter.

**Domitian** (81–96) was the first emperor to demand the title and worship of *Dominus et Deus* ('Lord and God'). All who refused were tortured to recant or killed.[2]

**Trajan** (AD 98–117) replied to Pliny, his governor in Bithynia who was unsure what to do with 'Christians'; Pliny had interrogated them, threatened them and executed those who refused to recant. He gives no indication of numbers. The emperor forbade any general persecution, but commended Pliny on his response to those who refused to recant when charged. Ignatius, the Christian leader at Antioch was was martyred on his watch.

**Above**
*The Trajan's column in Rome was completed in AD 113. It stands at 38m (125ft) and celebrates the victories of Trajan over the Dacians (Romania today) with over 2,600 figures of the battles and bridge-building. In 1588 the bronze figure of Trajan was replaced by St Peter*

**Left**
*A bust of Nero*

134

1. Marcus Aurellius, *Letter of Antoninus to the Common Assembly of Asia* (AD 161).
2. See more on Domitian in *Evidence for the Bible* p. 182–183.

# Persecution increases

## Before Septimus Severus, persecution was often local and sporadic; empire-wide edicts were ignored in some areas and applied vigorously in others

**S**eptimus Severus (AD 193–211), in order to maintain harmony in the empire, issued an empire-wide edict in AD 202 forbidding conversion to Judaism or Christianity. At this time Perpetua and her servant Felicitas courageously died for their faith and many others also.

**Decius** (AD 249–251) ordered an empire-wide persecution to restore the favour of the gods; sacrifice had to be made to the gods and the emperor, and a certificate (a *libellius*) obtained from a Roman magistrate. All who refused, Jews excepted, were killed. Many Christians died at this time.

**Valerian** (AD 253–260) blamed Christians for the increasing weakness of the empire and followed Decius' persecution. By now Christians were often in high office, including senators. Valerian targeted especially Christian leaders. Many were killed and others sent to the mines and their property was confiscated. Following Valerian's capture and death by the Persians, there was a time of peace for Christians.

**Diocletian** (AD 284–305) carried out the first empire-wide attempt to exterminate all Christians, from AD 303. Supposedly ignited by Marcellus, a centurion who refused to participate in a military celebration that demanded sacrifice to Roman gods, it was known as The Great Persecution and was the most severe. All worship was forbidden, churches destroyed and Christian books confiscated. Diocletian's own household staff and a whole congregation of Christians were burned alive in the town of Phrygia.

**Galerius** (AD 305–311) had been a successful general under Diocletian but was fanatically anti-Christian and is credited with persuading Diocletian to exterminate Christianity. As Junior emperor in the East he was especially cruel. Few survived the harsh conditions of *Damnatio ad metalla* (condemnation to the mines).

**The Roman Tetrarchy** ('four rulers') was Diocletian's way for dividing the empire into East and West for ease of government with two emperors, each with a Caesar. On his death Galerius and Severus in the East, and Constantius and Daza in the West were the last to persecute Christians.

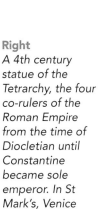

**Left**
A libellius (c AD 250 Egypt) for Aurelious Sarapammon confirming: 'Always sacrificing to the gods, now too, in your presence, in accordance with the orders, I sacrificed, poured the libations, and tasted the offerings, and I ask that you sign below. Farewell…'. It was signed by the two witnesses Aurelius Serenus and Hermas

**Right**
A 4th century statue of the Tetrarchy, the four co-rulers of the Roman Empire from the time of Diocletian until Constantine became sole emperor. In St Mark's, Venice

# The causes of persecution

**Throughout almost three hundred years of persecution, the church grew steadily and in places dramatically. Within a century and a half Christians were found not only among slaves and servants, but senators and senior military officers**

**Left**
*Publius Cornelius Tacitus (c. AD 56–120) is regarded as a most reliable Roman historian on the lives of emperors, including Tiberius, Claudius and Nero. His description of the treatment of Christians by Nero is unquestioned. His statue is outside the Austrian Parliament building in Vienna*

In spite of recent attempts to revise history[1], there is no question that persecution of the early church was at times bitter and widespread. The contemporary Roman historian, Tacitus, described the suffering of Christians under Nero: '*They died in torments, and their torments were embittered by insult and derision. Some were nailed on crosses; others sewn up in the skins of wild beasts and exposed to the fury of dogs; others, smeared over with combustible materials, were used as torches to illuminate the darkness of the night.*'[2]

The reasons for persecution varied across time. Pliny appears to have been annoyed at the stubbornness of Christians to recant. Writing to his emperor, Trajan, he admits he could find nothing wrong with their simple, honest life-style but: 'Whatever may be the principle of their conduct, their inflexible obstinacy appeared deserving of punishment.' Tertullian noted two enemies of the early church: 'Nero and rumour'. Without evidence, Christians were accused of 'chilling and monstrous charges', including incest, infanticide, adultery, cannibalism and worshipping the sun and even a donkey's head. Their seemingly 'secret' meetings, 'love feasts', the 'body and blood' eaten at the 'Lord's supper', and holy kisses between 'brothers and sisters' all gave rise to lurid and crude rumours of this new cult.

More significant was the fact that the Christians, like the Jews, worshipped only one God and despised the great pantheon of Roman gods; they were therefore despised as 'atheists'. This was disloyal to the emperor (treason), harmful to Roman identity (disruptive) and would seriously offend the gods (dangerous)— which is exactly what Valerian accused them of. Unlike the Jews, Christians had an evangelistic zeal to convert everyone—and that destabilised the harmony of the empire. Suetonius, the Roman lawyer and historian, referred to 'a new and mischievous superstition' and Tacitus called it 'a foreign and deadly superstition.' Their avoidance of the blood lust of the arena and the crudity of the theatre had the appearance of 'a hatred of the human race.'[3]

136

---

1. More recently: Candida Moss (a Professor at the University of Notre Dame) *The Myth of Persecution— how early Christians invented the story of martyrdom* (Bravo Ltd 2014). Her view has been largely dismissed.
2. Tacitus, *The Annals*, XV.44.
3. For evidence of martyrdom from the tomb inscriptions in the catacombs, see *Evidence for the Bible* p. 193.

# A bitter sweet peace **from Constantine**

**By the Edict of Milan in January AD 313, the emperors Constantine and Licinius allowed worship 'for any divinity whatsoever in the seat of the heavens.' However, this act of peace for Christians held within it the seeds of a bitter future**

Whatever the reality of Constantine's 'conversion' to the Christian faith after his victory at Milvian Bridge in AD 312, he encouraged Christianity and expressed his devotion to the cross, surmounting the Christian chi-rho symbol on his standard (the *Labarum*); he erected a portable chapel for prayer when he was on campaign. Constantine never again sacrificed at Jupiter's shrine in Rome. When, in AD 324, he clashed with Licinius who had resumed persecuting Christians in the East, his victory was seen as the triumph of Christianity over the traditional pagan gods. There were still many contradictions, and persecution would reappear before the end of the empire. [4]

## A bitter peace

Tragically, after the edict of Milan Christians found causes to divide. Some who had avoided suffering by purchasing a *libellius*, were refused fellowship by those who bore the scars of torture. Heretical sects, especially the Gnostics, found it safe to spread their views. The emperor now passed judgment on theological controversies, including Donatism, Arianism, and even the date of Easter.

With the popularity of Christianity, the churches were weakened by many 'pretenders'. The church in Rome owed much of its wealth to Constantine as gold, silver, lands and estates came into its possession. Church buildings became splendid palaces, ceremonies became royal processions and the church and its bishop in Rome slowly secured authority over the Western congregations. Power and politics corrupted the church in Rome. The historian Edward Gibbon concluded, 'During the ages of ignorance' following the fall of Rome in the fifth century, and the ascendancy of the power of the church in the once imperial city, 'Prosperity had relaxed the nerves of discipline. Fraud, envy, and malice prevailed in every congregation.' [5] Power, wealth and comfort replaced loyalty to Christ and its consequent martyrdom.

It is not possible to know how many Christians died for their faith in the first three centuries, but Gibbon reminds us that from the twelfth to the sixteenth centuries the Church

**Above**
*On one of the doors of Milan Cathedral at the central Piazza del Duomo, is a depiction of a seated Constantine the Great, holding the Milan edict in his hand; next to him is some of the text of the edict (inset)* (The relief is by Arrigo Minerbi 1948)

of Rome vigorously defended by violence and death 'the empire which she had acquired by fraud'. He concludes that this 'Christian' church tallied far more martyrs than pagan Rome had ever done.

4. For more on Constantine see *Evidence for the Bible* pp. 194–195.
5. Edward Gibbon, *The Decline And Fall Of The Roman Empire* ch. 16.

# Pioneers of archaeology
## Charles Leonard Woolley (1880–1960)

**Woolley is recognized as one of the first archaeologists to excavate methodically, keeping detailed records and using them to reconstruct ancient life and history**

*Woolley at Carchemish in 1912*

**Right**
*A photo taken by Woolley in the 1920s of the work at the Ziggurat of Ur at Tell el-Mukayyar, Iraq. This was jointly funded by the British Museum and the University of Pensylvania*

**Right below**
*A reconstruction of the Great Death Pit as it would have appeared before the death of the attendants. Drawn by Amedee Forestier in 1928*

After graduating from Oxford in 1905 Woolley became assistant keeper in the Department of Antiquities at the Ashmolean Museum. With little formal training, Woolley began his archaeological career in 1907. In both World Wars he worked in intelligence and from 1943 was chiefly involved in cataloguing, and where possible protecting, art and archaeological treasures from Allied and Axis damage

Woolley's first significant archaeological dig was in 1912 at the ancient Hittite site of Carchemish (Jeremiah 46:2) on the Turkey/Syrian border, where he worked with Thomas Edward Lawrence ('Lawrence of Arabia'). He also directed an excavation in Egypt at Tell el Amarna, the site of the pharaoh Akhenaten's capital city (see also Flinders Petrie here page 140).

He is chiefly remembered for his direction of the excavation at Ur of the Chaldees from 1922 to 1934. While on a dig he slept little and was often still at work in his study or in the catalogue room until the early hours. He refused to be rushed to discover great treasures and made his team work slowly and methodically. Woolley began working on the huge Ziggurat that Abraham would have been familiar with, since it was constructed only a century or so before his birth around 2000 BC. It was built for the worship of the moon goddess Nanna. The massive structure reached 30m (100ft) in height with three great staircases leading to the temple. Even the lower portion is calculated to contain three quarters of a million baked bricks with bitumen as the mortar.

It was also the burial site of many earlier Sumerians, the ancient civilization of that area, including royalty. Some predated Abraham by half a millennium. Woolley uncovered the graves of sixteen kings and their queens. In what he called 'The Great Death Pit', he found scores of soldiers, women attendants, carriage drivers and guards who had entered the tomb, taken up their respective stations, drank a potion (the cups were found beside them) to enter the next world and serve their king. A grim illustration of human sacrifice in the ancient world of Abraham.

# The hometown of Abraham

## The discoveries of Woolley and his teams reinforced the reputation of Ur of the Chaldeans in ancient Mesopotamia (southern Iraq) as the birthplace of civilization

Abraham was born in Ur of the Chaldeans (Genesis 11:27–31). According to Joshua 24:2 Terah and his family 'Long ago… lived beyond the River [Euphrates] and worshipped other gods.'[1]

The royal graves that Leonard Woolley found were filled with valuable treasures revealing the wealth, culture and craftmanship of the Sumerian civilization. The most lavish tomb was that of Queen Pu-Abi; a cylindrical seal bore her name in Sumerian. Exquisitely crafted jewellery and musical instruments came to light. Thousands of clay tablets in cuneiform writing, the earliest surviving literature and many still to be deciphered, reveal the Sumerian culture was highly skilled and advanced in knowledge.

They had a good understanding of astronomy, mathematics and geometry, including the theorem of Pythagoras nearly fifteen hundred years before the Greek philosopher; they understood the value of pi as 3 1/8, which is accurate to 0.06%! They were also familiar with quadratic equations to the 8th degree. They were the first people to design a calendar based on the phase of the moon and they developed a numerical system based on the number 60 (sexagesimal), which we still use to measure seconds and minutes and the 360

degrees in a circle. The death pit reveals some of the earliest known use of the wheel for their wagons.

In the large residential area of the city, houses in the time of Abraham were well-built two-story brick accommodation for the family, servants, and guests, with a lobby, courtyard, kitchen and toilet. Many included a chapel for their god. One fifth of all homes contained clay writing tablets, including marriage certificates, orders for goods and complaints for incorrect or inferior goods, revealing that trade was carried on through Syria and down to the Persian Gulf. [2]

Woolley's book *Ur of the Chaeldees* (1929) was the most widely read book on archaeology at the time. He later published *Volume II of Ur Excavations*. He was awarded a knighthood in 1935.

**Above**
*It is considered incredible that such intricate gold filigree could have been achieved half a millennium before Abraham*

139

**Top**
*A geometrical drawing from Ur*

**Above**
*Typical of the jewellery of Queen Pu-abi's attendants from the Great Death Pit*

1. A defence for Woolley's Ur of the Chaldeans being identified as the home of Abraham see A R Millard 'Where Was Abraham's Ur? The Case for the Babylonian City'. *Biblical Archaeological Review* May/June 2001.
2. For more details and illustrations of Woolley's work at Ur, see Edwards and Anderson, *Through the British Museum with the Bible* (Day One Publications 6th ed 2019), pp. 74–84.

# Pioneers of archaeology
## William Matthew Flinders Petrie (1853–1942)

**Petrie is known as 'The Father of Egyptology' and was one of the pioneers of the modern archaeological method**

Born in Charlton, Kent, Petrie was raised in a devout Christian household (his father belonged to the Plymouth Brethren and his mother to the Anglican Church), although his work was motivated more by a love of discovery than to defend Bible history.

Petrie was educated at home, and by the age of eight was being tutored in French, Latin and Greek; he was also encouraged from childhood to pursue archaeological interests. He travelled to Egypt in 1880, and when surveying the Great Pyramid at Giza he applied the same methods he had used at Stonehenge in England. Returning home later that year he wrote articles, gave lectures, and met Amelia Edwards, a journalist and patron of the Egypt Exploration Fund (now the Egypt Exploration Society). She later appointed him to her chair of Egyptology at University College, London.

In these early days there was no government aid to fund excavation; everything for travel, accommodation, food, transport and labour costs, photography, drawing and publication had to be raised from public subscription.

In Egypt, Petrie discovered the Merneptah Stela which contains the earliest known reference to Israel.[1] This is undoubtedly his most important discovery. In 1891/92 he worked at Amarna, the capital of Pharaoh Akhenaten, which he re-named Akhetaten.[2]

In 1890 his was one of the first digs in which the different layers of a large city mound were recorded to reveal the sequence of occupation layers, known as stratigraphy. Petrie is also known as the 'Father of Pots', because he was the first to appreciate the value of pottery in historical dating, and of keeping an orderly record of the progress of a dig.

When excavating, Petrie's simple lifestyle became the stuff of legend. Food hygiene was never a priority and James Quibell recalled how one was expected to eat food out of half-empty tins left over from the previous day. T.E. Lawrence (Lawrence of Arabia) was one of Petrie's students and commented that 'a Petrie dig is a thing with a flavour of its own.'

Flinders Petrie was knighted for services to British archaeology and Egyptology in 1923. He died on 29 July 1942 in Jerusalem.[3]

**Above**
*An encaustic portrait of a bearded man on a mummy excavated by William Flinders Petrie in 1911 at the site of a pyramid bult by Pharaoh Amenemhat III in the 19th century BC at Hawara, Egypt*

1. See *Evidence for the Bible* p. 32.
2. See *Evidence for the Bible* p. 29.
3. Margaret S. Drower, *Flinders Petrie A life in Archaeology* (London Victor Gollancz Ltd 1985).

# Howard Carter and 'Wonderful things'

## The discovery of the tomb of the young Egyptian Pharaoh Tutankhamun reverberated around the world

Howard Carter in Chicago, Illinois

**H**oward was the son of Samuel John Carter, a successful artist, and at an early age Howard himself showed an aptitude for drawing. This, coupled with his interest in Egyptian antiquities, led him to travel to Egypt in 1891 at the age of seventeen. Though born in Kensington, London, he spent his youth in Swaffham, Norfolk, where he received a modest education.

From 1891 to 1899 Howard Carter served with the Egyptian Exploration Fund, working with Flinders Petrie at Amarna and, as a member of the team, making an epigraphic recording (the study of inscriptions) of the Temple of the Egyptian queen, Hatshepsut at Deir el-Bahri. In 1900 Carter was appointed Chief Inspector of Antiquities to the Egyptian Government with responsibilities for Upper Egypt. He stayed in this post until late in 1904 when he moved to the post of Chief Inspector for Lower Egypt.

Famously, with the Earl of Carnarvon funding the dig, on 4 November 1922 Howard Carter discovered the first steps leading to the tomb of Tutankhamun, in the Valley of the Kings. Carter immediately sent a telegram to Carnarvon in England and waited anxiously for his arrival. Carnarvon made it to Egypt by November 26th and watched as Carter made a hole in the door. Carter leaned in, holding a candle to take a look. Behind him Lord Carnarvon asked, 'Can you see anything? Carter answered, 'Yes, wonderful things.' Work on the clearance and recording of the contents of the tomb continued until the concession ran out in 1929. Unfortunately, failing health and other commitments meant that Carter never published a detailed scholarly account of the tomb.[4] He died on 2 March 1939, in Kensington.

**Below**
The mortuary temple of Queen Hatshepsut (1479–1458 BC) at Deir el-Bahri in Egypt where Carter worked with Petrie

4. TGH James, *Howard Carter the path to Tutankhamun* Kegan (Paul International Ltd 1992).

# Pioneers of archaeology
## Austen Henry Layard (1817–1894)

**Layard is known best for his discovery of the massive city of Nineveh mentioned nearly twenty times in the Bible but lost for 2,500 years**

**M**any of the early archaeologists were not orthodox Christians and did not realize how much their discoveries would help to confirm the reliability of the biblical record. Though brought up in the Church of England, Layard was a religious sceptic and his primary interest in the artefacts he found was their artistic merit. After a period as an MP he became an Ambassador in Madrid and then in Constantinople. On a trip to join the civil service

in Ceylon (Sri Lanka) the young Layard (pronounced 'Laird') stopped to explore Persia and was given financial assistance by the British Ambassador to Constantinople to search for antiquities.

Digging into mounds near Mosul (Iraq), Layard discovered several buried Assyrian cities, including Nimrud and the lost city of Nineveh (2 Kings 19:36; Jonah 3:2).[1] Large alabaster reliefs and sculptures were removed to the British Museum in London. His published work, *Nineveh and Its Remains'* (1849) became one of the bestsellers of the Victorian age.

At the mound that preserved the remains of Nineveh, Layard excavated the palaces of Sennacherib (reigned 705–681 BC) and found wall reliefs depicting the fall of Lachish described in

2 Chronicles 32:9.[2] In the palace of Shalmaneser III (reigned 859–824 BC) at nearby Nimrud, Layard also found a black obelisk inscribed with tribute from subject nations, including Jehu the Israelite king.[3]

Layard was not trying to prove the Bible, he thought what he had found at Nineveh only illustrated the biblical text. One historian notes, Layard and Rawlinson 'had underestimated the extent to which these findings related to stories in the Bible.'[4] Later scholarship would come to recognize how these discoveries would verify the accuracy of the biblical accounts.

**Bottom left**
*Part of the library of Ashurbanipal at Nineveh on display at the British Museum*

**Bottom right**
*A drawing by Solomon Caesar Malan in 1850 of Layard drawing at Nineveh. These early pioneers had to rely on their ability to draw and copy with meticulous accuracy*

---

1. See pages 34, 51, 64, 80-82 here for Nineveh.
2. See *Evidence for the Bible* pp. 65,70,71.
3. See *Evidence for the Bible* pp. 50–52.
4. Timothy Larsen, 'Austen Henry Layard's Nineveh: The Bible and Archaeology in Victorian Britain', *Journal of Religious History*, Vol. 33:1, March 2009, 66.

# 'Leaving Nineveh utterly desolate'

## When Layard discovered the lost city of Nineveh in 1847 it made international news as a Bible story re-emerged out of the ground

In 1842, the Louvre museum in Paris had commissioned Paul Botta to excavate an Assyrian city which he misidentified as Nineveh. In fact, it was Khorsabad.[5] Layard, inspired by what Botta had found, located the true site of Nineveh. Several ruined towns existed in close proximity near Mosul in modern day Iraq. It was at a site called Kuyunjik that Layard found the remains of Nineveh.

- The palace of King Sennacherib (reigned 705–681 BC) was found with its seventy-one rooms and remarkable wall reliefs.

  A prism containing the annals of King Sennacherib includes a reference to King Hezekiah and siege of Jerusalem (2 Kings 19).[6]

- In the palace of Sennacherib Layard found reliefs depicting the fall of Lachish with Jews being taken into captivity by the Assyrians (2 Chronicles 32:9).

- The remains of the library of Ashurbanipal (668–627 BC) preserved over 30,000 cuneiform tablets and included the Epic of Gilgamesh account of the flood. Ashurbanipal is mentioned in Ezra 4:10.

- During recent destruction of Nineveh by the terrorist group Isis, the 'tomb of Jonah' was blown up. However, tunneling into the mound beneath also revealed the palace of

Esarhaddon (reigned 681–669 BC) who is mentioned three times in the Bible (2 Kings 19:37; Isaiah 37:38; Ezra 4:2).

Layard misunderstood the size of the city. In reality, the walls of Nineveh were almost eight miles long and covered an area of 1,850 acres. Jonah refers to a visit taking three days (Jonah 3:3) which describes how much time would be taken to explore such an enormous city. See here pages 80–81.

Despite its great strength and power, the Assyrian empire ended in 612 BC with the destruction of Nineveh. The biblical prophets Nahum and Zephaniah predicted: 'Leaving Nineveh utterly desolate, and dry as the desert" (Zephaniah 2:13).[7]

Which is exactly how Austen Henry Layard found it almost two and a half thousand years later.

143

**Top**
*When Layard excavated the Lion Hunt palace wall reliefs at Nineveh, he recognised the importance of keeping the sections together as a single piece as shown in the British Museum display*

**Above**
Refugees from Lachish showing the effects of the siege in the ribs of the animals! From the wall relief of Nineveh

5. See *Evidence for the Bible* p. 61.
6. See *Evidence for the Bible* pp. 70–75.
7. See *Evidence for the Bible* p. 79.

# Pioneers of archaeology
## Henry Rawlinson (1810–1895)

**Sometimes referred to as the 'Father of Assyriology', his training in the Persian language would open up the world of the Ancient Near East**

**Right**
*Plates from Rawlinson's* The Persian Cuneiform Inscription at Behistun *published in 1846,*

**Below right**
*His careful copying of the Behistun text perched on his precarious ladder!*

Henry Creswicke Rawlinson's ability with language and literature was evident at an early age. When he and a friend were caught breaching a school regulation they faced expulsion unless they learned off by heart all 476 lines of a Roman poem in Latin. While his friend failed and was duly expelled, Rawlinson recited it perfectly.[1]

Rawlinson served as an army officer with the British East India Company in Persia. When he arrived there at the age of seventeen, he began a ten year tour of duty. Having already gained a knowledge of Persian and a passion for history, he was well placed to try and decipher the mysterious ancient inscriptions found throughout the region.

One particularly important inscription had long been known high on a cliff face at Behistun in modern day Iran. While records of this inscription appear as early as the sixteenth century no one had deciphered its meaning.

From 1835 Rawlinson began to copy the texts from the cliff. Using ladders and a narrow ledge 200 feet high in the rock, he took considerable risks over more than ten years to make sense of the inscription. Despite illness and interruption because of war he devoted himself to the task, knowing that it could prove to be the key to unlocking the meaning of cuneiform.

Rawlinson became the consul general at Baghdad in 1851 and was able to continue the productive work of Austen Henry Layard in securing artefacts for the British Museum. Having donated his own collection of Babylonian antiquities to the museum he became one of its trustees in 1876 until his death in 1895. His pioneering work would lead to the greater interest in, and recovery of many more, cuneiform tablets and inscriptions from Persia.

Rawlinson had managed to carefully record an almost inaccessible inscription of a thousand lines and decipher not one but three ancient, disused, languages. He did all this while also serving in the Anglo-Afghan War and fulfilling his role as a soldier and diplomat in the region.

1. Lesley Adkins, *Empires of the Plain: Henry Rawlinson and the Lost Languages of Babylon*, (Harper Collins, 2004). p. 21.

# The Key to Cuneiform

## The rock inscription in three languages (trilingual), high on a cliff face in Persia proved to be for cuneiform what the Rosetta Stone was for hieroglyphs

It unlocked the meaning of many ancient texts and eventually allowed us to read the literature of Sumer, the birthplace of civilization and hometown of Abraham (see here Leonard Woolley pp. 138–139). Cuneiform is not a language but a script, or writing system, that can convey many different languages. Impressing a stylus into wet clay, or chiseling onto stone, produced the cuneiform ('wedge shaped') signs that represented sounds.

For three thousand years cuneiform was used by many different empires with their own languages. Unlike our alphabet of only twenty-six signs, cuneiform would sometimes need several hundred signs. It lasted until the spread of Greek in the 4th century BC.

The inscription at Behistun [2] had long been known to travellers. 100m (328ft) above the valley floor it covered a surface 15m (29ft) high and 25m (82ft) wide. Early attempts to read it had identified the names of the Persian kings Darius and Xerxes, who were also known from the Bible. Darius I (522–486 BC) assisted in the rebuilding of the Temple in Jerusalem (Ezra 6); what we now know of his reign from Persian texts confirms the fact that this pagan king did support the distinctive worship of his subject people.[3] Esther was the Queen for Xerxes.

What Rawlinson revealed was an identical text in three different languages all using the cuneiform script. One of these proved to be Old Persian, the native language of King Darius who had commissioned the inscription in c.520 BC. The other languages were Babylonian and Elamite. Rawlinson shared in unlocking these earlier languages with other scholars. Edward Hincks, an Anglican minister in Ireland, although he never visited the Behistun rocks was able to publish a guide to cuneiform in 1847. Hincks was also able to identify, from further inscriptions, a much earlier use of cuneiform in the unrelated language of Sumerian.[4]

145

**Top**
*An engraving from 1895 of Rawlinson perched high on a ladder to copy the Behistun inscription from the rock face*

**Above**
*The Behistun Inscription from the time of King Darius I*

2. See also *Evidence for the Bible*, p. 9.
3. Kitchen, *On the Reliability of the Old Testament*, (Eerdmans Publishing Company, Grand Rapids and Cambridge, 2003) p. 77.
4. Alan Millard, *Discoveries from Bible Times*, (Lion Publishing: Oxford), pp. 29–31.

# Pioneers of archaeology
## Charles Warren (1840–1927)

**General Charles Warren brought his natural investigative skills to bear in archaeology, helping it become the scientific discipline of today**

Warren was an officer in the British Royal Engineers, a role that equipped him for his later archaeological work in Jerusalem, and carried out his survey of the Rock of Gibraltar from 1861–1865. As a member of the Church of England he had an interest in the historical background to the Bible.

The Palestine Exploration Fund was founded in London on 22 June 1865. The principles of the Fund were to enable research in the Holy Land 'carried out on scientific principles.' Avoiding religious prejudice or controversy it sought to establish an objective approach to archaeology. Warren had an ideal background to be appointed by the Fund to head up a new expedition to the Holy Land. Among his many accomplishments:

- He carried out the first excavations at Tell es-Sultan (Jericho).
- Published the first accurate topographical map of the old city of Jerusalem including its cisterns and tunnels.

- Correctly identified a pool in the old city as the location of the Struthion Pool from the time of King Herod.
- Carefully explored the wall and gates of the Temple Mount, making sense of an architectural protrusion called Robinson's Arch.
- Uncovered fortifications to the south of the Temple Mount that we now know as the City of David.
- Found the Gihon spring and a vertical tunnel leading from it, which is still called 'Warren's Shaft'.
- Investigated the phenomena known as the 'Holy Fire' that appears in the Church of the Holy Sepulchre.

In 1882 Warren led an expedition to the Sinai desert to investigate the murder of a team of archaeologists. His success led to him receiving the royal order of a Knight Commander (KCMG) and probably led to his appointment in 1885 as commissioner for the London Metropolitan Police. His appointment was during the time of Jack the Ripper and the failure of the police to capture the killer contributed to a shadow left over Warren's reputation.

**Above**
*A plan of the Temple Mount enclosure from Charles Warren's* A Survey of Western Palestine-Jerusalem *(1884)*

146

# A Mole in Jerusalem

## Having been continuously occupied for millennia, the streets and walls of the old city of Jerusalem are a patchwork from different periods and it requires a cautious mind to interpret their significance

Religious sensitivities in Jerusalem made it impossible for Warren to excavate on the Temple Mount itself. Instead, he carried out excavations around the outside edges of the walls and further south on a hill called the Ophel.

Warren realized that what was above ground was only part of a more significant structure that extended far below ground. To reach the pavement as it was at the time of King Herod it would be necessary to dig down through almost 23m (75ft) of debris. The authorities were concerned that Warren's excavations could have undermined the integrity of the Temple platform and so he dug vertical shafts some distance from the walls and then created horizontal tunnels to reach the walls. This method earned him the nickname 'the Mole'. It would not now be considered good practice because today archaeologists carefully expose each strata (level) of occupation, rather than tunneling toward a target and potentially damaging information along the way.

Charles Warren was able to identify the architecture from the period of King Herod. He identified the purpose of 'Robinson's arch' when he excavated a support pier for a huge monumental stairway that led to the Temple. It is Charles Warren's careful surveys (he meticulously recorded every small find) that provided a framework for understanding the location of the Temple at the time of Christ.

South of the Temple Mount, outside the mediaeval city walls, were the ruins of an ancient city that Warren identified as the Jerusalem from the time of King David and before. While exploring its hidden water source he found the Gihon spring. He thought a 15.8m (52ft) vertical shaft might have been the one used by Joab to infiltrate the city (2 Samuel 5:8) and it is still named after Warren.

Excavations around the Temple Mount and at the City of David continue to this day. They have revealed much more about the Temple, its environs and the city even in Canaanite times. But Warren's survey remains exemplary and, despite some mistakes in his conclusions, he is considered a pioneer of archaeology as a scientific discipline.

147

**Above**
*Deep beneath the old city of Jerusalem, tunnels continue to reveal the foundation walls of Herod's Temple*

**Below**
*An artist's impression of Robinson's Arch as it joins the Temple mount from a supporting pier the base of which was found by Charles Warren*

# Pioneers of archaeology
## William Mitchell Ramsay (1851–1939)

**Ramsay was the foremost authority in his day on the history, geography and epigraphy (inscriptions) of Asia Minor and their relation to the New Testament**

**B**orn in Glasgow, Ramsay became a fellow of Exeter College, Oxford and subsequently a fellow and Professor of Lincoln College, Oxford and Regius Professor of Humanity at the University of Aberdeen. His degrees came from British, Continental and North American universities and he was an honorary member of almost every archaeological society.[1]

Ramsay saturated himself with the geography and history of the Graeco-Roman world and mastered it more than anyone before or since. He insisted on original research, and his knowledge of first-century literature and the historical and geographical background of Asia Minor (modern Turkey), is unequalled. He published widely on the history, geography and epigraphy (inscriptions) of Asia Minor, and his two volumes on *The Cities and Bishoprics of Phrygia* (1895 and 1897) remain standard works today.

He had little doubt that Paul was the author of the thirteen letters attributed to him, and his extensive research and publications bring Paul and his travelling companions to life by accurately providing the background of the Acts and Paul's letters; much of this is found in two of his many publications: *St. Paul the Traveller and the Roman Citizen*[2] and *The Cities of St. Paul*.

Ramsay was knighted in 1906 for his service to archaeology and he died in 1939. His legacy in New Testament archaeological research has never been surpassed. Prof FF Bruce was correct when he commented: 'I am repeatedly amazed by modern writers who deal with areas of New Testament scholarship to which Ramsay made contributions of peculiar value, with hardly so much as a hint that such a person ever lived.'[3]

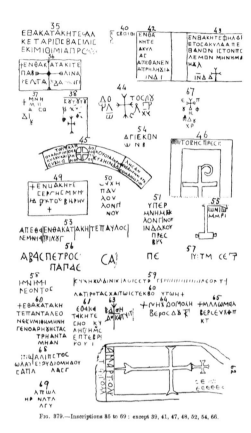

Fig. 379.—Inscriptions 35 to 69 : except 39, 41, 47, 48, 52, 54, 66.

**Above**
*This is a typical page of the detailed notes Ramsay kept. Many of the original inscriptions he copied have since been lost. (From* The Thousand and One Churches *by William Ramsay and Gertrude Bell 1909)*

**Far left**
*Ramsay's wife, Jane, often accompanied and assisted him and also published. Ramsay and Jane outside their tent at Binbirkilise (Lycaonia) in 1907*

---

1. For a detailed survey of Ramsay's contribution to New Testament scholarship see W. Ward Gasque, 'Sir William M. Ramsay: Archaeologist and New Testament Scholar—A Survey of His Contribution to the Study of the New Testament', *Baker Studies in Biblical Archaeology* (Baker Book House Grand Rapids, Michigan 1965). For a summary see Brian Edwards *Nothing but the Truth* (Day One Publications, Leominster 2020). pp. 543–552.
2. Possibly the most popular of all his titles, from 1895 to date 156 editions in 3 languages.
3. Prof F F Bruce in *The Acts of the Apostles—The Greek text with introduction and commentary* (The Tyndale Press, London 1962). p. 17. See also Gasque (above) in footnote 4: 'One of the surprising facts in the history of New Testament criticism is the small amount of attention that has been given to the work of Sir William Mitchell Ramsay.'

# Ramsay's radical change of mind

**Ramsay concluded: 'You may press the words of Luke in a degree beyond any other historian's and they stand the keenest scrutiny and the hardest treatment.' But he did not always believe this**

As a student, Ramsay spent a long vacation at Göttingen learning Sanskrit under the scholar, Prof. Theodor Benfey. Here, 'I gained some insight into modern methods of literary investigation.' He later studied under Ferdinand Baur, a founder of the Tübingen University in Germany, and accepted Bauer's view that the New Testament could not be relied on as an historical document and that there was a fundamental difference between the theology of Paul and Peter. Ramsay admitted he 'worshipped Wellhausen', the German scholar who equally dismissed the historical accuracy of the Old Testament.

When Ramsay began his research in Greece and Asia Minor, he expected to support the supposed inaccuracy of the Acts of the Apostles. Instead, he became convinced of its historical truth. His conclusion was that Luke, the author of the Gospel and Acts wrote, 'with such judgement, skill, art and perception of truth as to be a model of historical statement... I set out to look for truth on the borderland where Greece and Asia meet, and found it there [in Acts].' [4]

### What changed his mind?

In Acts 14:6 Paul and Barnabas fled from Iconium 'to the Lycaonian cities of Lystra and Derbe' which implies that they crossed a frontier

**Above**
*An inscription at the base of a statue refers to the diuumvirate of Publius Sulpicius Quirinius; discovered outside Antioch in Pisidia in 1912*

into Lycaonia. However, it was assumed that Iconium was in fact the chief city of Lycaonia. Therefore, the author of Acts had made a plain historical error. Ramsay discovered that until AD 372, Iconium was not a part of Lycaonia but belonged to Phrygia, an entirely different district of Asia Minor with a different language. He concluded that perhaps Luke was as meticulously accurate elsewhere.

That is precisely what he found in Luke's equal exactness in the issue of the two censuses by Quirinius referred to in Luke 2:1–5 and Acts 5:37. Quirinius, was the senior (a Legate/Consul) in a diuumvirate (dual control) with Sentius Saturninus in Roman Syria during the two censuses.[5] He found Luke equally precise in all his details relating to people, customs, geography, local officials and historical events.

Ramsay's conclusion still stands: 'Christianity did not originate in a lie, and we can and ought to demonstrate this, as well as to believe it.'

**Left**
*An inscription from the tomb of Quintus Aemilius Secundus, a Roman officer who conducted a census for the city of Apamea in the Roman Province of Syria c. AD 14 on behalf of 'Publio Sulpicio Quirinio Legate of Caesar Augustus'*

149

4. Ramsay, *The Bearing of Recent Discovery on the Trustworthiness of the New Testament* (First published 1914), pp. 85,89.
5. See above pp. 275–300. For a summary see *Evidence for the Bible* pp. 203–204.

# Religion in Israel

**At the time of Jesus' birth, factions within Judaism vigorously competed against one another for influence. The life and teaching of Jesus interacted with most of these, and even drew some together**

## Mainstream parties

The **Pharisees** developed from those who had taken a firm stand against Antiochus Epiphanes (175–164 BC) who, towards the end of the Seleucid (Syrian) rule, tried to impose the culture and religion of Greece upon Israel, sold the high priesthood to the highest bidder, and desecrated the Temple. This led to the Maccabean Wars (167–161 BC).[1] The name Pharisee is probably best understood as 'separatist'.

The Pharisees promoted piety, learning and a rigid obedience to the Jewish law (Torah). Not to know the Law was to be accursed (John 7:49). However, they added oral law passed down through the generations.[2] One historian records, 'Every one of their own interpretations of the Law was stereotyped. Their traditions were regarded with greater veneration than the original Law. In the accumulated mass of precepts all sense of proportion was lost. All true spirituality was in danger of suffocation under the complex of ritual and ceremonial'[3] It was these subsidiary rules, many of which were foolishly and tediously extreme, that Jesus opposed (eg. Matthew 23:4,23).[4] This Pharisaic rigidity led to the first theological conflict in the church between the Christian Judaizers and the Gentile converts (Acts 15).

By Jesus' day, the Pharisees were the largest and most popular party. At one time they had a missionary zeal (Matthew 23:15; cf. Philippians 3:5–6) but later became more exclusive. Their emphasis focussed on the synagogue for teaching rather than on the Temple for ceremonial, therefore they survived the destruction of the Temple in AD 70. The popularity and teaching of Jesus presented a real threat to the Pharisees and, apart from a few like Simon, Joseph and Nicodemus, most were relentlessly opposed to him and wished him dead (Mark 3:6; 11:18).

The **Scribes** were the lawyers of the day. Because they were professional copyists of the sacred Hebrew Scriptures, they were considered the best to interpret and apply the Law of God—and therefore to invent those subsidiary rules. This gave them their reputation and influence. They were also the teachers in the schools to instruct the boys (Luke 2:46?). After a lengthy training, the Scribe was given the title 'Rabbi' (Teacher). Some Scribes were Sadducees, although most were Pharisees (Acts 23:9). On points of detail, they were divided between the two schools of Shammai and Hillel. Gamaliel, under whom Saul was educated, was a renowned Pharisee Scribe (see here page 161).

At the time of Christ although not all the priests were **Sadducees**, certainly the high priests were (Acts 5:17).[5] They were likely the priests descended from Zadok (2 Samuel 8:17); they were few but elite and therefore influential. With the High Priest as

---

1. See *Evidence for the Bible* pp. 114–115.
2. This fundamental difference from the Sadducees is made clear by Josephus *Antiquities of the Jews*, Book XIII.10.6.
3. Hastings, *Dictionary of the Apostolic Church* (T & T Clark, Edinburgh 1918) Vol. 2 p. 210.
4. For examples of this foolishness in the later Talmud see Alfred Edersheim, *The Life and Times of Jesus the Messiah* (Pickering and Inglis, London 1959), Vol. 2, pp. 56–59.
5. Also Josephus, *Antiquities*, XX.9.1.

**Below**

*A model of the temple and part of Jerusalem as it was in AD 66, the year of the revolt that led to the final destruction of the city in AD 70. The full model was completed in 1966 at a scale of 1:50. At the time, the city was 445 acres*

a member of their party (Acts 5:17), the Sadducees controlled the Sanhedrin (see below). They insisted on the letter of the Law (the Torah of Moses), and this alone— in contradiction to the Pharisees.[6] Also, unlike the Pharisees, they did not believe in the immortality of the soul, the resurrection, a future judgement, or angels and spirits (Luke 20:27; Acts 23:6–8). They believed the Messiah would come from the line of Aaron. The Sadducees apparently died out after the destruction of the Temple in AD 70.

Most of Jesus' criticism was levelled at the Pharisees, and his judgement against the human traditions of the Pharisees would have pleased the Sadducees: 'You have let go of the commands of God and are holding on to the traditions of men.' (Mark 7:8). However, they appear to be at the forefront of opposition to the young Christian church of Acts (4:1; 5:17; 23:1–10). According to Josephus, they ordered the death of James, the brother of Jesus in AD 62.[7] From John 18:15, 16, some

believe the apostle John may have once supported the Sadducees, hence his acquaintance with the High Priest.

## Splinter groups

The **Zealots** were the passionate and often brutal nationalistic terrorists; the overthrow of Roman domination was their single goal. Theirs was a revolutionary Messianic hope. A rigid, legalistic offshoot of the Pharisees, some were also known as the *Sicarii*—'dagger men' from the name for a small curved dagger. Josephus refers to them as a 'fourth sect of Jewish philosophy' and founded by Judas the Galilean (Acts 5:37); this would place their origin around 6 BC,

**Above**

*The final stand of the Zealots*
*took place in AD 73 on Herod's luxurious fortress palace in the arid desert of the Dead Sea (the hill top left). Inset: the Roman encampments at the base of the fortress and their surrounding wall to seal-off escape; the remains of their siege ramp on the western face* [8]

6. *Antiquities*, XIII.10.6
7. *Antiquities*, XX.9.1.
8. See *Evidence for the Bible* p. 181 for more on the final defeat of Massada.

# Appendix 01

instigated by Quirinius's first census. Josephus also comments that they accepted no authority but God alone as their ruler and they despised death in themselves or their friends or relatives in pursuit of their goal.[9] This was seen clearly in their fanatical defence of Jerusalem against the Roman legions of Titus in AD 70 and their final stand and eventual suicide on Masada in AD 73.[10] Very likely the *Sicarii* planned the assassination of Paul (Acts 23).

Remarkably, Jesus called Matthew, a tax agent for the Roman government, and Simon, a member of this terrorist group, to be his disciples (Luke 6:15).

To the north of Judah were the **Samaritans**. Their origin was the divided kingdom during the time of Rehoboam (1 Kings 12) but their capital, Samaria, was not built until the time of Omri (1 Kings 16:23–24). Their first king, Jeroboam I, and all kings who followed, led the people in idolatrous worship and there was constant conflict between Samaria and Judah. In 722 BC Sargon II of Assyria defeated the north, took many into exile and replaced them with foreigners who mixed their gods with Yahweh worship.[11] The Jews never considered Samaritans belonging to God's people, and this is reflected in Ezra 4:1,2. Sanballat, soon to be governor of Samaria, threatened the work in the time of Nehemiah (2:20).

By the time of Jesus, the Samaritans were in some ways orthodox: strictly monotheistic, rejecting idols and following carefully the Jewish ceremonial law. However, their only Scripture was an edited version of the Pentateuch (the five books of Moses); this, and their temple on Mount Gerazim,[12] meant that they would never be accepted by the Jews. They had imbibed a Messianic hope, though different, from Judaism (John 4:25). A very small number of Samaritans live in Israel today.

Jesus' initial limit to the evangelism of his disciples (Matthew 10:5) was because they could not grasp his full mission at that stage. The phrase 'Jews do not associate with Samaritans' (John 4:9) was an understatement because Jesus' mission was at a time when the relationship between Jew and Samaritan was at its most bitter and violent, as illustrated in Luke 9:51–56 and John 8:48. This antagonism continued long into the years of the early church and, in the time of the emperor Claudius in AD 51, even led to a local civil war that the Romans had to quell. All of which makes Jesus' gentle conversation with the Samaritan woman (John 4:1–26), his frequent commendation of Samaritans (John 10 and 17), and the Gospel offer to 'all Judea *and Samaria*', the more radical and beautiful (Acts 1:8).

**Above**
*The Kidron Valley was 21m (70ft) deeper in the time of Jesus and was a place to deposit rubbish (2 Kings 23:6). The deep ravine separated the City from the Mount of Olives (John 18:1). Jewish, Christian and Muslim traditions see it as the place of the final Judgment and many Jews want to be buried there as is evident here in the background*

9. *Antiquities* Book XVII.1.6.
10. See here p. 118 for the siege of Jerusalem and *Evidence for the Bible* p. 181 for Masada.
11. See *Evidence for the Bible* pp. 60,106.
12. See *Evidence for the Bible* p. 106.

152

The **Essenes** are not mentioned in the Bible and, in spite of the imagination of some critics, it is very unlikely that either John Baptist or Jesus ever met them, and they were certainly not influenced by Essene teaching. The Essenes were an unorthodox sect and lived apart from mainstream Judaism, rejecting the Temple and all that it stood for. It is generally agreed that a monastic group of Essenes provided the Dead Sea Scrolls that were discovered at Qumran.[13] They appear to have originated around 150 BC and lived as celibate monastics in a common community of strict piety. Whilst similar to the Pharisees, they differed in some fundamental doctrines and practices.

The **Sanhedrin** was not a separate religious group, but the supreme council and court of justice in Jerusalem during the Greek and Roman era. It was composed of *the chief priests,* who were the most important members, with the High Priest as the president. Hence the strong influence of the Sadducees. Other members were Pharisees, Scribes and leading men (Elders) in the community. The function of the Sanhedrin was largely judicial and, apart from capital offenses, its judgements and punishments were final. However, the Roman Governor or Tribune had the right to summon the Sanhedrin and withdraw a prisoner from their jurisdiction (Acts 22:30). The Sanhedrin suffered a long and turbulent period of in-fighting; however, under the Romans, so long as they kept the people under control, they were allowed a large degree of internal government. Tragically, the Sanhedrin was unable to halt the Zealot rebellion that led to the final destruction of the city by the Romans.

153

*The narrow streets and bustling markets of today in Jerusalem are little different from the time of Jesus, dress and commodities excepted*

13. See *Evidence for the Bible* pp. 112–113.

# Rome in Israel

**Throughout the world of the New Testament the influence of Rome was everywhere. Rome in Israel was undoubtedly part of God's preparation for the coming of Jesus Christ and the spread of his good news**

Roman armies first entered Jerusalem under Pompey in 63 BC, and stayed there for almost four hundred years. By the time Paul embarked on his missionary journeys around AD 46, the Roman Empire controlled over two million square miles of land and possibly almost a fifth of the world's population. In today's terms, the empire reached out from Rome to Germany (to the Rhine) and Britain (to the Thames) in the north, Spain in the West, Syria in the east, and from Egypt along the north African coast to Morocco in the south. The Mediterranean was encircled by Rome.

For ease of travel and military deployment Roman engineers constructed well-built and straight roads across the empire, dotted with hostelries to enable fast and convenient travel. Around 50,000 miles of stone paved roads were built across the Roman Empire of which 4,000km (2,500mi) were in Britain where Watling Street travels 444km (276mi) from Dover (Kent) to Wroxeter (Shropshire). The Fosse Way from Exeter to Lincoln (293km) never deviated more than 10km from a straight line.

Pompey had freed the Mediterranean from pirates by 66 BC, and trade flourished. It was an empire of huge wealth for the rich, and extravagant mansions, villas and temples were built. Before his death in AD 14 Augustus could justifiably claim 'I found Rome a city of bricks and left it a city of marble.' In spite of its many deficiencies, the empire benefited throughout by the efficiency and ingenuity of Roman engineers, architects, builders, administrators, lawyers and doctors. They widely used concrete, invented the underfloor heating (hypocaust) and developed many engineering techniques.

**Above**
*Trajan's Column in Italy (completed AD 113) depicts various scenes to illustrate the emperor's military victories; one section shows Roman engineers (pioneers) building a road*

It is estimated up to half a million men under arms maintained law and order and kept the borders of the empire relatively secure. For most, *pax romana* was a reality. The whole empire was generally united by Latin as the language for law and government and Greek for trade.

Israel benefitted from all of this and the elite, whilst complaining against the imperial taxes, profited more than most.

**Centre**
*A Roman milestone in Capernaum*

**Above**
*The best-preserved Roman road in Britain is considered to be Wade's causeway in Yorkshire, though it has changed since a picture in 1912*

## The Politics of Rome

Politically, everything changed after the civil wars of 44 BC.[1] **Octavian** (Augustus Caesar, 27 BC to AD 14), softened the pure dictatorship of Julius Caesar and reformed the Senate, slimmed down the army and settled veterans in colonies throughout the empire. He introduced many good laws, even encouraging marriage for stability, and his forty-one years of leadership built a solid foundation for the Roman empire. The chaos of the democracy under the Republic appeared to be history.

Unfortunately, when **Tiberius**, his adopted son and successor, came to power, many of the gains were lost. Tiberius' initial natural political experience and wisdom gave way to a sour, suspicious and malicious temper. The Senate was glad when he died in AD 37. However, Gaius **Caligula** was worse. He demanded worship as a god, offended the Jews and emptied the imperial treasury. Fortunately, when **Claudius** was elected after the assassination of Caligula in AD 41, Rome had an emperor who, though physically weak, was mentally strong and able. It was Claudius who expelled all Jews from Rome (Acts 18:2) and added *Provincia Britannia* to the empire in AD 43. In AD 54 **Nero** began well but degenerated to the point at which he would have been executed by the Senate had he not arranged his own death first. Tradition claims that under Nero both Paul and Peter were martyred.

Grasping corruption still pervaded much of government. Back-stabbing (often literally) and corridor whispering, removed state officials with alarming ease. Much of the land was in the hands of the rich who farmed it with the harvest of slave labour that resulted from Roman military expansion. Poverty struggled alongside wealth and Rome was forced to feed thousands of its citizens with grain from Egypt.

1. See here p. 86.

# Appendix 02

**Left**
*A marble bust of Jupiter, chief of the Roman gods, in the Capitoline Museum*

156

## Greek and Roman religion

Rome could tolerate all religions provided they were peaceful. Even the Jews were allowed to worship freely throughout the empire. The gods rarely took much interest in life here, being preoccupied with squabbling for power. The emperor himself had a wider sphere of influence than most of the gods, and in the time of Augustus the imperial religion of worshipping the emperor as a son of the gods was established. The gods offered no moral or spiritual foundation for mortals living on earth. They were frequently envious, greedy, lustful, revengeful and cruel. The chief of all Greek gods, Zeus (Jupiter for the Romans), destroyed his father Kronos, was deceitful, licentious and unfaithful to his wife Hera, who schemed against him and punished his mistresses. Anger, pride and broken promises littered their mythological lives. For

centuries, religion in Greece and Rome, waited for something real and substantial to take its place.

This moral and spiritual vacuum in the heavens inevitably led to the same on earth. Morality slid steadily down. Marriage was downgraded in preference for licentious freedom. Literature and art revealed the low morality and the widespread enjoyment of the vulgar. Entertainment depended upon the crudity of the theatre and the cruelty of the arena.

## Culture

Three fine universities at Alexandria, Athens and Tarsus allowed orators (Cicero), poets (Horace and Virgil), historians (Sallust and Livy) and philosophers (of whom there were many schools) to gain a valuable education. It also allowed a large degree of freethinking, and by no means all were committed to the worship of the gods—many philosophers scorned them. However, even when they offered, as Epicurus and Seneca did, some excellent moral advice, it was countered by the insistence that personal happiness was all that really mattered. The moral state of the Roman Empire at the time of Christ and the apostles proves that there is no necessary connexion between fine education, intellectual freedom and pure morality.

# Roman Administration[2]

Even under the firm imperial power of the Caesar, Rome did not practice a central administration imposed on every part of the empire. Wherever Rome found a satisfactory and working authority, it was left in place and Roman laws were rarely imposed beyond those that united the empire. Once conquered, Rome preferred to absorb its subjects and bind them by treatise of peace for mutual advantage.

Broadly, Rome divided its provinces between those governed directly by the Emperor and those under the rule of the Senate with a proconsul in charge locally. Provinces often changed their status between Imperial and Senatorial. Luke is correct in referring to both Sergius Paulus in Cyprus and Gallio in Achaia (Greece) as proconsuls; in fact, Achaia had only transferred its status from Imperial to Senatorial a few years before Paul arrived in Corinth in AD 51. In addition, there were client kingdoms whose local king was given significant freedom under the authority of a local Roman Governor answerable directly to the Emperor. This was the case in Judea under the rule of Herod the Great and his grandson Herod Agrippa I (Acts 12:1).

In each region, local affairs were governed by a 'town council', although they all had their own designation that Luke is careful to observe[3]. In Judea it was the Sanhedrin, which had no authority in Samaria or Galilee. The local authorities had three essential responsibilities towards Rome: maintaining peace and order, collecting revenues, and upholding law. Only if they failed here would Rome take direct control. All three are repeatedly illustrated in the Gospels and Acts, and in the letters of Paul and Peter.

The privileges of Roman Citizenship were significant, and citizenship was by birth, payment or

**Above**
*The ruins on the Palatine Hill, once the elite residential quarter of Rome where Augustus was born and lived, and many emperors who followed him*

**Below**
*A room inside the house of Augustus on the Palatine Hill*

---

2. For the military arrangements see here 'Soldiers of the Empire' pp. 106–107.
3. See *Evidence for the Bible* p.158

reward. No 'Roman' could be crucified or flogged, and it removed him from the jurisdiction of the Sanhedrin. The death sentence was reserved for the Imperial representative (John 18:31). A Roman citizen could appeal directly to the Emperor (Acts 25:11). See here page 117.

## Summary

With possibly some exaggeration, Sir William Ramsay summarised the state of the empire at the time of the mission outreach of the apostles:

'Many writers who came into contact with the real facts of the Imperial world expressed their admiration of the Imperial peace and its fruits. The sea was covered with ships interchanging the products of different regions of the earth, wealth was vastly increased, comfort and well-being improved, hill and valley were covered with the dwellings of a growing population, wars and pirates and robbers had been put an end to, travel was free and safe, all men could journey where they wished, the most remote and lonely countries were opened up by roads and bridges. It is the simple truth that travelling, whether for business or for pleasure, was contemplated and performed under the Empire with an indifference, confidence, and, above all, certainty, which were unknown in after centuries until the introduction of steamers and the consequent increase ease and sureness of communication.'[4]

The Stoic philosopher Epicetus (AD 50–135) wrote: 'There are neither wars nor battles, nor great robberies nor piracies, but we may travel at all hours, and sail from east to west.' And the Christian leader, Tertullian, agreed. However, For many, travel by sea was still considered dangerous and even foolhardy.

When Paul lists his own dangers in 2 Corinthians 11:25–27, we must remember that they cover two decades during which 'I have been constantly on the move.' From Luke's account alone, it has been estimated that Paul travelled at least 16,000km (10,000mi) in his missionary journeys.[5]

Unknown to itself and its multiplicity of deities, imperial Rome had established a stable empire reaching some two and a half thousand miles east to west, connected with excellent roads, secure trade routes, free passage, the minimum of disruption, firm local government and the common trade language of Greek— all in preparation for the Gospel of peace.

However, whilst Rome unwittingly opened the door wide for the message of Jesus Christ, it would soon close it firmly on the messengers.

**Left**
*A bronze certificate for the year AD 90 during the reign of Domitian, stating that the owner (his name is missing) was honourably discharged and granted Roman citizenship after 25 years military service. Stationed in Judea, he likely saw action in the horrors of the siege of Jerusalem in AD 70. Citizenship was a huge prize with many benefits that he could pass on to his children*

4. William Ramsay, The Letters to the Seven Churches of Asia (Hodder and Stoughton 1940). p. 13.
5. For this subject see Edwin M. Yamauchi, *On the Road with Paul* - 'The Ease - and dangers - of Travel in the Ancient World'.

## Rome in Egypt

After the death of Anthony and Cleopatra following the sea battle of Actium in 31 BC, Octavian (later Caesar Augustus) added Egypt to the expanding empire of Rome. Many of the magnificent buildings of Egypt admired by tourists today could have been familiar to the Romans two millennia ago

**Left**
The Great Sphinx of Gaza is the most notable and the oldest monolithic sculpture in Egypt. Dating from the Old Kingdom (2558—2532 BC) its origin and purpose is uncertain. It was cut from the limestone bedrock and it, and the Great Pyramid of Gaza behind it, would have been known to Abraham

**Above**
Many obelisks were quarried from the red granite at Aswan. This one was ordered by Queen Hapshepsut (1508–1458 BC), the mother of Tuthmosis III. The largest ever attempted at 42m (138 ft) and weighing over 1,000 tons, it was cut from the bedrock but cracked and was abandoned

**Above**
The Great processional Way at the Karnak Temple in Luxor was begun during the New Kingdom (1550-1077 BC). Here, the Procession includes rams representing Amun-Re, the god of Thebes

**Left**
The Hypostyles (meaning, many columns) at the Karnak Temple at Luxor consist of 138 massive columns

**Left**
The obelisk of Tuthmosis III (1479-1425) at Luxor stands 21.7 m (71ft) high and was carved from red granite at Aswan; it weighs 143 tons

# Annas, Caiaphas and Gamaliel

**In the light of what we know about them, Jesus was not extreme in his condemnation of many High Priests and rabbis of his day**

The office of High Priest was traced back to Moses. In 539 BC when the Jews returned to Jerusalem after the exile, it was revived and at first it was religious, hereditary and for life. Gradually this changed and it became an important secular role at the disposal of the Roman procurator.

According to Josephus there were twenty-eight High Priests from the time of Herod in 37 BC to the destruction of Jerusalem in AD 70.[1] During the life of Christ, the high priesthood had become the preserve of elite families who jealously guarded their privilege and power. Five of Annas' sons and his son-in-law became High Priests. This power was chiefly political; the High Priest conducted sacrifices only on special occasions, such as the Day of Atonement. In the Gospels, the title 'High Priests' and 'chief priests' refer to the same exclusive families since previous High Priests retained significant influence. The High Priests belonged to the Sadducees (Acts 5:17) [2].

**Annas** was appointed High Priest in Jerusalem by Quirinius in AD 6. He was known for his arrogance, injustice and greed. He undoubtedly made a significant income from turning the temple court into a market for the sale of animals required for sacrifice (Matthew 21; John 2). They were known as the 'bazaars of the sons of Annas'. Annas was deposed by the Roman procurator Valerius Gratus in AD 15 and three replacements, all related, were appointed and deposed

in as many years. In AD 18 Joseph Caiaphas, son-in-law of Annas, [3] was the fourth.

Annas continued to be the most powerful man in the Sanhedrin even after his deposition; significantly on each occasion where he is mentioned in the Gospels—Luke 3:2, where Luke deliberately used the singular 'High Priest', and John 18:13,24—he is placed before his son-in-law and successor **Caiaphas**. John accurately refers to Caiaphas as the High Priest 'that year' but notably, Jesus was first taken before Annas. Similarly, in Acts 4:6 Luke pointedly refers to 'Annas the High Priest and Caiaphas, John, Alexander and the other men of the High Priest's family' in that order, and in 5:17 John refers to 'the High Priest and all his associates' (literally 'all who were with him'). The high priesthood was bitterly unpopular. Many in Israel would look forward to the 'Kingdom of Heaven' that Jesus preached, not merely to remove the Romans!

It was Caiaphas who prophesied more than he understood (John 11:49–53; 18:14), who held the first trial of Jesus, and who finally condemned him (Matthew 26:65–66). For more on the house of Caiaphas and the ossuary containing his bones see *Evidence for the Bible* pages 136 and 142.

The Jewish *Talmud* describes the high priesthood during this period as guilty of simony, greed, violence, injustice and even indecency: 'Morals were corrupted, judgement perverted, and the Shekinah withdrawn

1. Josephus, *Antiquities of the Jews* XX.10.
2. See also *Antiquities*, XX.9.1.
3. *Antiquities* XVII.2.2.

161

from Israel.'⁴ Josephus describes the High Priest Ananias, who in AD 62 ordered the death of James the brother of Jesus and writer of the New Testament book, as 'a great horder of money'. He used this for bribery, and his servants stole from and beat the populace. Nicodemus, Joseph of Arimathea, and even Gamaliel would be powerless to confront the violence and corruption of the high priesthood.

**Gamaliel** was the opposite of Annas and Caiaphas. All that we know of him confirms Luke's reference that he was 'a teacher of the law, who was honoured by all the people' (Acts 5:34). With Gamaliel on his CV, the apostle Paul could be sure of a hearing (22:3). Gamaliel is described as representing a broader, more liberal and tolerant school among the Pharisees. His approach to the apostles is evidence of his wisdom and

Non novi illum.
Lc 22, 57

4. The *Talmud* contains the exhaustive teaching on morality, philosophy, history, legend and much more, from thousands of rabbis from BC to the 5th century AD. Alfred Edersheim in *The Life and Times of Jesus the Messiah* vol 1 p. 263, refers to this claim by the *Talmud*.

tolerance (5:34–40); unfortunately, this tolerance does not appear to have rubbed off on his most significant student (22:4–5). Gamaliel encouraged his students to study Greek literature and followed a more spiritual interpretation of the law of Moses, urging the Jews 'to friendly intercourse with foreigners.' Unlike the High Priests, he concerned himself with relief, providing for the poor, the widows, and the protection of wives from the harshness of the divorce laws.

The Jewish Mishna indicates that during his lifetime the Sanhedrin made very few important decisions without consulting Gamaliel; it is therefore unsurprising that his brief advice in defence of the apostles persuaded the Sanhedrin (Acts 5:40). The Mishna also comments that with the death of Gamaliel 'the reverence for the law ceased and purity and abstinence died away.' He was the first among only seven teachers who received the special title *Rabban*, a higher form of Rabbi.[5] It is the word Mary used recorded in John 20:16; it was a word of great honour and reverence, much more than simply 'my teacher'—it could be translated, 'My Lord and Master.' The only other use in the New Testament is by the blind man in Mark 10:51.

Gamaliel died c. AD 57. There is no support for the legend that he was a secret Christian who was later baptized by Peter and Paul.

**Left and above**
*The Western Wall, often incorrectly referred to as the Wailing Wall, is almost all that remains of the great retaining wall of the Temple Mount on which Herod built his magnificent Temple begun c.19 BC and destroyed in AD 70. Only the large blocks at the lower level are from Herod's time. However, seventeen courses are below ground level and excavations have revealed some of them. See* Evidence for the Bible *p. 121*

5. Hastings, *Dictionary of the Apostolic Church*, Vol.1 p. 440. The Mishna is a highly significant collection of Jewish oral law from 536 BC to 70 AD compiled in the third century AD.

163

*The Nazareth Village in Israel offers authentically recreated scenes that would have been familiar to Jesus when he lived there*

# The seven Herods of the New Testament

## It can all be very confusing! Six Herods are descendants of Herod the Great and four are referred to as 'Herod'

Although they are not all referred to as Herod in the New Testament, they were all sons or grandsons of Herod the Great. Here they are in brief with reign dates:[1]

**Herod the Great** (34–4 BC) at the time of Jesus' birth (Luke 1:5).

**Herod Archelaus** (4 BC to AD 6). A son of Herod the Great who took control of Judea, Samaria and Idumea. (Matthew 2:22).

**Herod Antipater (Antipas)** (4 BC to AD 39). A son of Herod the Great who ordered the death of John Baptist; Pilate sent Jesus to him (Luke 3:1 and 23:7).

**Herod Philip I** (Mark 6:17–18). A half-brother of Antipater.

**Herod Agrippa I** (AD 41–44). A grandson of Herod the Great and tetrarch of Judea (AD 41–44). He ordered the death of James and the imprisonment of Peter (Acts 12:1). He met a gruesome death (Acts 12:19–25).

**Herod Agrippa II** (AD 50–93). The son of Agrippa I and tetrarch of Roman territories outside Judea. He was present at Paul's trial in Caesarea (Acts 25–26).

**Herod Philip** (4 BC to AD 33). The son of Herod the Great and tetrarch of territories north of Galilee (Luke 3:1).

In all the references to these Herods, Luke the historian has the correct men in the correct place at the correct time and, where relevant, with the correct title and area of control described.

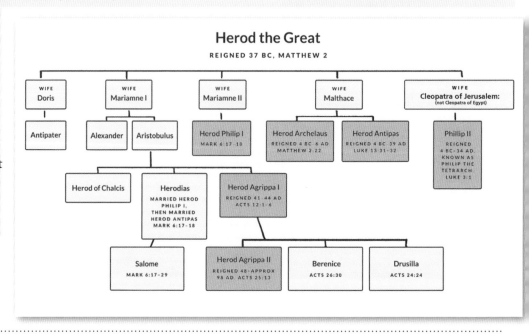

### Herod the Great
**REIGNED 37 BC, MATTHEW 2**

| WIFE Doris | WIFE Mariamne I | WIFE Mariamne II | WIFE Malthace | WIFE Cleopatra of Jerusalem: (not Cleopatra of Egypt) |
|---|---|---|---|---|
| Antipater | Alexander / Aristobulus | Herod Philip I MARK 6:17-18 | Herod Archelaus REIGNED 4 BC-6 AD MATTHEW 2:22 / Herod Antipas REIGNED 4 BC-39 AD LUKE 13:31-32 | Phillip II REIGNED 4 BC-34 AD, KNOWN AS PHILIP THE TETRARCH: LUKE 3:1 |

Herod of Chalcis

Herodias MARRIED HEROD PHILIP I, THEN MARRIED HEROD ANTIPAS MARK 6:17-18

Herod Agrippa I REIGNED 41-44 AD ACTS 12:1-6

Salome MARK 6:17-29

Herod Agrippa II REIGNED 48-APPROX 98 AD. ACTS 25:13

Berenice ACTS 26:30

Drusilla ACTS 24:24

---

1. For more on the Herods, see *Evidence for the Bible* pp. 120–123.

**Herod the Great** (34–4 BC). The first reference in Matthew 2:1.

When the Roman general Pompey entered Jerusalem in 63 BC, Herod's father Antipater gained significant political influence. After the death of Pompey, Julius Caesar appointed Antipater procurator of Judaea, and Antipater appointed his eldest son, Phasael, as governor of Jerusalem and committed Galilee to his second son Herod, who was then about twenty-five years of age.

Herod immediately and ruthlessly suppressed bands of robbers who had been troubling the country and this strengthened his relationship with Rome. However, the Sanhedrin in Jerusalem intended to try and punish Herod for murdering the leader of the robbers without a trial. Herod threatened Jerusalem with an army but was dissuaded by his father and his brother. After the murder of Julius Caesar in 44 BC and the poisoning of Herod's father, there seemed little future for Herod. He supported the ill-fated Anthony and Cleopatra, and after their defeat by Octavian (later proclaimed Augustus) he saved his life by assuring Octavian of his loyalty and that he would serve well as king in Jerusalem.

He raised an army, and by 37 BC again laid siege to Jerusalem. During this siege he divorced his first wife and married Mariamme. Jerusalem surrendered and immediately on entering the city Herod executed forty-five members of the Sanhedrin.

Herod reigned in Jerusalem for thirty-four years and maintained control only with Roman support and an iron fist. He was never popular generally and the Zealots were his arch enemies. Since his ancestors came from Idumea, he was never considered a true Jew.

In an attempt to win favour, Herod provided for the people during famine, cared for Jews in the dispersion, at times reduced part of the burden of taxation, and above all, restored the Temple. He began this is 19 BC although it was not until the early AD 60s that the work was completed. He also built the harbour at Caesarea and at various times entertained Anthony, Cleopatra, Agrippa and Augustus as royalty. He also built a magnificent palace for himself in Jerusalem. However, by placing a golden eagle in honour of the Romans above the temple gate, building a theatre, amphitheatre and hippodrome near Jerusalem for Greek plays and games, and constructing temples for the Emperor Augustus, Herod only increased the common hatred—especially among the strongly religious Pharisees.

Herod's entire life was spent discovering intrigue against him and dispensing with all who he suspected. His obsessive, and at times irrational cruelty, led to the murder of Mariamne, whom he genuinely loved, on suspicion of her attempt to poison him. This nearly drove him insane and Josephus suggests it was 'divine vengeance' on him for the murder. The latter years of his reign were immersed in court intrigue with deadly consequences.

Apart from countless political and religious opponents, Herod murdered his wife Mariamne, her two sons, her brother, mother and his own first-born son. These families were almost all involved in court intrigue. Little wonder that the Emperor is supposed to have commented that it was better to be Herod's pig than his son.

With advancing age Herod became more bitter and cruel, and when news of his incurable illness spread, the popular rejoicing embittered him even more. When the eagle above the temple gate was cut down, Herod ordered forty-two of those he held responsible burned to death. Josephus records that, shortly before his death, Herod bemoaned, 'What principally troubles me is this, that I shall die without being lamented.' To avoid this, he gave orders for 'all the principle men of the entire Jewish nation' to be gathered in the hippodrome at Jericho, and at his death they would be killed so that the people would have cause to mourn his passing—an order that was, mercifully, not carried out.[2]

Herod died in 4 BC[3] and he was buried in Herodium where his tomb and likely sarcophagus was discovered by archaeologist Ehud Netzer in 2007 (see here page 128).

Apart from Matthew 2:16, there is no other contemporary reference to the slaughter of the infants in Bethlehem. However, this would have seemed a trivial act of cruelty compared with the horrors of his vengeance throughout his reign.

**Above**
*King Herod's construction work at Caesarea Maritima included a harbour, aqueduct, palace, hippodrome and this impressive 4000 seat theatre*

**Left**
*The remains of Herod's palace at Herodion*

2. For the gruesome details of Herod's final suffering, his sinister cruelty, and his death and burial see Josephus, *Antiquities of the Jews*, XVII.6.5 and XVII 7 and 8.
3. The reference to the death of Herod in 4 BC may seem confusing in the light of Matthew 2:19 that Mary and Joseph returned from Egypt to Nazareth 'after Herod died'. When our present dating system was fixed by a monk in the year AD 533, he made a few mistakes in his calculations—including the fact that the Emperor Augustus reigned under his name Octavian for four years before assuming the title 'August'. Christ's birth is probably to be dated in the year 5 BC.

**Left and below**
*The remains of the incredible harbour built by Herod at Caesarea Maritima with the aid of Roman engineers; it included artificial islands and breakwaters, Inset: the quay where Paul would have landed and left (Acts 9:30; 18:22)*

**Herod Archelaus** (4 BC to AD 6). The only reference in Matthew 2:22.

The son of Herod the Great and Malthace (a Samaritan). On his father's death he took control in Jerusalem but, in spite of his early concessions, was unpopular because he was half Idumean and half Samaritan—and a divorcee. The people clamoured for a High Priest 'of greater piety and purity' and the punishment of those who killed the forty-two under the orders of Herod the Great.[4] Archelaus failed to appease them and eventually ordered out the military who, according to Josephus, slaughtered three thousand and cancelled Passover.

Archelaus immediately travelled to Rome to claim his right, by Herod's (disputed) will, to rule Judaea, Samaria and Idumea. The objection of his brother, Antipas, was overruled by Caesar Augustus and Archelaus was appointed tetrarch.[5] However, his continued unpopularity and cruelty—Josephus says he treated both Jews and Samaritans 'barbarously'[6]—led directly to an appeal to Augustus, resulting in Archelaus being recalled to Rome and banished to Vienna in Gaul in AD 6. From this year Judea became a Roman province.

The slaughter of the three thousand would explain Joseph's fear of returning to Judea with his young wife and child. Matthew 2:22 is the only reference to Archelaus in the New Testament. It is likely that Jesus' parable about a nobleman who travelled to a far country to 'have himself appointed king' and was hated by his subjects, had an allusion to Archelaus; especially as the parable was told in Jericho, the city in which Archelaus's father died (Luke 19:12–27).

4. Josephus, *The Wars of the Jews* II.1.2.
5. Originally the word 'tetrarch' referred to the ruler of one fourth of a country or province; however, by the first century it simply referred to a ruler installed by, and answerable to, Caesar. The populace frequently used the title 'King' though tetrarch was never independent of Rome.
6. *Wars* II.7.3.

# Appendix 04

**Above**
*A coin of Archelaus*

168

**Herod Antipas** (4 BC to AD 39). The first reference in Matthew 14:1.

The second son of Herod the Great and Malthace under whose will he was given Galilee and Perea as tetrarch. Josephus tells us little about him, but we do know he built Tiberius on Galilee as his capital and named it after the emperor and fortified two other cities.

He was a half-brother to Herod Philip I, the son of Herod's second Mariamne (Mark 6:17). This is not the Philip referred to in Luke 3:1 (see below). While staying with Philip in Rome, Antipas persuaded Herodias, Philip's wife, to marry him. To do so, he divorced his present wife who was the daughter of Aretas, king of the Nabataeans. This inevitably led to a breach with Aretas and finally a war that Antipas lost. Josephus adds that many Jews saw this defeat as a 'mark of God's displeasure against him.'

Josephus and all four Gospels record the death of John Baptist under the orders of Herod Antipas (eg. Matthew 14:3–12). Josephus refers to John as 'a good man, [who] commanded the Jews to exercise virtue both as to righteousness towards one another and piety towards God...'[7]. Josephus suggests Herod's 'suspicious temper' ordered John's execution because of his growing popularity with the people. It is the Gospels that give the immediate cause. We do not know how long John was imprisoned in the fortress of Macherus (according to Josephus), but Herod met with him on a few occasions (Mark 6:17–20) and his own disciples had access to him (Matthew 11:2–3).

Herod Antipas was responsible for Galilee throughout the entire life of Jesus, although there is no record that Jesus ever visited Tiberius. Interestingly when Jesus heard that Herod had shown interest in him, he withdrew into the region of Tyre and Sidon which was part of the Roman province of Syria. Jesus warned his disciples against the bad influence of Herod Antipas (Mark 8:15) and referred to him as 'that fox' when warned that Herod was set on killing him (Luke 13:31–33). The only time Herod Antipas came face to face with Jesus was when Pilate sent Jesus to him at his trial (Luke 23:6–12). Jesus' refusal to respond to Herod's questioning, or to perform a miracle to entertain him, clearly infuriated Herod who mocked him and set his soldiers on him. Presumably the violent action of Pilate against some Galileans had estranged Pilate and Herod and their common scorn of Jesus united them (13:1). The disciples clearly implicated Herod Agrippa in the conspiracy against Jesus (Acts 4:27). Intriguingly, the Manaen of Acts 13:1 was a foster-brother (the word *suntrophos* can also be an intimate childhood friend) of Antipas.

The Herodian family 'civil war' continued when Herod Agrippa levelled charges before the emperor Caligula against Antipas for embezzlement; in AD 39 Antipas was banished to Gaul and Herodias voluntarily accompanied him into exile. Agrippa took over his territory.

7. See *Antiquities of the Jews* XVIII.5.2.

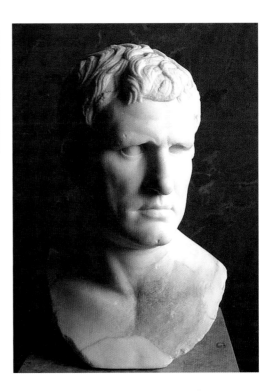

**Herod Philip I.** A half-brother of Antipas who married Herodias, the High Priest's daughter, until Antipas enticed her away (Matthew 14:3–4 and Mark 6:17–18). It was their daughter, Salome, whose dance before Herod Antipas led to the death of John the Baptist. In the New Testament he is not called 'Herod'.

**Herod Agrippa I** (AD 41–44). The first reference in Luke 3:1.

A grandson of Herod the Great, both his early life and the end were turbulent and tragic. His father had been executed and he fled to Rome. His extravagant lifestyle led him into more trouble and debt, and for a while he stayed with Antipas in Galilee. Agrippa was imprisoned by Tiberius for an incautious remark but released by his old friend Caligula and given the tetrarchy of Iturea, Traconitis (Luke 3:1) and Abiline, vacant since the death of Philip II. To this was added the tetrarchy of Galilee and Perea when Antipas was exiled. After AD 41 Claudius added Samaria and Judea. Herod Agrippa considered himself now truly a king. Josephus writes well of him as much more generous and compassionate than his predecessor to both Jew and foreigner.[8] Agrippa was scrupulous in observing the Jewish law and ceremony and, to please the Jews, arrested some of the followers of Jesus, executed James and imprisoned Peter (Acts 12:1–5).

His pride was his end. Acts 12:19–24 is mirrored in the account given by Josephus who adds many details including that his robes sparkled in the sunlight and that he saw an owl which was considered an ill-omen. From that day Herod was taken ill and five days later died in great pain at the age of fifty-four.[9]

169

8. Josephus, *Antiquities* XIX.7.3.
9. *Antiquities* XIX.8.2.

**Herod Agrippa II** (AD 50–93). Never in full charge of Judea. The only reference in Acts 25 and 26.

He was seventeen years old and in Rome for his education when his father Agrippa I died. The emperor Claudius did not immediately allow him to inherit his father's rule offering him only the tiny Chalcis but with the right to superintend the Temple and appoint the High Priest. Later, he received parts of Galilee and in AD 56 Nero extended his territory. A Roman at heart and by education, he always supported the emperor, although he made himself fully acquainted with the Jewish faith (Acts 26:3). He tried to avert the rebellion that led finally to the destruction of Jerusalem in AD 70. He was in Rome in AD 75 and received the pretorian rank. He died sometime before AD 100.

In AD 60 Paul was on trial before Porcius Festus, the Roman procurator for Palestine, and Agrippa II (Acts 25:13 to 26:28). The expression in 26:28 is literally 'in a short time' and not 'almost'. Clearly the word 'Christian' was becoming widespread—cf. Acts 11:26. At this trial Agrippa was accompanied by his sister Bernice; twice widowed and once divorced she lived much of her time with Agrippa. After the destruction of Jerusalem by General Titus, Bernice lived in his palace in Rome, which became a public scandal; she was dismissed when Titus became emperor. The 'great pomp' with which she appeared at Paul's trial (Acts 25:23) is in keeping with what we know of her.

**Left**
*Herod Agrippa II*

**Herod Philip II** (4 BC to AD 33). The only reference in Luke 3:1 but the title Herod is not given.

A son of Herod the Great, at his father's death he was made 'tetrarch of Iturea and Traconitis' among other small territories, all of which were chiefly non-Jews. His reign was 'mild and peaceful' and he rebuilt Pania re-naming it Caesarea Philippi in honour of the emperor (and himself)[10]; he also rebuilt Bethsaida on Galilee. He married his niece Salome, the daughter of Herodias and Herod Philip, who is mentioned, though not by name, in Matthew 14:6 and Mark 6:22. On his death, his territory was given to Herod Agrippa.

Jesus entered Herod Philip's territory when he travelled north from Galilee (Matthew 16:13).

10. See *Evidence for the Bible* p. 130.

**Left**

*Pania had been dedicated to the Pan god for centuries before Philip II rebuilt the town and dedicated it to Caesar, renaming it Caesarea Philippi. These niches would have been filled with images of Pan*

**Below**

*The more recent text of Nymphaios discovered at Souq Wadi Barada, the site of ancient Abila (18mi from modern Damascus), the capital of the tetrarchy of Abilene*

**Lysanias** 'tetrarch of Abilene' (Luke 3:1) was not a member of the Herodian family. There has been some unnecessary debate around Luke's reference here. A Lysanias, the son of Ptolemy, is known to have been king (not tetrarch) of Iturea between 40–36 BC; he was put to death by Mark Anthony on the insistence of Cleopatra. Since we knew little of another Lysanias it was assumed that Luke was in error, in spite of Luke's known scrupulous accuracy in his historical writing. If Luke was confusing with the earlier Lysanias he would have referred to him as 'King' not 'tetrarch'.

Among the evidence supporting Luke's accuracy is an inscription discovered in the nineteenth century, from the time of Tiberias some fifty years after the death of the first Lysanias, from an otherwise unknown Nymphaios. He built a road and a temple,

which he dedicated to the 'salvation of the Augustan Lords' and described himself as 'a freedman of Lysanias the tetrarch.' The only time that phrase 'Augustan Lords' (Lords Imperial) could be used of a tetrarch of Abilene was between AD 14–29. This inscription is now lost and only copies remain. However, more recently what appears to be an identical inscription has come to light.[11]

171

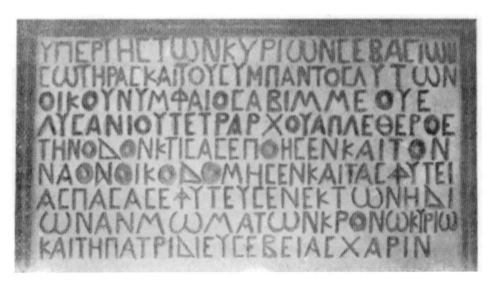

11. For a discussion of the issues see Hastings, *Dictionary of Christ and the Gospels*. vol.2 pp. 95–96, and William Ramsey, *The Bearing of Recent Discovery on the Trustworthiness of the New Testament*. pp. 298–300. For the recent inscription see online the blog post: 'The Complete Text of the Abila Inscription Concerning Lysanias' by Raphaël Savignac.

# Appendix 04

## Royal connections

We have already noted that the **Manaen** of Acts 13:1 was a foster-brother or close childhood friend of Herod Antipas. His full story would be intriguing since, in AD 46, only seven years after the banishment of his childhood friend, Manaen had come to faith in Christ and was a leader in the church at Antioch.

'**Joanna** the wife of Chuza, the manager of Herod's household' (literally: 'a manager/steward of Herod'), is named as one of the 'women who had been cured of evil spirits and diseases' and who supported Jesus out of their personal means (Luke 8:1–3). Her husband Chuza held a position of high responsibility as house-steward for Herod Antipas (see above). Chuza may have been a Nabatean who married a Jewish wife. Joanna was also one of the women who came early to the tomb to anoint the body of Jesus (Luke 24:10).

Paul's greetings to the Christians at Rome (written c. AD 57) reveal even closer ties to royalty. In 16:10,11 Paul does *not* use the word 'household' (as he does, for example, in 1 Corinthians 1:16 and 2 Timothy 1:16) but literally 'those of (ie belonging to)' Aristobulus and Narcissus. Both these men are clearly important. An **Aristobulus** was a grandson of Herod the Great who was known to have lived the end of his life in Rome as a close friend of the emperor Claudius; if he bequeathed his estate to Claudius, his household of servants and slaves would carry the name *Aristobuliani*. Similarly, **Narcissus** was a well-known, wealthy, corrupt and powerful freedman and close friend of the emperor Claudius; he was executed by the scheming of Nero's mother, Agrippina, only three or four years before Paul wrote this letter. His estate would pass to the emperor Nero, but the household would carry the name forward.[12]

Significantly, between the two is **Herodion** (v.11) who was almost certainly a slave or freedman belonging to a Herodian family. The guarded reference to the unnamed mother of **Rufus** (16:13), might be a way of protecting Pomponia Graecina, the wife of General Plautius who led the victorious Roman army into Britain for the emperor Claudius in AD 43. She was later charged with adopting a 'foreign superstition', at that time a certain reference to Christianity; she had a son named Rufus.[13]

Elsewhere, Paul sends greetings from '**those who belong to Caesar's household**' (Philippians 4:22). Paul is writing from Rome, and Philippi was a Roman colony (see here pages 86–87), therefore, the reference to those in the imperial service, which could mean anyone from slaves to managers, would resonate with the recipients.

All this is evidence of how deeply the gospel was already penetrating the heart of the empire.

**Left**
*Two years after his accession, the emperor Trajan (AD 98–117) built Trajan's Market. Some of those who received Paul's letter to the church in Rome may have lived to see this magnificent complex of 150 shops and offices that became one of the wonders of the ancient world*

12. This link is made in Hastings, *Dictionary of the Apostolic Church* art. on Narcissus. Also the New Testament scholar Bishop Lightfoot, *Epistle to the Philippians* (Macmillan and Co. 1878). p. 174–5, and as far back as Calvin.
13. For an interesting discussion on the possibility of the family of Caratacus, the British chieftain, being committed into the care of Pomponia and a reference to her and her son in Romans 16:13, see 'The Early Writing of the Gospel' by W R Cooper in *The Tyndale Society Journal* (Oxford, No. 37, Autumn 2009). pp. 32–39. However, others believe Rufus was the son of Simon of Cyrene (Mark 15:21), so F F Bruce, *The Epistle to the Romans*, Tyndale Commentaries 1963. p. 274.

172

## Herod the builder

*Herod the Great built Caesarea Maritima on the site of an ancient Phoenician town. He named it Caesarea in honour of the emperor. Its freshwater aqueduct (See* Evidence for the Bible *p.120), deep water harbour, Hippodrome, swimming pool and splendidly decorated palace, all enhanced his reputation as an imaginative builder. Caesarea became the headquarters of the Roman governor and military in Judea*

**Top**
*The tiered seating for the Hippodrome (from the Greek* hippos, *horse) where the city dignitaries would watch the chariot racing*

**Above**
*The palace included a magnificent hall, probably the 'audience room' where Paul made his appeal to be tried before the Emperor Nero (Acts 25:11-12,23)*

**Left**
*The swimming pool was once part of the splendid palace and included changing rooms and heating*

# What is the *Apocrypha?*

**The close of Malachi to the Gospel of Matthew covers four hundred years of Israel's history. These were tumultuous years in the life of the Jewish nation, and during this 'intertestamental period' fourteen or fifteen books were written, collectively known as the *Apocrypha*—from a Greek adjective meaning 'hidden'**

The *Apocrypha* is a mixture of history and legend. It is a useful collection of books to help us understand the hopes of the Jews for the coming of the Messiah and their struggle to remain pure and loyal to their religion in an alien society. Some of the books that make up the *Apocrypha* are concerned with stories already found in the Bible. For example, *1 and 2 Esdras* deal with the events of rebuilding the city after the exile, recorded in Ezra and Nehemiah. *The Rest of Esther* retells the Bible story of Esther, whilst *Tobit* and *Judith* are accounts of life after the destruction of Jerusalem by Nebuchadnezzar; and *The Song of the Three Holy Children* is concerned with the three friends thrown into the furnace by Nebuchadnezzar. *The History of Susanna* and *Bel and the Dragon* are both stories of Daniel. The two books of *Maccabees* record some of the Maccabean wars, before the birth of Christ, when many nationalistic Jews fought hard for their independence against the Syrians and later the Romans.

## Who accepts the *Apocrypha?*[1]

The *Apocrypha* has never been accepted by Protestant Christians as part of the Bible. In 1643 a preacher before the Commonwealth Parliament in London denounced 'that wretched *Apocrypha*'. However, others have been more generous towards it, whilst never accepting its authority. Even John Bunyan, the courageous Puritan Baptist author, spoke of the benefit he had gained by reading from *Ecclesiasticus*.

On the other hand, the Roman Catholic church attributes to some of the *Apocrypha* the same authority as it does to the Bible. They include: *Tobit, Judith, Wisdom, Sirach, Baruch, I and II Maccabees* and the additional stories of Daniel and Esther. They do not consider the two books of *Esdras* and the *Prayer of Manasses* as canonical. The Roman church took a while to decide on the *Apocrypha*. In AD 405 Pope Innocent I endorsed the *Apocrypha*, even though Jerome, who was translating the Bible into Latin, wanted to exclude it. In AD 600 another pope excluded it, as did Cardinal Ximenes in the sixteenth century. Finally, at the Council of Trent in 1546, Rome made up its mind and a curse was placed upon all who reject the *Apocrypha*.

Sometimes the Russian and Greek Orthodox churches make a distinction between the *Apocrypha* and Scripture, although in practice they treat them as equal, and most Orthodox priests will insist that the *Apocrypha* is part of their Bible, even though there are few official statements to this effect. Some Orthodox Bibles include the books of the *Apocrypha* scattered through the Old Testament, which implies an equal status.

Because it was translated into Greek in the third century BC along with the Old Testament Scriptures, some of the early church leaders referred to the *Apocrypha* in much the same way that they quoted from the Old Testament itself. On the other hand,

---

1. For more on the *Apocrypha* see Brian Edwards, *Nothing but the Truth* (Day One Publications 2020). pp. 271–276. Also *Evidence for the Bible* p. 111.

many of the leaders, such as Melito of Sardis, Origen and Athanasius of Alexandria, Cyril of Jerusalem and John of Damascus all rejected the *Apocrypha* as being inferior to the Scriptures. However, there were sufficient leaders in its favour, including the influential Augustine of Hippo, for many in the church, both in the east and in the west, to accept the *Apocrypha* as Scripture right up until the time of the Reformation in the sixteenth century. But there was little certainty about it, and much confusion.

The *Apocrypha* has influenced art and poetry. Familiar hymns such as 'Now thank we all, our God' and 'It came upon a midnight clear' were evidently influenced by passages in the *Apocrypha*. Toby, Judith and Susanna are old English Christian names.

### Why reject the *Apocrypha*?

1. Jesus and the New Testament writers all had access to the *Apocrypha*. Although they were constantly quoting from the Old Testament as authoritative, and occasionally made reference to other books (Acts 17:28; 1 Corinthians 15:33; Titus 1:12 and Jude 14–15), they never once quote directly from the *Apocrypha*. There are a few expressions in the New Testament that are found in the *Apocrypha*, for example: 'I gathered you together as a hen gathers her chickens under her wings' (2 Esdras 1:30, compare Matthew 23:37). 'The innumerable multitude of angels' (2 Esdras 6:3, compare Hebrews 12:22). 'There was a voice that spoke, and the sound of it was like the sound of many waters' (2 Esdras 6:17, compare Revelation 1:15). Hebrews 1:3 may reflect 'The Wisdom of Solomon' 7:26 where wisdom is described as 'The brightness of the everlasting light, the unspotted mirror of the power of God, and the image of his goodness'. Some of these expressions may have been in common use, and it is likely that Jesus and the apostles, familiar with the language of the *Apocrypha* employed it to their own end. However, the books of the *Apocrypha* were never mentioned as the source or used as an authority.

2. The first century Jewish historian, Josephus, and the Jewish Talmud were quite clear that the books of the *Apocrypha* formed no part of the Hebrew Scriptures. Josephus believed that nothing could be added to or taken from the canon of the Hebrew Scriptures.[2]

3. The community who copied out the Dead Sea Scrolls never referred to these books with the special phrases, 'It is written', or 'God says', and therefore clearly they did not accept them as part of the Hebrew Scriptures.

4. Philo, the Jewish Philosopher writing from Alexandria in AD 40, quoted from, or referred to, all but five Old Testament books, but the *Apocrypha* was never mentioned or quoted. Similarly, the Jewish Council of Jamnia, five decades after Philo, rejected the *Apocrypha*.

5. None of the books of the *Apocrypha* ever claims inspiration or a divine origin. The phrase 'Hear the word of the Lord', so familiar in the Old Testament, does not occur in the *Apocrypha*. The writers were careful to avoid their work being confused with Scripture. On three occasions, the first book of Maccabees states that a prophet was no longer available in Israel. In 1 Maccabees 9:27 the writer records the terrible sufferings of the Maccabean wars and claims, 'So there was a great affliction in Israel, unlike anything since the time a prophet had ceased to be seen among them' (see also 1 Maccabees 4:46; 14:41).

6. Some parts of the *Apocrypha* contain historical errors and even contradict the teaching of the Old Testament. The 'Prayer of Manasseh' includes the statement: 'You therefore, O Lord, who is the God of the just, have not appointed repentance to the just, to Abraham and Isaac and Jacob, which have not sinned against you…' All scholars admit the many errors in 'Tobit' and 'Judith'. The opening verse of 'Judith' refers to the Babylonian king Nebuchadnezzar as king in 'Nineveh', which was the capital of the Assyrian empire and totally destroyed

175

---

2. Josephus, *Against Apion* (1.8,42), where Josephus claims the Jews have only 22 books (equivalent to our 36). Translated by William Whiston. (Ward, Lock & Co. London. No date given).

by the Babylonians in 612 BC. 2 Maccabees 12:40–45 claims not only the right, but the great value, of praying for the dead, 'that they might be delivered from sin'—a claim found nowhere in Scripture but valuable to the Roman Catholic church. Although the two books of the 'Maccabees' are of historical value, most of the stories in the *Apocrypha* are fables with little historical base.

7. In AD 170 Melito, the leader of the church at Sardis, travelled to Jerusalem to assure himself of the exact limit of the Jewish Scriptures. He came back with a list precisely as our Old Testament, with the exception of Esther, which he seemed to have omitted in error and, for some reason, added 'The Wisdom of Solomon'. Augustine is an important exception by including the *Apocrypha*, but even he admitted that the Jews did not accept the *Apocrypha* as part of the canon of the Old Testament.

8. The Greek translation of the Hebrew Old Testament, the *Septuagint*, was completed around 250 BC and was known by Jesus and the apostles. The only complete copies of the *Septuagint* available today are from the Christian era in the fourth and fifth centuries

**Left**
*A page from the Geneva Bible 1560. It marks the opening of the* Apocrypha *(between Malachi and Matthew) with the preface ensuring that it is not confused with Scripture. By the end of the 16th century the* Apocrypha *was no longer included in copies of the* Geneva Bible

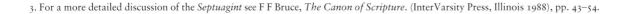

3. For a more detailed discussion of the *Septuagint* see F F Bruce, *The Canon of Scripture*. (InterVarsity Press, Illinois 1988), pp. 43–54.

AD and these do contain some of the books of the *Apocrypha*. However, since many of the Apocryphal books were written after 250 BC, it is unlikely that the original *Septuagint* could have included all the apocryphal books. Josephus did not include them in his list of Jewish Scriptures.[3]

All the available evidence is that the Jews, Jesus and the apostles, the Reformers and the Puritans never accepted the *Apocrypha* as part of Scripture. The earliest English translations of John Wycliffe (1380) did include the *Apocrypha* as a separate section, though with an introductory note that they are 'without the authority of the Bible', and the same was true of the Dutch translations (1526) and German-Swiss (1527–1529). Tyndale did not live to complete the translation of the Old Testament, and therefore John Rogers, who compiled *Matthew's Bible* (1537) from Tyndale's work, simply added the translations of Miles Coverdale to complete the Old Testament and the *Apocrypha*.

The *Geneva Bible* (1560) — the Bible of the early Protestants, the Puritans and the Pilgrim Fathers — included the *Apocrypha*, though with a disclaimer, until an edition appeared in 1599 without the *Apocrypha*. The *Authorised Version* (1611) originally contained the *Apocrypha*, although the Church of England in the *Thirty-Nine Articles* of 1563 had rejected them from belonging to the canon. The Puritans in their *Westminster Confession of Faith* in 1647, concluded, 'The books commonly called Apocrypha, not being of divine inspiration, are no part of the canon of the Scripture; and therefore are of no authority in the Church of God, nor to be any otherwise approved, or made use of, than other human writings.'[4]

---

4. For a full discussion on the *Apocrypha* in early editions of English Bibles see David Daniell, *The Bible in English*. (Yale University Press, New Haven and London 2003).

# Appendix 06

# Letters from the heretics

**As the New Testament was being written, some of the unorthodox groups were inventing their own books, at times pretending to be from apostles**

Paul was aware of this (2 Thessalonians 2:2). Most came from a group known as the Gnostics. They dismissed the Old Testament and its 'god' and selected only the books they wanted from the New Testament. Salvation was through self-enlightenment and freeing oneself from the body which was the prison house of the soul. The Gnostics believed that Jesus was the one to give this enlightenment; however, their Jesus was very different from the one portrayed in the four New Testament Gospels. Most Gnostics believed that the Christ only *seemed* to be a real man—a view known as Docetism from the Greek verb *dokein* 'to seem'—and that he was substituted by another at the cross; some believed this was Simon of Cyrene.

These Gnostics and others produced their own 'gospels' and letters. This is known as *pseudepigrapha*, meaning 'false writing'. Irenaeus, the second century church leader, summed them up by referring to their 'mighty fiction' adding:

> 'Since they differ so widely among themselves both as respects doctrine and tradition, and since those of them who are recognized as being most modern make it their effort daily to invent some new opinion, and to bring out what no one ever before thought of, it is a difficult matter to describe all their opinions.' [1]

Here are a few examples of their false 'gospels', none of which were considered by the mainstream churches across the empire to be part of the New Testament.

### The Gospel of Judas

Discovered in Egypt in the 1970s and launched into the world by the *National Geographic Magazine* in April 2006, with the foolish prediction that it 'could create a crisis of faith'; others suggested that we may have to rethink the story of Christ in the light of this new revelation. It was a copy made around AD 280 of an original probably written just prior to AD 180 when Irenaeus referred to it and summarised it accurately as 'a fictitious history … which they style the Gospel of Judas.' [2] Judas becomes the hero of the story and the only one who knew who Jesus really was. It is clearly a Gnostic work, with its esoteric (cryptic) language throughout. [3]

**Right**
*The first page of the Gospel of Judas. When discovered it was in very poor condition and around fifteen percent is irretrievably lost*

1. Irenaeus, *Against Heresies*, Book I, Ch.18:1.
2. Irenaeus, *Against Heresies*, Book 1, Ch. 31:1.
3. For details of all this and examples of other *pseudepigrapha* see Brian Edwards, *Nothing but the Truth* (Day One Publications, 2020) pp. 363–379.

178

## The Infancy Gospel of Thomas

Not to be confused with the *Gospel of Thomas* (see below). The only copy is from the sixth century, although the original may have been written in the middle of the second century. It fills the gap for the early life of Christ with such stories that at the age of five Jesus fashioned sparrows out of clay that flew away, and a young lad who, having spoiled one of Jesus' miracles, was punished by Jesus and he promptly 'withered up wholly'. Irenaeus and Eusebius both condemned it as spurious and heretical.

## The Gospel of Pseudo Matthew

Two documents are involved, both copies from the fifth century and it is clearly influenced by the cult of Mary. She is presented as a perfect child who received her food from the angels who talked often with her. Mary determined to remain a virgin all her life and eventually was committed to the care of Joseph, along with five other virgins. She becomes pregnant by the Holy Spirit and, with many embellishments, the story runs more or less parallel to the Gospels at this point until the flight to Egypt where, on the way, even lions and leopards adored him 'showing subjection by wagging their tails.' Various miracles follow including the idols of Egypt falling down.

There are many more like this, including *The Arabic Gospel of the Infancy* (probably written in the eighth century to exalt Mary), *The Gospel of Peter, The Preaching of Peter, The Acts of Peter, The Apocalypse of Peter*—obviously some thought Peter should have written more—*The History of Joseph the Carpenter,* and a very late *Epistle to the Laodiceans*—to supply the missing letter of Colossians 4:16.

Other *pseudepigrapha* provided letters written by Paul, Peter, Herod, Pilate, Joseph of Arimathea, the woman healed from an issue of blood (Matthew 9:20–22), and by Jesus himself! There is even a little correspondence between Paul and Seneca, the Roman Philosopher and Nero's tutor.

# The *Nag Hammadi Library*

**Above**
*Some of the codices (books) of the Nag Hammadi library*

In 1945 an Arab peasant discovered a collection of old books close to Nag Hammadi, on the east bank of the Nile in Upper Egypt. It consisted of sixty-one fragments covering fifty-two separate documents in thirteen codices (books). They had been written sometime in the fifth century, although are probably copies from the third century. They are in Coptic, an old Egyptian language written mostly with Greek characters, and are now in the Coptic Museum in Old Cairo. For the most part we have only fragments or badly damaged copies. The Gnostics largely died out by the sixth century. The early church leaders who wrote against them are seen to have given an accurate assessment of Gnostic beliefs. They are 'tedious and verbose', and only a sample is presented here. The literature of the *Nag Hammadi Library* is part of the 'mighty fiction' that Irenaeus wrote about in AD 180.

## The Gospel of Truth

This is the fullest expression of the Gnostic mind of all the books in the *Nag Hammadi Library*, and some believe that it was written around the middle of the second century by the influential Gnostic, Valentinus. It reveals the Gnostic love of the obscure. The theme is that ignorance of the Father is darkness and the darkness is dispelled only by attaining true knowledge of oneself and the world. It bears no resemblance to the New Testament record of salvation and presents a philosophy that is not remotely Christian. Irenaeus was aware of this so-called 'gospel' since it had just begun circulating when it came to his attention. He wrote:

'Indeed, they have arrived at such a pitch of audacity, as to entitle their comparatively recent writing *The Gospel of Truth*, though it agrees in nothing with the Gospels of the Apostles, so that they have really no Gospel which is not full of blasphemy.'[4]

### The Gospel of Thomas

The *Gospel of Thomas* (not to be confused with the *Infancy Gospel of Thomas* described earlier) contains one hundred and fourteen sayings, supposedly of Jesus, revealed to the apostle Thomas. Some bear similarities with the teaching of Jesus. Others are straightforward quotations, which clearly reveals a knowledge of the Gospels. Thirteen parables are included that, though much shorter in Thomas, are paralleled in the Gospels. Much else is vague and obscure, for example:

'Jesus said to them: "When you make the two one, and when you make the inside like the outside and the outside like the inside, and the above like the below, and when you make the male and the female one and the same, so that the male not be male nor the female female; and when you fashion eyes in the place of an eye, and a hand in place of a hand, and a foot in place of a foot, and a likeness in place of a likeness; then will you enter the kingdom"'[5]

It has been suggested that one reason why the Gnostic gospels were destroyed was because they revealed the 'true' story of the leadership of women in the first century church. If this is so, what should we make of this in the *Gospel of Thomas*?

'Simon Peter said to them, "Let Mary leave us, for women are not worthy of Life." Jesus said, "I myself shall lead her in order to make her male, so that she too may become a living spirit resembling you males. For every woman who will make herself male will enter the Kingdom of Heaven."'

Irenaeus made no direct reference to the *Gospel of Thomas*, and since he was familiar with most of the Gnostic writings, it suggests that this one was written after AD 180.

### The Gospel of the Egyptians

This is the most bizarre of all the documents in the Hammadi Library. Some of the early church leaders were aware of it, but all rejected it entirely as spurious. Large sections are missing and it gives the impression of the ramblings of an unsound mind.

### The Apocryphon of James

These are secret revelations to James (the brother of Jesus) and to Peter. They are things that Jesus 'did not wish to tell to all of us, his twelve disciples.' We may question whether Jesus would ever have said, either openly or in secret: 'The Father has no need of me, for a father does not need a son, but it is the son who needs the father, though I go to him. For the Father of the Son has no need of you.'

**The Gospel of Mary** contains mystic teaching of Mary Magdalene. The book reveals Mary Magdalene as a favourite of Jesus and one who possessed a knowledge and spirituality superior to that of the Apostles. Nothing more is written about her relationship to Jesus than this.

4. *Against Heresies*, Book III, ch.11:9.
5. Quotations from the *Gospel of Thomas* from The Gnostic Society Library on line. James M Robinson. ed.

## The Gospel of Philip

The *Gospel of Philip* is a handbook of Gnostic thinking and does not claim to be the teaching of Jesus. Much of it is obscure. For example:

> 'Light and Darkness, life and death, right and left, are brothers of one another. They are inseparable. Because of this neither are the good good, nor evil evil, nor is life life, nor death death. For this reason each one will dissolve into its earliest origin. But those who are exalted above the world are indissoluble, eternal.'[6]

Much is heretical: 'Some said, "Mary conceived by the Holy Spirit." They are in error. They do not know what they are saying. When did a woman ever conceive by a woman?'

And of creation: 'He who created it wanted to create it imperishable and immortal. He fell short of attaining his desire. For the world never was imperishable, nor, for that matter, was he who made the world.'

Wild claims are made suggesting that the *Gospel of Philip* reveals that Jesus and Mary Magdalene were married. In fact, there is not one word or phrase in any literature of the first four centuries that makes this claim.

### The value of the Pseudepigrapha?

Not one was ever considered by the churches for inclusion in the New Testament; their late date of writing, their strange Gnostic teaching and their often foolish and heretical content betrayed them. Their only value was to help the churches to distinguish what one early writer called 'gall from honey'.

181

6. The *Nag Hammadi Library*. Revised edition (HarperCollins, San Francisco, 1990). Translated by Thomas O Lambdin.

# Some valuable letters

## Not all writing outside the apostolic letters was bad. Many able and godly Christian leaders wrote to encourage the church, teach the truth, expose error and defend the Christian faith

However, not one of them ever found its way into the permanent collection of New Testament books, nor did their writers intend them to; they frequently denied any apostolic authority for themselves.[1]

The *Didache*, or the 'Teaching' of the twelve apostles, is possibly the earliest non-canonical Christian document on record. It is thought to have been written somewhere between AD 50 and 80. The author is unknown and it is not a book of theology but of pastoral advice dealing with the Way of Life and the Way of Death, baptism, fasting, and Communion, caring for travelling prophets and teachers, and finally a brief warning about the coming anti-Christ before the return of the Saviour.

We cannot be certain who **Clement of Rome** was, but he is thought to have been the third leader of the church at Rome and possibly the 'fellow-worker' with Paul referred to in Philippians 4:3. Writing before the close of the first century, in a lengthy pastoral letter to the church at Corinth he complained that some of their abuses were even worse than when Paul dealt with the same church: 'The shameful and detestable sedition, utterly abhorrent to the elect of God, which a few rash and self-confident persons have kindled to such a pitch of frenzy'. Clement turned his readers to Christ to encourage them:

> 'Let us look steadfastly to the blood of Christ, and see how precious that blood is to God, which, having been shed for our salvation, has set the grace of repentance before the whole world.'

He promised them full forgiveness if they follow this path. Finally, he called the troublemakers to repentance. His letter, full of wisdom and Scripture, was still being read decades later.

**Ignatius** was the leader at Antioch in Syria. During his journey under guard to Rome, where he knew he would be martyred in AD 115, Ignatius wrote six letters to churches and one to his friend Polycarp at Smyrna. The letters reveal a man living close to Christ who encourages the Christians, pleads for harmony and truth among the churches, and warns against false teachers:

> 'Some most worthless persons [who] are in the habit of carrying about the name of Jesus Christ in wicked guile, while yet they practise things unworthy of God, and hold opinions contrary to the doctrine of Christ.'

His friend, **Polycarp,** was soon also to meet a martyr's death and his only extant letter, to the church at Philippi, is a warm pastoral encouragement for the Christians at Philippi to stand firm in the faith, avoid heresy and to maintain a life of good works. He would also like to receive any news of the welfare of Ignatius—if he has not already died. Like Ignatius, he made no apostolic claims, but he was aware of Paul's letter to the Philippians and encouraged them to re-read it.

**Justin Martyr** of Rome was born around AD 114 and, as a well-educated philosopher, his writing was a vigorous defence of the Christian faith addressed to

---

1. For examples of these excellent letters and defence of the truth see Brian Edwards *Nothing but the Truth* pp. 343–362. (2020).

the emperor and senate, especially contrasting the high morality of Christian faith with the lives of pagans and protesting against the treatment of Christians. He also engaged in a lengthy response to a Jew named Trypho and capably challenged the empty philosophy of his day. Justin was the first great apologist for the Christian faith and his work is full of Christ.

Around AD 180, **Irenaeus** became a leader at Lyons, where the Christian church was well established, although it was soon to be decimated by persecution. He published five volumes against the heretics of his day. Irenaeus had sat under the teaching of Polycarp, but he also knew first-hand the teaching of the Gnostics and others who perverted the truth. The later discovery of Gnostic writing, including the Nag Hammadi collection, revealed how accurate Irenaeus was. He insisted that all the churches were united in their proclamation of the truth, and therefore heretics must prove that the universal church was in error. Irenaeus was aware of the subtleties of heretical teaching that made it so attractive to many:

> 'Error, indeed, is never set forth in its naked deformity, lest, being thus exposed, it should at once be detected. But it is craftily decked out in an attractive dress, so as, by its outward form, to make it appear to the inexperienced (ridiculous as the expression may seem) more true than the truth itself.'[2]

**Clement of Alexandria,** born in AD 153 and converted from paganism, became a great apologist to win pagans to Christ. His *Exhortation to the Heathen* was effective and it was followed by the *Instructor,* to enable the converted heathen, who were mostly leaving a life of wasteful licentiousness, to continue in Christ, who is the great Instructor by his life and teaching; it is minutely practical in its application. Clement's eight books in *Miscellanies*, reveal his wide learning (one scholar has recorded almost 360 classical and other non-Christian authors quoted in his work) and exposed the false theology and philosophy of the Gnostics, which he dismissed as disciples of the philosopher Plato in a new guise. All his work was Christ-exalting as the fount and foundation of all truth.

Beyond these, in the third and fourth centuries, men like Tertullian, Cyprian, Hippolytus, Origen and later still, Eusebius and Athanasius were able defenders of the faith against the growing influence of the Gnostics and others.

2. Irenaeus *Against Heresies* Book I, Preface 2.

# Fakes, Fabrications and Relics

## Caution must be exercised when using archaeological discoveries to interpret or affirm the biblical record. Whether deliberate or accidental, not all artefacts and claims are what they appear to be

Archaeology involves the interpretation of material remains from the distant past. While these interpretations can be faulty, it is worse still when deliberate hoaxes can fool even the experts.

### Fake news

A famous example is the discovery of human remains at Piltdown, East Sussex, announced in 1912. The skull fragments were estimated to be 500,000 years old, and the find was hailed as a 'missing link' between apes and humans. It was not until 1953 that it was exposed as a deliberate hoax. Piltdown Man was a fabrication of human and orangutan remains. Not only were some palaeontologists involved but even a theologian and priest, Teilhard de Chardin, has been implicated in the hoax. The prime culprit is now generally considered to be Charles Dawson who was an amateur collector in search of academic acclaim and did so through creating fake evidence in support of a theory.

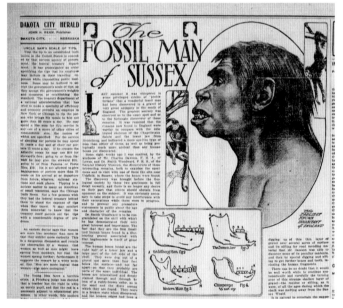

**Top right**
*How the 'discovery' of Piltdown Man was reported in a newspaper in 1913. Forty years later it was finally dismissed as a hoax*

**Right**
*Excavations at Piltdown in 1913, Charles Dawson, seated on the left, is considered the most likely man to have planted the fake materials*

Sometimes evidences for the Bible have been based on **wildly sensational claims**. One researcher claims to have discovered Noah's Ark, Egyptian chariot wheels on the Red Sea floor and the Ark of the Covenant, supposedly hidden in Jerusalem. None of his claims have borne scrutiny.[1] Grainy photographs purporting to be the Ark of the Covenant or underwater images of chariot wheels do not themselves count as evidence. In the case of the chariot wheels they are more likely to be images of coral formations or modern debris unless scientific testing can show otherwise. Such imaginative claims have been compounded by the modern use of software to enhance or distort photographs. Images of giant skeletons in the earth, purporting to be examples of the Biblical Nephilim, only testify to the power of photo manipulation.

Headlines were made in 2007 when it was claimed that **the family tomb of Jesus** had been discovered. The Talpiyot Tomb in Jerusalem had been excavated in 1980 and ten ossuaries recovered. A number of the names on these ossuaries were associated with the family names of Jesus, such as Joseph, Mary and Judas. One even bore the name Jesus. The claim made by two film makers was that this was the resting place of Jesus of Nazareth. A number of academic scholars were deceived by the film makers to lend credibility to their sensational claim. The film gave the misleading impression that these scholars supported their outlandish claim, forcing the scholars to release a joint public statement pointing out that the probability of the Talpiyot tomb belonging to the family of Jesus 'is virtually nil.'[2]

Another sensational news story was made in 2012 when a Harvard University Professor announced the discovery of what she called **'The Gospel of Jesus' Wife.'** On a small ancient fragment she had deciphered a Coptic text in which Jesus spoke of Mary Magdalene as his wife. Within days of the announcement the

**Above**
*Ossuaries from the Talpiyot Tomb on display in the Israel Museum in 2012*

fragment was identified as a hoax. The forger turned out to be a German pornography film maker with an interest in Egyptian art and sales. Using ancient blank papyrus, he had created the ink and written the text that had fooled one of the world's leading experts.[3]

Museums can also be deceived by clever fakes. The British Museum displays a good example with **a crystal skull** that inspired a Hollywood movie involving Indiana Jones. The stunning sculpture of a full-sized skull is carved from rock crystal and was claimed by a collector to have come from Mexico. It had been bought in New York in 1890 before being passed among collectors and arriving in the hands of the British Museum. It had been considered an example of pre-Columban Aztec or Inca art until testing revealed that almost certainly it had been produced with more modern tools. It is now generally considered a modern fake.

1. Alan Millard, 'Is the Bible Fake News? The Verdict of Biblical Archaeology', *Perspectives*, No. 68 Spring 2020, 32–35.
2. For a full discussion see Mark Goodacre, 'The Talpiyot Tomb and the Bloggers', in Eric Meyers and Carol Meyers (eds.), *Archaeology, Bible, Politics, and the Media*, Penn State University Press (2012). pp. 56–68.
3. Ariel Sabar in *Veritas: A Harvard Professor, a Con Man, and the Gospel of Jesus's Wife*, Scribe Publications, London and New York (2020).

**Below**
*The Crystal Skull is still displayed at the British Museum, though with an accompanying inscription that draws attention to the fact it was probably a relatively recent fabrication*

**Left**
*A fake tablet, part of the Michigan Relics, created around 1890 to depict the Biblical account of the Flood. Although wholly dismissed by scholarship, it has deceived the gullible with its striking images of scenes associated with Genesis*

Another example of a deliberate hoax was used to attempt to prove pre-Columban contact between the Americas and the Ancient Near East. The **Michigan Relics,** found in North America in 1890, were a collection of inscribed tablets and other artefacts. They included cuneiform inscriptions and unique hieroglyphs. They were dismissed as fraudulent by academics almost as soon as they were made public—even photographs revealed enough to undermine their credibility. However, in 1960 a Mormon researcher took a renewed interest in the relics. He was intent on proving the claim of the Book of Mormon that a lost tribe of Israel had settled in America long before Columbus. He assembled the Michigan Relics as a collection which were then displayed in a Utah museum for several decades. The Church of Jesus Christ of the Latter Day Saints sponsored an official investigation into the finds in 2001 which concluded that they were, as suspected, poorly manufactured fakes.

Exaggerated or invented claims, even if in a good cause, are always dishonest and counter-productive. They undermine trust and confuse our understanding. Those interested in the background to the Bible should be careful to avoid allowing their enthusiasm to cloud their judgement.

The **'Ivory Pomegranate'** held by the Israel Museum has been considered part of the High Priest's scepter from the time of Solomon's Temple. Carved from hippopotamus bone it bears an inscription in early Hebrew script declaring 'Belonging to the House of Yahweh, Holy to the Priests.' It was purchased from the antiquities market in 1979 and eventually made its way into the Israel Museum collection. However, in 2004 suspicion arose over its authenticity and some scholars claimed that while the carved pomegranate itself is ancient the inscription is a modern forgery. While debate over the artefact continues,[4] with some scholars still maintaining that it is authentic, the Israel Museum has chosen to remove it from display.[5]

4. *Shmuel Ahituv; Aaron Demsky; Yuval Goren; André Lemaire (2007). "The Inscribed Pomegranate from the Israel Museum Examined Again". Israel Exploration Journal.* **57** *(1): 87–95.*

5. Hershel Shanks, 'A New Target', Biblical Archaeology Review, November/December 2014, p. 6, 64.

**The manufacture
of fake antiquities is
as old as antiquities
themselves.** In the
ancient world it was not
uncommon for people
to create objects that
resembled something from earlier times. This may not
have been deliberate deception but an interest in the
past, much as modern mock Tudor styles or replica
Greek statues can reflect our love of history. However,
this can create confusion in the archaeological record.
Scarabs could be carved bearing the name of a
Pharaoh who lived long before, potentially misleading
archaeologists. The British Museum has a display
of antique fakes. These include poorly made tablets
designed to resemble cuneiform documents. To the
trained eye they are easily dismissed, but Victorian
collectors were duped. Internet based auction sites have
been flooded with crude fakes or replicas sold as if they
were genuine ancient artefacts.

It is beyond our scope to consider the psychology
of why people might deliberately deceive others
with such fakes and forgeries.[6] But when scholars
are misled by them this highlights the danger. If an
expert wants to prove something, they may ignore
their doubts. On a positive note, all of these examples
have eventually been identified and rejected by the
scholarly community. It only required time. Even if
a museum paid $550,000 for an object, as the Israel
Museum did for the Ivory Pomegranate, they will
remove it from display if its authenticity is shown to be
dubious. However, it is a lesson for us not immediately
to embrace sensational claims or the latest headline.
Whether it is an evidence for the Bible or an alleged
refutation of the Bible, often we only need wait to
discover the truth.

## Relics

**From the time of Helena, the mother of
Constantine, Christians have been interested in
physical, tangible remains that connect us directly
to people in biblical history. But hunting for relics
should not be confused with archaeology.**

Constantine was the first Roman emperor to
embrace the Christian faith, and early in the fourth
century his mother, Helena, set out to discover
identifiable places in the Holy Land connected with the
biblical narrative.

When she had the site of the crucifixion excavated,
Helena exposed a Roman period stone quarry with
tombs that may fit the site described in the Gospels.
However, as evidence for the location, it was claimed
she found fragments of the Holy Cross which were
then distributed to churches for their veneration. By
the early Middle Ages pieces of the cross were to be
found in churches throughout the Christian world. The
earliest historical source for the excavation of the site
and building of the Church of the Holy Sepulchre is
from the church historian Eusebius of Caesarea (c.AD
260–339) and he makes no mention of the discovery
of crosses. However, in the century that followed the
construction of the church, there were claims to have
also found the crown of thorns and the nails used at the
crucifixion along with the cross of Christ. During the
Reformation, John Calvin dryly observed that if all the

---

6. Clearly fame and fortune have sometimes played a part, documented in Nina Burleigh, *Unholy Business: A True Tale of Faith, Greed and
Forgery in the Holy Land,* Harper Collins, 2008.

fragments of the Holy Cross found in churches were re-assembled they 'would form a whole ship's cargo.'[7]

Other relics to be found in Churches include the head of John the Baptist, the finger of the apostle Thomas, and the lance that pierced the side of Jesus at his crucifixion. Such claims are not helped by the fact that there are multiple relics claiming to be the same thing – four different Churches claim to have possession of the head of John the Baptist.

## The Turin Shroud

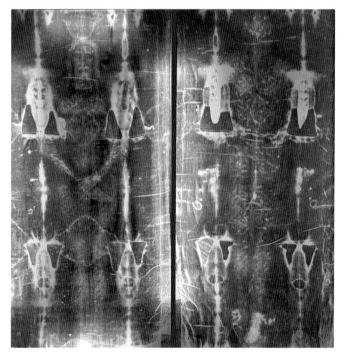

188

**Above**
*The Turin Shroud, front and back, as it appears in a photo negative*

The fact that an artefact is venerated as a relic does not mean it must be a fake. Perhaps the most intriguing relic is the Shroud of Turin. Bearing the faint image of a disfigured human body, it has been venerated as the shroud of Jesus since at least its earliest appearance in the historical record in AD 1390. It was the invention of photography that brought the shroud to greater notice. A photographic negative taken in 1898 revealed far more details than had been visible to the naked eye. The photographic negative image resembles an X-ray and reveals a badly bruised face including a swollen nose, distorted cheeks and torn eyelid. If this were a fake, then the fraudster was so clever that they faked elements that would not even be detected until centuries after its creation.

An attempt to carbon date the Shroud in 1988 indicated a date in the thirteenth century (c.1260–1390) and seemed to confirm it as a mediaeval hoax.[8] However, interest in the Turin Shroud and analysis of its features has continued. Modern attempts to recreate the Shroud using techniques that might have been available in the Middle Ages have not come close to replicating the details. Studies have shown that the 1988 carbon dating of the Shroud had used a fragment from a medieval repair to fire damage making the dating unreliable.[9] A long-lost Byzantine shroud called the Mandylion of Edessa has been suggested as the earlier name for the Turin Shroud before it entered western history, though this is disputed by many.[10]

Whether the Shroud belongs to the first century and whether the image could be that of Jesus may never be proven or disproven. But the relic will probably always remain intriguing and is not lightly dismissed as a hoax. Along with fakes and fabrications the realm of relics is to be treated with some caution for its value in understanding the Bible.

7. John Calvin, *Treatise on Relics,* Johnstone, Hunter & Co (1870), p. 127.
8. Damon, P. E. (et. al.), 'Radiocarbon Dating of the Shroud of Turin', *Nature* 1989, 337, pp. 611–615.
9. T. Casabianca (et. al.), 'Radiocarbon Dating of the Turin Shroud: New Evidence from Raw Data', *Archaeometry*, University of Oxford, 2019, pp. 1–9
10. That the Mandylion of Edessa could not have been the Turin Shroud is discussed at length in Andrea Nicolotti, *From the Mandylion of Edessa to the Shroud of Turin*, Brill: Leiden/Boston, 2014.

## The Ossuary of James the brother of Jesus

In 2002 a bone box (ossuary)[11] came on to the antiquities market inscribed 'James, son of Joseph, brother of Jesus'. It would be most unusual for a brother to be named on the ossuary unless he was someone very significant. Scholars on both sides argued whether or not it was a forgery. After five years of debate and examination, an Israeli court concluded that it was not a forgery. It remains possible that the ossuary really is a physical object associated directly with a member of the family of Jesus and the first leader of the Jerusalem Church. But it is also a good example of the uncertainty that surrounds objects that are found on the antiquities market. Devoid of context, which an archaeological excavation would provide, there will always be concern that the dating may be mistaken or the object been tampered with.

## The Ark or what?

An unusual formation at Durupinar, on Mount Aararat in Turkey, has been thought to be the resting place of Noah's Ark. It is named after the Turkish airforce pilot who spotted it in 1959. In the 1980s Ron Wyatt made a more concerted effort to prove that the formation really was the remains of an ancient boat.

Wyatt claimed to have tested the structure, found wooden remains and even anchor stones that would have helped give the boat stability. None of his claims have withstood scrutiny. In fact, a Google Earth search of the vicinity shows that there are similar formations in the vicinity. It is a geological formation created by mud moving past uplifted rock.[12]

189

**Left**
*The structure claimed to be Noah's Ark, Durupinar, photographed in 2007*

11. For more on this ossuary and others see *Evidence for the Bible* p. 143.
12. Andrew Snelling, 'Special Report: Creation Ark Expose', *Creation* 14:4, September 1992.

## Here are some questions to help us discern what is reliable

- **When and where was the discovery made?**
  Has there been time for proper scrutiny and discussion or is this a latest press release designed to sell papers or serve as online click bait? If the discovery was made at a genuine archaeological site, that gives it credibility. But some claims are made on the basis of items bought on the antiques market or from photographs shared online. These should be handled with caution.

- **Who is associated with the discovery?**
  Has the claim been made by people with appropriate credentials and training to make sense of it? Astonishing finds have been made by amateurs and enthusiasts but those with training have always been necessary to scrutinize their claims – even though, as we have seen, they too can sometimes be deceived!

**Above**
*Spot the difference. One of these cuneiform tablets is the original Babylonian map of the world from the sixth century BC. The other is a cheap modern replica. When sold as a replica these can be useful educational tools or attractive decoration but when passed off as genuine they defraud collectors and confuse historians. The replica with text that is a little too clear (right) is an imitation of the genuinely antique script of the original (left)*

- **Where is this material published?**
  The internet has created a context where fake news, conspiracy theories and satire rub shoulders with genuine discovery. We would recommend the *Biblical Archaeology Review* and its associated Biblical Archaeology Society as a popular level, accessible magazine. While the contributors come from many different perspectives, it provides a convenient window into academic study. The Associates for Biblical Research have a useful website and publish a magazine, *The Bible and Spade*, from an evangelical perspective. Genuine discovery and authentic artefacts will usually be widely published in a range of books and journal articles.

- **Where can I see them?**
  Museums are a fabulous resource because their exhibits will have been scrutinized by the scholars employed by them. Many of them have a good range of exhibits relevant to biblical background. Even museums have made mistakes from time to time and had to remove objects from display, but this only serves to confirm their commitment to authenticity. The Ancient Near East offers a wealth of opportunity to see the world of the Bible and various companies provide reliable tours of Egypt, Israel and Jordan that help explain the value of archaeology. Search, for example, under Day One Tours.

# **Museums**—a relic from the past?

Gertrude Bell was born in 1868. Known as the 'Desert Queen', she became something of a legend in her day as one of very few women in the world of archaeology. Her passion for travel led her to the Middle East where, among many notable achievements, she provided military intelligence for T. E. Lawrence (Lawrence of Arabia). Perhaps her greatest achievement was to establish the National Museum in Baghdad, which received its permanent home in 1926, the year of her death. [1] The last three years of her life were devoted to the creation of this archaeological museum. Gertrude Bell insisted that antiquities should stay in the country of their origin and this ensured that the National Museum of Iraq, which is her monument in the land she loved, possessed an invaluable collection of Iraq's own antiquities. Sadly, the National Museum was looted in the aftermath of the Gulf War in 2003 and thousands of its artefacts are still missing.

**Below**
*Under the face of the Sphinx. A few of the thirty-nine participants of the Conférence du Caire in Cairo March 1921. Winston Churchill is third rider from left and beside him Gertrude Bell and T.E. Lawrence*

1. Janet Wallach, *Desert Queen. The extraordinary life of Gertrude Bell Adventurer, Advisor to Kings, Ally of Lawrence of Arabia* (Weidenfeld & Nicolson 1996).

The first library to contain all knowledge

The Reference

The story of Gertrude Bell illustrates a major issue today in the world of museums and archaeology: should items taken from their homeland be returned? Are museums both necessary and relevant today, or are they an unwanted reminder of colonial looting? Some of the finest museums across the world hold hundreds of thousands of cultural items mostly gathered during the years of occupation by Western powers. Should artifacts always stay in the country of their origin?

**Collecting items from previous ages is nothing new**. King Ashurbanipal of Assyria (668–627 BC) is credited with assembling the oldest surviving royal library in the world. It is a set of at least 30,000 cuneiform documents written in the Akkadian and Sumerian languages, which was found in the ruins of the Assyrian city of Nineveh. He set out to collect copies of all known cuneiform tablets to enhance his and his people's knowledge. Texts ranged from government records to works of literature and technical instructions. He had the known towns of Babylonia searched for them, and one collector reported his joy on discovering a tablet from the time of Hammurabi,

**Above**
*A small part of the Library of Ashurbanipal in the British Museum*

over a thousand years before. Ashurbanipal is also famous for claiming to have read them all!

**Admittedly there has been some plundering**. The Koh-i-noor diamond was seized by the British East India company in 1849 and is now part of the British crown jewels; the Benin Bronzes, looted from the capital of Benin (in modern Nigeria) by British soldiers in 1897, are now spread across several museums in Europe and America. Reparation or repatriation may be the discussion point for some items. However, at the end of World War I, the British, administering Mesopotamia, protected archaeological sites and prohibited looting and exporting antiquities.

**Successful repatriations** of recent looting have occurred. For instance, in 2011, the Museum of Fine Arts Boston returned a Roman sculpture of Herakles to Turkey from which it had been stolen. In 2018

The National Gallery of Australia returned to India a bronze statue of the god Shiva which had been looted from a Hindu temple in Tamil Nadu. In 2020 The Museum of the Bible in Washington, D.C. returned a few thousand looted objects to Iraq and Egypt, including papyri fragments and clay tablets.

**However, there are many reasons why museums generally consider their acquisitions should remain where they are**:

- All major museums have the **facilities and experience to conserve, protect and display** artifacts from the rich heritage of the past which might otherwise be lost to private collectors or to the erosion of time. Without museums we would certainly have lost many tangible links to the past.

- In our multicultural Western societies many, whose ancestral roots go far back—for example to Africa or Asia—may never have **the opportunity of experiencing their cultural history** if they cannot visit a world-class museum in their country of adoption. The value of museums and their highly skilled conservationists scattered across the globe, means that millions will have access to the ancient cultures of history without having to travel far.

- The issue is not simply where items 'belong' but **where they can be most culturally and educationally visible**. For example, more people are able to admire the Parthenon Marbles in the British Museum each year (six million) than visit the Parthenon in Athens (one and a half million). Even if ancient artifacts are returned to their land of origin, they will never be exactly in their original setting. The world of the Egyptian pharaohs or the Assyrian, Babylonian and Persian rulers is two or three thousand years removed from the culture, language and religion of today. Almost all artifacts would simply be returned from one museum to another, they can rarely go back to their original location.

- The question must be asked of many museum exhibits: **what state were they in before they were rescued from destruction**, and how much would have remained unless discovered by foreign archaeologists? Most of the Egyptian royal tombs were plundered by grave robbers in antiquity. Since we all know the immense treasure of the tomb of Tutankhamun, a relatively unimportant pharaoh who died in his teens, what might the tombs of Ramesses II and Tutmosis III have contained—two of the greatest and long-lived pharaohs—if they had not been robbed before archaeologists found them?

- One example among many of uncovered ruins is the façade of a Greek funerary temple to the sea-god Nereus, built for king Arbinas c.390–380 BC. It was nothing more than a scattering of rubble eroded and covered by time and the elements when discovered by Charles Fellow between 1838 and 1842. It came to England with the permission of the Ottoman rulers.

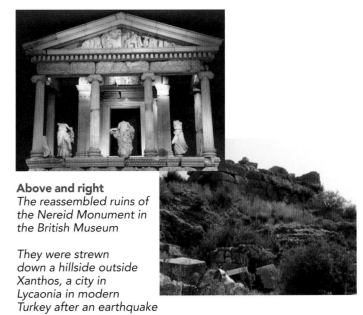

**Above and right**
*The reassembled ruins of the Nereid Monument in the British Museum*

*They were strewn down a hillside outside Xanthos, a city in Lycaonia in modern Turkey after an earthquake*

A more celebrated example is the story of the Parthenon Marbles (Elgin Marbles).

The Parthenon, dedicated to the goddess Athena, was the central focus on the Acropolis in Athens and was completed by 438 BC. In the sixth century AD the building was used as a Christian church, and at the time of the Ottoman empire it became a mosque and later a fortress and a munitions store. An explosion in 1687 destroyed a large part of it, and scattered remains were looted for building material or burned for lime. Between 1801 and 1812 agents of Lord Elgin removed many of the remaining marble sculptures from the ruins and they were brought to England where they finally came into the possession of the British Museum in 1816. Some of these sculptures in the Museum depict scenes from mythology, but the procession that makes up the frieze illustrates the Panathenaic festival commemorating the birthday of Athena. Whether Elgin removed the marbles illegally (he strongly denied this) is still debated; however, he at least rescued them for posterity, since only in this century has the Greek government begun to restore the Parthenon and place remaining sculptures in the Athenian Museum to preserve them.

- It was only **the understanding of early foreign explorers** that saw the intrinsic value of many items. Local workers actually broke-up the Mesha Stela (Moabite Stone c.840 BC) to access the 'treasure' inside—there was none. It was the text written on the outside of the solid block of black granite that was its value—an early extra-biblical Moabite reference to Yahweh, the kings of Judah and Israel and 'the house of David'. This item remains in Egypt with so much more. The story of the Dead Sea Scrolls is similar, with so many valuable manuscripts broken-up to be sold by the Bedouin.

- **Many items were not 'stolen'** but came to museums with legal documentation/permission of the time, as the Nereid Monument above. However, it is often impossible to determine the true provenance of many items two or more centuries later.

- **Returning items to fragile governments,** volatile areas of the world or simply where they cannot be either conserved or displayed may lose them for ever.

As an example of what can happen in a volatile country.[2] Of the ruins left by Austen Henry Layard at Nineveh (see pages 65, 143), it is estimated that 90% were blown up and destroyed by 'Islamic State'. Equally tragic, the Mosul Cultural Museum was the second largest museum in Iraq (after the Iraq National Museum in Baghdad) when it was badly looted during the second Gulf War in April 2003; fortunately, some 1,500 movable pieces were sent into storage in the Iraqi National Museum of Baghdad days before the looting. However, when 'Islamic State' took control of the museum in June 2014 the Hatra sculptures were 'all brutally smashed with sledgehammers', and most of the Assyrian items from the Mosul Museum disappeared and are probably being trafficked by IS on the antiquities market.

One acquisition is a particular loss. The bronze panels of the Balawat Gate, built during the reign of Shalmaneser III (859–824), were excavated by the British School of Archaeology in Iraq under the direction of Max Mallowan

2. Paolo Brusasco, 'The Assyrian Sculptures in the Mosul Cultural Museum: A Preliminary Assessment of What Was on Display Before Islamic State's Attack', University of Genova (*The Journal of Near Eastern Studies* 2016).

in 1956. They had been badly damaged by fire in antiquity and were sent to the British Museum for conservation and study in 1965; the reconstructed gates were then returned to the Mosul Cultural Museum in 1974. During the second Gulf War from 2003, the Mosul Museum was looted and the gates were largely lost. The 2009 UNESCO report stated 'the largest single loss from the looting was thirty bronze panels. Forty-five other panels from the same gate were left behind, although the looters damaged some

trying to remove them.' Fortunately, a replica of these gates, together with a few of the original bronze panels are on display in the British Museum.

- Positively, **antiquities are frequently loaned between museums**. Many of the fine exhibits from the tomb of Tutankhamun have travelled to the UK, USA, USSR, Japan, France, Canada and West Germany. The iconic Cyrus Cylinder has been loaned twice to Iran (1971, 2010), once to Spain (2006) and once to the USA (2013).

- Frequently the question has to be raised: **exactly where is the home country** of some items? For example, the Cyrus Cylinder is considered an icon in Iran since it contains an order from Cyrus the king of Persia in 539 BC; however, in 1879 it was discovered in the ruins of Babylon in modern

**Left**
*The replica of the huge Balawat Gates in the British Museum. Sadly, most of the remaining original bronze bands in the Mosul Cultural Museum have been stolen or damaged. One of the original bronze panels preserved in the British Museum shows the cruel treatment of prisoners in the time of Shalmaneser III*

Iraq. Even more bizarre are the world travels of the four copper 'Horses of Saint Mark' dated to classical Greek (or Roman?) antiquity: from the Hippodrome of Constantinople in the fourth century AD, to Venice by the Crusaders, to the Arc de Triomphe in Paris by Napoleon and back to Venice after Waterloo! Where do they belong?

- **Many countries are a treasure-trove of discovered, and as yet undiscovered, antiquities,** Egypt and Greece especially. It would be tragic if the world had to travel to those countries before they could visibly connect with the past. These countries have yet much more to discover.

- The argument that the way many exhibits were acquired is a reminder of the 'cultural imperialism' of a colonial past that must be deleted, is an unfortunate distraction. Granting the negative side of colonialism, **the significant benefits that conquering nations brought to their empires are currently ignored.** For example, Ruth and Vishal Mangalwadi researched the Indian legacy from the Baptist Missionary, William Carey:[3]

William Carey introduced the steam engine to India, built a paper mill and what was then the largest press in India. He printed the first newspaper in any oriental language and introduced the idea of Savings Banks. To the sciences he introduced the Linnaean system to gardening and published the first books on science and natural history in India; he founded the Agri-Horticultural Society to maximise usage of the land and taught and wrote about the cultivation and use of timber. He taught that the stars and planets were not deities that governed our lives, but were created by God to help us keep time and travel the world. To education and literature he started dozens of schools for Indian children of all castes, and translated and published some great Indian classics such as the *Ramayana*, and wrote the first Sanskrit dictionary for scholars; he also introduced the idea of lending libraries. To the medical and ethical world he campaigned for the humane treatment of lepers and cared for the suppression of women by working against polygamy, female infanticide, child marriage, widow-burning, euthanasia and forced female illiteracy; he opened schools for girls. Through his position of professor in Fort William, Carey influenced the ethos of the British East India Company and turned the British administration from imperial exploitation to a civil service.

More profitable than the debate about repatriation would be a serious discussion to encourage prestigious and well-stocked museums to share their rich surplus harvest, which is often in store and out of sight, with emerging museums in countries which have few. In this way many more millions will be able to enjoy, not simply their own history, but that of other nations across the world.

Nicholas Thomas, Director of the Museum of Archaeology and Anthropology in Cambridge, has wisely concluded: 'The issue is not in the end where artefacts 'belong' but where they can be culturally and socially beneficial. Some collections should be returned to their nations of origin, but communities in Africa, Oceania and elsewhere should have access not only to their own heritage but also to the world art that is so accessible to multicultural publics in Europe. Historic artefacts are representative not only of humanity's achievements, but of the travel and traffic that have formed the world order we all now inhabit.'[4]

3. Ruth and Vishal Mangalwadi, *Carey, Christ and Cultural Transformation* (OM Publishing 1997). They show how Carey was the central character in the story of the modernization of India.
4. See also Tiffany Jenkins, *Keeping Their Marbles: How the Treasures of the Past Ended Up in Museums – and Why They Should Stay There* (Oxford, 2016).

# Biblical Chronology

'How old is it?' is one of the most common questions ever asked in matters related to archaeology. In this survey of the background to the Bible it has been crucial to try and identify how old an artefact or a site is in order to relate it to the chronology of the Bible. Although this is one of the most important and fascinating topics, there are frequently uncertainties even among scholars.

Chronology refers to the sequence of events as they took place in history. The Bible is written as a linear narrative with a clear sequence running from Creation to the time of the Patriarchs, through the Exodus, to the monarchy and beyond. The order of the events is relatively straightforward and the interest in genealogies by Bible writers reinforces the importance of the narrative following a historical progression.

Occasionally uncertainties emerge when we try to synchronize this biblical narrative with events in the rest of the world, such as the chronologies of Egypt, Assyria, Babylon, Persia, Greece, and Rome. However, these uncertainties need never undermine our confidence in the biblical record. While we may not be dogmatic about exactly which year a certain king reigned, archaeology has confirmed the reliability of the Bible's historical record.

## Tools and technology

The broadest system of dating for ancient history refers to the tools and technology that were in use at that time. This system was proposed in 1836 by a Danish scholar, Christian Thomson, as a way of organizing exhibits in a museum. The earliest period of human history discovered by archaeology is characterized by the use of stone. In the Fertile Crescent the Stone Age drew to an end around 3800 BC with the first uses of copper (Chalcolithic). This does not mean that metal was not used in earlier periods (Genesis 4:22), only that it is less common in the archaeological record. The Chalcolithic Age lasted until the development of Bronze in 3300 BC. This is followed by the Iron Age (from 1200 BC) and then the various dominant empires enable scholars to date the historical periods that follow.

| | |
|---|---|
| Bronze Age | 3300–1200 BC |
| Iron Age | 1200–586 BC |
| Neo-Babylonian | 586–539 BC |
| Persian | 539–332 BC |
| Greek | 332–198 BC |
| Late Hellenistic | 198–63 BC |
| Roman | 63 BC – AD 360 |
| Byzantine (Christian) | AD 360–640 |

It is important to note that these dates describe developments in the Fertile Crescent but not necessarily elsewhere in the world. For example, the Iron Age is dated from 1200 BC in Canaan but in Britain the Iron Age did not begin until 800 BC and does not end until the Roman invasion in AD 43.

## Pottery

Apart from tools and metals, pottery has been the most important diagnostic tool for helping to date archaeological excavations. In 1890 Flinders Petrie (see page 140) proposed 'Sequence Dating' using

**Below**
*A pottery assemblage from the Israel Museum showing the various styles and functions, including oil lamps, that are invaluable for dating when a site was in use*

pottery types. The gradual changes in the form and function of pots and bowls enable archaeologists to find the relative date for a site. In modern times the development of techniques like carbon dating has confirmed that, despite a few anomalies, pottery has been a reliable guide to understanding the past.

## Empires and astronomy

However, we need even more precision if we want to fix a date for an event or a person described in the Bible. The Bible makes a number of references that we can compare with the histories of other records from the ancient world in order to establish such a date. For example, Luke refers to the 'fifteenth year of Tiberius' (Luke 3:1) which, by Roman chronology, would have been AD 29. In the Old Testament the Babylonian attack on Jerusalem happens in the 'nineteenth year' of Nebuchadnezzar's reign (2 Kings 25:8) which, according to Babylonian dating, would have been 586 BC.

The Egyptians kept many records of their history. One of the most important is that of Manetho, an Egyptian priest in the late 4th century BC who catalogued thirty Pharaonic dynasties that told the story of their history from Narmer (c.3300 BC) to Alexander the Great (c.363 BC). His original writings are lost but his histories are known through later references to his work. Most scholars consider the earliest dynasties in this list to be less precise but after about 1500 BC the chronology is regarded as reliable.[1]

Astronomical data has provided an important means of cross-checking the absolute dates in a chronology. The Egyptians often refer to celestial events (such as an eclipse) and developed an annual calendar fixed by the position of the star Sirius (called Sothis by the Egyptians). This 'Sothic calendar' can be accurately dated by astronomers.[2]

There are also extensive lists of kings in the Babylonian and Assyrian records. Ptolemy, a Greek astronomer resident in Egypt during the Roman period, drew up a record of the Babylonian kings from the time of Nebonassar in 747 BC. More recent discoveries in cuneiform documents, such as the Babylonian Chronicle[3], have only served to confirm the general reliability of these historical records.

Using the Babylonian, Assyrian and Egyptian records we can arrive at absolute dates for the major events of Old Testament history.[4] Of course, those dates are not always beyond criticism and the further back we go, the more contested they become. In particular, the dates for the period of Moses and the conquest of Canaan are subject to some debate.[5]

1. See also *Evidence for the Bible* p.217.
2. See also the ancient reference to what we know as 'Halley's Comet' in *Evidence for the Bible* p.iv.
3. See the value of the Babylonian Chronicle for biblical dating in *Evidence for the Bible* pp.80–81.
4. Edwin Thiele, *The Mysterious Numbers of the Hebrew Kings* (1951). Widely regarded as the definitive work on the chronology of the Hebrew Kings.
5. This issue is discussed in *Evidence for the Bible* pp. 22–23; 198–200.

**Above**
*The Egyptian god, Amun, in the form of a great ram, protects pharaoh Taharqa*

## Clarity or confusion?

Mainstream scholarship accepts a fairly complete set of chronologies for the kings of the ancient world, and biblical scholars have found that the history given in the Bible fits well with those chronologies.[9] However, there are a number of different chronologies that have been proposed for Egyptian history which lower these dates by anything from a few years to several hundred years. One particular challenge to the chronologies of ancient kings is whether they are consecutive or whether there may have been overlapping periods of coregency which serve to lower the dates.

David Rohl, an English Egyptologist, has developed an alternative chronology of the Ancient Near East that lowers the dates of many of the Egyptian Pharaohs by as much as 350 years. Rohl argues that Shishak should not be identified with Pharaoh Shoshenq I but with Ramesses II. Traditionally, Ramesses II's reign is dated to 1279 to 1213 BC.

According to Rohl, the period of Amarna and Pharaoh Akhenaten correspond to the time of David and Saul. He proposes that the Amarna tablets are read as correspondence from the time of the united monarchy in Israel.[10] This has not met widespread support because many scholars see such a proposal as creating far more problems than it solves. Information in the Amarna correspondence fits well with what we know from Assyria or Hittite culture enabling us to fix their dates to the 14th century BC.

There are other scholars who also voice doubts about the mainstream chronology of Egypt; for example, John Bimson suggests a lowering of the dates given by as much as 250 years.[11] In particular some draw attention to how little we know of 'Dark Ages' or Intermediate periods in ancient records. However, using the conventional chronology it is perfectly

## Foreign Kings

A number of kings from the surrounding nations, referred to in the Old Testament, can be correlated with references from sources outside the Bible. An Egyptian pharaoh called Shishak (1 Kings 14:25) mounted an attack on Jerusalem in 925 BC and this finds confirmation in an Egyptian victory inscription at the Temple of Karnak from the time of Pharaoh Shoshenq I (c.945–924 BC).[7] Taharqa was a Pharaoh of the 25th Dynasty who began to reign around 690 BC.[8] The Bible makes reference to him at the time of King Hezekiah, and the invasion of Sennacherib which took place in 701 BC (2 Kings 19:9). This may mean that Tirhakah was only a prince at the time of Sennacherib and that the biblical writer is referring to him by the title he would take by the time of writing.

7. See *Evidence for the Bible* pp. 42,47.
8. See *Evidence for the Bible* p. 73.
9. K. A. Kitchen, *On the Reliability of the Old Testament*, Eerdmans. (Grand Rapids, Michigan/Cambridge, U.K., 2003).
10. For the Amarna letters see *Evidence for the Bible* p. 29.
11. John J. Bimson, *Redating the Exodus and Conquest*, Journal for the Study of the Old Testament: Sheffield, 1978.

**Right**
*A clay tablet from the Amarna letters from Yapahu, King of Gezer, to Pharaoh Akhenaten, begging for help against the 'Hapiru'. Key references in the Amarna letters make it difficult to date them later than the 14th century BC*

possible to align biblical history with the records of neighbouring empires.[12]

There are also internal questions regarding the numbers given in the biblical texts and whether they can simply be added together to arrive at fixed dates. For example, in 2 Kings 15:2 we read that Azariah reigned for 52 years. But most chronologies will give his reign as c. 767–740 BC; the earlier twenty-five years are considered a period of coregency with his father, Amaziah. For reasons like this, a chronology cannot be created merely by adding together the reigns of various kings; the Biblical writers were aware of such coregencies even if they treat their reigns independently of each other.[13]

While it may be unwise to be dogmatic in our use of a particular chronology to date early Old Testament history the broad picture is clear. What we read in the Bible fits with what we know of that time. As the story moves closer to the New Testament period, and more data becomes available, the reliability of the biblical text is confirmed even more clearly.

12. Ken Kitchen, *The Third Intermediate Period (1100–650)*, Aris and Philips: Warminster (1973).
13. On the important example of Nabonidus and Belshazzar see *Evidence for the Bible* pp. 92–93.

# Maps

Full timelines of Israel and Judah and the surrounding nations, throughout the Old and New Testaments, will be found in *Evidence for the Bible* pp. 220-231

## The Fertile Crescent at the time of the Patriarchs

## The Land of Israel and Judah in the Old Testament surrounded by its neighbours

# Empires at the time of the Exodus

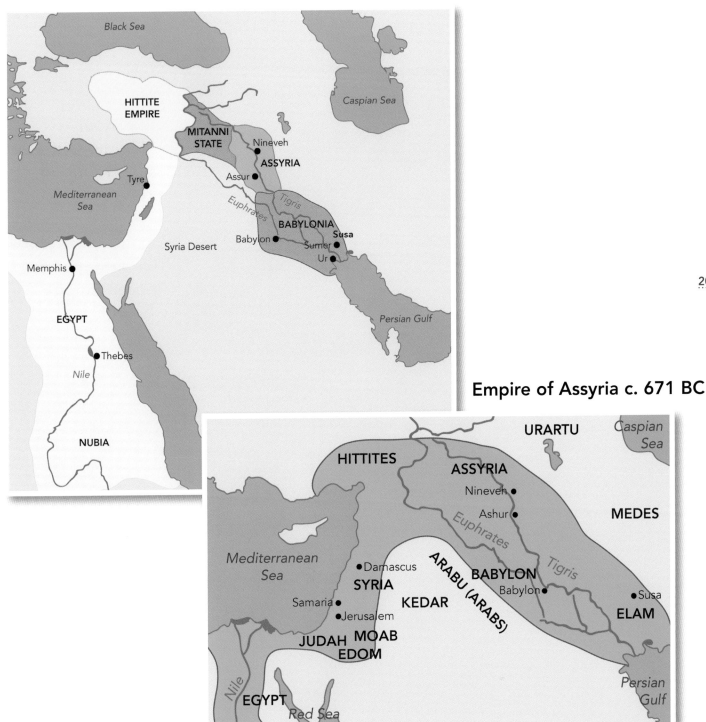

## Empire of Assyria c. 671 BC

# The extent of the Babylonian Empire c.605 BC

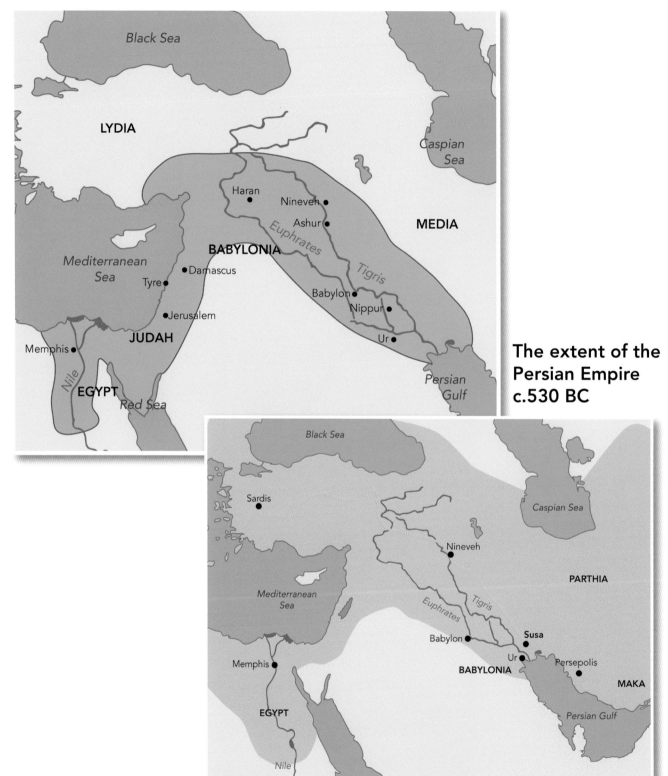

## The extent of the Persian Empire c.530 BC

# The Greek Empire between the Testaments c.330 BC

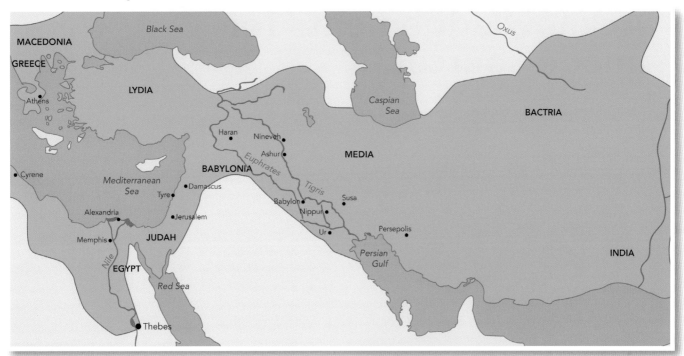

**Right**
*A tombstone portrait of a freedman and his wife. As freed slaves they enjoyed a new life as Roman citizens and most bankers, merchants, shippers, factory owners and craftsmen came from this class. Their children were also full Roman citizens. See pages 110–111 for first century slavery*

# The Roman Empire in the second century

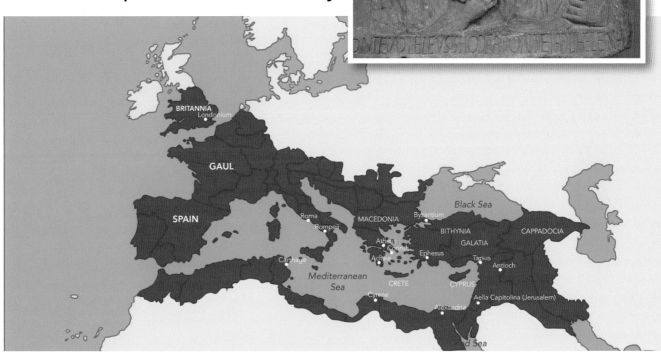

# Acknowledgements for image sources

The authors express their appreciation for all whose images have been used in this book. If we have inadvertently overlooked a copyright acknowledgement we will be glad to rectify this in any subsequent publication.

## List of illustrations

**page number**–*position on page*–picture credit–photo credit

2– – –Brian Edwards
4–*Left*–Israel Exploration Fund–
7–*Right*– –Brian Edwards
7–*Below*– –Chris Sinkinson
8–*Top*–Public Domain–
9–*Top*–Wikimedia Ceative Commons–Greg Schechter
9–*Above*– –Chris Sinkinson
9–*bottom image*– –Ian Scott
12–*Right*–The Ashmolean Museum, University of Oxford–
13–*Left* –Courtesy of the British Museum–
13–*Below*–Wikimedia Creative Commons–
14–*Top right*– –Gary Todd
15–*Above*–Wikimedia Creative Commons–Mehmetkrckrc.
15–*Left*–Wikimedia Creative Commons–Eric de Redelijkheid from Utrecht, Netherlands
16–*Above*–Arabian Rock Art Heritage–
17–*Above*–Courtesy of the British Museum–Brian Edwards
18–*Left*–Wikimedia Creative Commons–D. Denisenkov
18–*Below*–Wikimedia Creative Commons–
18–*Below*–Musée du Louvre, Paris–
21–*Left*–Wikimedia Creative Commons–
22–*Left*–used with permission Sue Bayfield–
23–*Above*–Courtesy of the British Museum–
24–*Top*–Israel Museum–Mike Brookbank
24–*Middle & Bottom*–Wikimedia Ceative Commons–
25–*Top*–Musée du Louvre, Paris–Jastrow
25–*Bottom*–The Pergamon Museum, Berlin–Marcus Cyron
26–*Left*–Wikimedia Creative Commons–A Parrot
26–*Right*–Courtesy of the British Museum–
27–*Above*–Courtesy of the British Museum–
28–*Right*–Wikimedia Creative Commons–Manna Nader, Gabana Studios Cairo
29–*Above left*–Wikimedia Ceative Commons–Manna Nader, Gabana Studios Cairo
29–*Above right*–Courtesy of the British Museum–Brian Edwards
29–*Right* –Musée du Louvre, Paris. Wikimedia Commons–Jalviar

30–*Above*–Courtesy of the British Museum–
31–*Above and below*–The Metropolitan Museum of Art–
31–*Left*–Brooklyn Museum. Creative Commons–
33–*Right*–The State Museums, Berlin.–Marburg/Art Resource, New York
33–*Background*–Cairo Museum–
34–*Above* –Courtesy of the British Museum–
35–*Above and Below*–Courtesy of the British Museum–
36–*Above*–Courtesy of the British Museum–
37–*Above*–Timna Park, Israel–
38–*Left*–USCD Levantine Archaeological Laboratory–K Smith
39–*Above*– –Thomas R Levy)
40–*Far left*– –Brian Edwards
40–*Top left*–Courtesy of the British Museum–
40–*Left*–Wikimedia Creative Commons–Amanda Slater
41–*Top left*–Metropolitan Museum. Wikimedia Creative–
41–*Far left*– –Chris Sinkinson
41–*Left*–A private collection–
42–*Left*–Musée du Louvre, Paris–Todd Bolen/BiblePlaces.com
43–*Above*–Courtesy Israel Antiquities Authority–
43–*Below*–Ben Gurion University–Dani Machlis
44–*Left*– –Giraud Patrick
45–*Right*– –Giraud Patrick and George Bernard
47–*Left below*–The Israeli Museum–
48–*Left*– –Brian Edwards
49–*Below left*–Archaeological Museum of Epidaurus, Greece.–Mike Tookey
49–*Below right*–Wikimedia Creative Commons–Zunkir
51–*Below left*–With permission Mike Tookey
51–*Below right*–Wikimedia Creative Commons–Zunkir
52–*Left*–Wikimedia Creative Commons–
52–*Below*–Wikimedia Creative Commons–Ad Meskens
53–*Left and above*–Courtesy of the British Museum–Brian Edwards
54–*Right and inset*–Musée du Louvre, Paris–

56–*Above*–O.Rouault and M G Masetti-Rouaylt 1993–
57–*Below*–The Istanbul Archaeology Museum –Ahmed Turp
58–*Above*–Wikimedia Creative Commons–
59–*Above*–The Israeli Museum–
59–*Left & Below left*–Courtesy of the British Museum–Brian Edwards
60–*Above*–Wikimedia Creative Commons–
60–*Below*–The Berlin Museum–
61–*Above*–Wikimedia Creative Commons–Carole Raddato
66–*All pictures*–Courtesy the British Museum–Brian Edwards
67–*Top right*–Courtesy the British Museum–
67–*Top*– –Brian Edwards
67–*Bottom right*–Courtesy the British Museum–Brian Edwards
69–*Right*– –Brian Edwards
69–*Bottom right*–Courtesy the British Museum–Brian Edwards
70–*Above*–Cairo Museum–
70–*Right*–Courtesy of the British Museum–
71–*Above*–Courtesy of the British Museum–
72–*Left*–The Hebrew University–
73–*Left*–With permission Y Garfinkel–
74–*Left & Above*–The Iraq Museum, Baghdad. Wickimedia Creative–Osama Shukir Muhammed Amin
75–*Above & Below*–Courtesy of the British Museum–
76–*Left*– –Chris Sinkinson
77–*Above*– –Ian Scott
78–*Above*– –Aren Maeir
78–*Top*–Wikimedia Creative Commons–
80–*Top*–Wickimedia Creative Commons–Courtesy the Beirut National Museum
80–*Left*–Courtesy of the British Museum–Brian Edwards
81–*Left & Right*–Courtesy the British Museum–Chris Sinkinson & Brian Edwards
81–*Above*–The monuments of Nineveh (London 1853)–
82–*Above left & right*–Courtesy of the British Museum–
83–*Left* –Wikimedia Ceative Commons–Osama Shukir Muhammed Amin
84–*Left*–Wikimedia Creative Commons–

84–*Below*–Courtesy of the British Museum–Toby Sinkinson

85–*Above and below left*– –Brian Edwards

86–*Above*–Division of Humanities, Macquarie University–

86–*Below*– –Mcleclat

87–*Above*– –Clive Anderson

88–*Left*– –Brian Edwards

88–*Below*– –Chris Sinkinson

88–*Bottom*–Israel Antiquities Authority–

89–*Right*–Wikimedia Ceative Commons–Graham Racher

89–*Below*– –Chris Sinkinson

90–*Above*– –Chris Sinkinson

91–*Left*– –Chris Sinkinson

91–*Above*–Wikimedia Ceative Commons–

92–*Right*–Steve Caruso/Aramaic New Testament. Design by Auras

95–*Above*–Courtesy The Faculty of Classics, Cambridge–Alessandro Launaro

95–*Below*–Courtesy of the Egyptian Museum, Cairo–

96–*Above & Below*–Courtesy of the British Museum–Toby Sinkinson

97–*Above*–Courtesy of the British Museum–Toby Sinkinson

97–*Below left*–Courtesy of the British Museum–Toby Sinkinson

97–*Below Centre*–Public domain–

97–*Below right*–Metropolitan Museum of Art. Public Domain–

98–*Left*–Metropolitan Museum. Public Domain–

98–*Below*–Courtesy of the British Museum–Toby Sinkinson

99–*Below*–Public domain–

100–*Above & Below*–Wikimedia Creative Commons–Below: Grant Barclay

101–*Above & Below*– –Chris Sinkinson

102–*Left*– –Chris Sinkinson

103–*Above*– –Chris Sinkinson

103–*Below*–Used with permission Rami Avav–Rami Arav

104–*Above*– –Gary Wilkinson

104–*Below*– –Mike Brookbank

106–*Left*– –Brigitte Stamm

108–*Above*–Stanza della Segnatura in the Vatican– Erich Lessing/Art Resource, New York

109–*Left*–Wikimedia Creative Commons, Museo del Prado–

111–*Above*–Wikimedia Creative Commons–The Ashmolean Museum, Oxford

112–*Above*–The archaeological museum in Konya–Photo by Ferrell Jenkins

113–*Above*–The Palatine Museum, Rome–

117–*Right*–The Romer Museum, Weissenburg, Germany–Livius.org Jona Lendering

118–*Above*–The Israeli Museum–Brian Edwards

119–*Above*– –G Alföldy

120–*Left*– –Chris Sinkinson

120–*Bottom left*–Courtesy the Madain Project–

121–*Top right*–Wikimedia Creative Commons–Oren Rozen

123–*Top*– –Hannah Taylor

125–*Below*–Wickimedia Creative Commons–Joonas Plaan

126–*Above and inset*– –Chris Sinkinson

126–*Below*– –Chris Sinkinson

127–*Left and below*– –Chris Sinkinson

128–*Left*– –Ny Carlsberg Glytotek, Denmark

128–*Below*–Wikimedia Creative Commons–Oren Rozen

129–*Top & Above*– –Chris Sinkinson

131–*Left*– –Bernard Gagnon

132–*Above & Below*–Courtesy of the British Museum–Brian Edwards

134–*Above (inset)*–Shutterstock–

135–*Left*–Luther College Decorah Iowa–

137–*Above*– –Bianca Cadore

138–*Right & Right below*–Courtesy the British Museum–Brian Edwards

139–*All pictures*–Courtesy the British Museum–Brian Edwards

141–*Below*– –Brian Edwards

142–*Bottom left*–Courtesy the British Museum–Brian Edwards

143–*Top*–Courtesy the British Museum–Toby Sinkinson

143–*Above*–Courtesy the British Museum–Brian Edwards

144–*Right & Below right*–Public Domain–Brian Edwards

145–*Top & Above*–Wickimedia Creative Commons–

151–*Below*–The Israeli Museum–Brian Edwards

151–*Above* – –Brian Edwards

152–*Above* – –Brian Edwards

153–*All pictures*– –Brian Edwards

159–*All pictures*– –Brian Edwards

161–*Left and below*– –Brian Edwards

162–*Above*– –Brian Edwards

163–*All pictures*– –Brian Edwards

166–*Above*–Wikimedia Creative Commons–

166–*Left*– –Mike Brookbank

167–*Left & below*– –Brian Edwards

170–*Left* –Altes Museum, Berlin–

172–*Left*– –Brian Edwards

173–*All pictures*– –Brian Edwards

174–*Left*– –Brian Edwards

178–*Right*–The Gospel of Judas. Critical Edition. Washington 2007 –Wolfgang Rieger

179–*Above*–Institute for Antiquity and Christianity, Claremont, CA–

184–*Top right & Right* –Public Domain–

185–*Above*–Wikimnedia Creative Commons–Tamarah

186–*Below*–Courtesy of the British Museum–Toby Sinkinson

186–*Left*–Public domain–

187–*Right* –Courtesy Madain Project–

188–*Above*–Public domain–

189–*Left* –Wikimedia Creative Commons–

190–*Above*–Courtesy of the British Museum–Toby Sinkinson

193–*Above*–courtesy the British Museum–Toby Sinkinson

194–*Above and right*–Courtesy the British Museum–Brian Edwards

196–*Left* –Courtesy the British Museum–Toby Sinkinson

199–*Below*–Wikimedia Creative Commons–

200–*Above*–Courtesy the British Museum–Toby Sinkinson

201–*Right*–Courtesy the British Museum–Toby Sinkinson

204–*Right*–courtesy the British Museum–Toby Sinkinson

213–*Main picture*– –Brian Edwards

213–*Inset*–courtesy the British Museum–

# Scripture Index

211

212

213

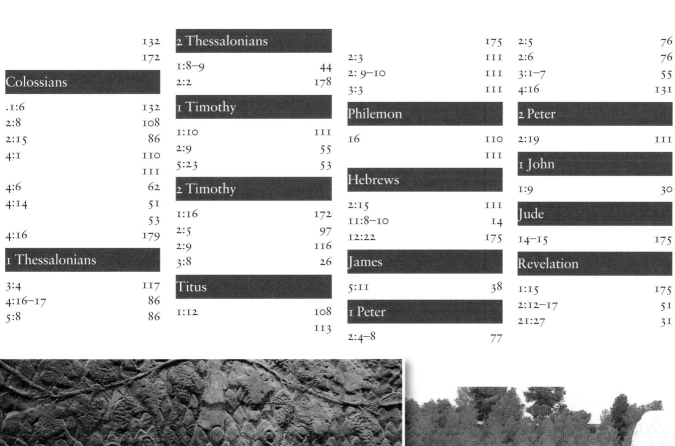

**Above**

*The Assyrian reliefs of the siege of Lachish show grape vines above the stone-slingers. Almost 3,000 years later a vineyard is still evident below the ruin mound of Lachish. (See here pp. 142-143 and* Evidence for the Bible *pp. 70-74)*

# General Index

This index is not comprehensive; only the more significant uses of a word are included.

215

216

# Evidence for the Bible

**Clive Anderson**
**Brian Edwards**

## The essential 'twin' for Background to the Bible

**A** unique volume in the field of biblical archaeology and a valuable resource for all who preach or teach the Bible at whatever level.

- Accurate and accessible. Large format hardback of 253 pages. Over 200 colour plates
- Timelines of Ancient Near East empires place biblical events in context
- Articles on some critical issues
- An assessment of fallacies in the world of biblical archaeology

The evidence of archaeology authenticates and illustrates the Bible, lifting people and events from its pages and setting them in the context of time and place.

# Nothing but the Truth

**Brian Edwards**

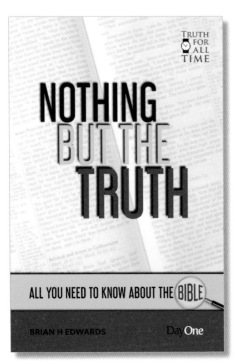

**N** *othing but the Truth* answers, in an accessible and accurate way, the many questions that are asked about the Bible: What does it claim for itself? Who wrote it and when? What Bible did the Jews, Jesus and the apostles have? Was anything left out? How can we respond to its critics? How can we choose a translation and read it with understanding? And much, much more….

- A chart of the Old Testament books and their main preparation for the Messiah
- A harmony of the Gospels. An outline of the Acts and where the letters were written
- A plan to read the whole Bible in eighteen months
- Using your Bible for a daily time with God

Hardback 766 pages with source references and a full index

'A tour de force and a marvellous gift to the church in our secular age. I could not commend it more warmly or enthusiastically.'
**RICHARD CUNNINGHAM**, *Director, Universities and Colleges Christian Unions.*

'A wealth of material in readable style, it is a rich resource, giving fresh confidence in the reliability and authority of the Scriptures.'
**BILL JAMES**, *Principal, The London Seminary*

# Through the **The British Museum** with the **Bible**

T he British Museum is visited by six million people annually from every continent and country. *Through the British Museum with the Bible* centres on the items that are related to the history recorded in the Christian Scriptures. Here is all that you need to make your tour both enjoyable and relevant. The past is brought to light in front of you.

A room-by-room Bible-related tour. Concise and accurate explanations. Around 150 photographs. An index of Bible references. A valuable reference guide, packed with information for those who may never be able to visit the Museum in London

'The British Museum is a great storehouse of treasures from the past. This guide brings them together in a concise way that will help readers to understand more clearly what each has to offer.'

**ALAN MILLARD,** *Rankin Professor Emeritus of Hebrew and Ancient Semitic Languages, the University of Liverpool. Formerly Assistant Keeper of Western Asiatic Antiquities at the British Museum*

'This guide enables anyone, either alone or with a group, to identify Bible related items accurately. It is both reliable and easy to use.'

**DONALD J WISEMAN,** *Late Professor Emeritus of Assyriology in the University of London, formerly Assistant Keeper in the Egyptian and Western Asiatic Antiquities at the British Museum*

221

# Other **DayOne** titles in this series

## Edited by Brian Edwards

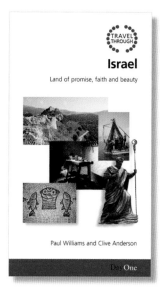

**Israel**
Land of promise, faith and beauty

Paul Williams and Clive Anderson

Day One

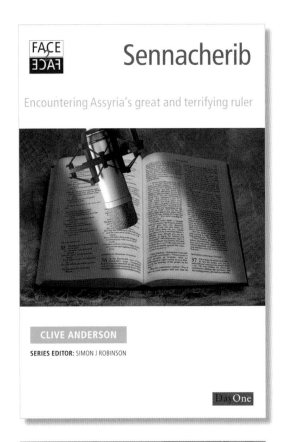

# Sennacherib
## Clive Anderson

Sennacherib was once a name to send a chill down spines, yet today, relatively few have heard of him, and even fewer know much about him. Lord Byron immortalized one part of his life in a poem, but there was much more to this man than king and fearsome warrior. Coming face to face with him in this book not only reveals a complex and multi-talented man, but also the formidable enemy that the land of Judah, its king, Hezekiah, and prophet, Isaiah, were confronted with at a time of national crisis. Today, many Christians across the world find themselves faced with situations that appear to be beyond their control. How should they react in such circumstances and what help can they expect to receive? This book, while dealing with real history, also focuses on life in the twenty-first century and gives pointers towards being faithful witnesses of Jesus Christ.

# Time Travel to the Old Testament
Inter Varsity Press

## Chris Sinkinson

*Time Travel to the Old Testament* deals with many of the confusing or mysterious elements of the Bible that can make it a difficult book to read.

In an accessible and engaging way, the reader is shown how the cultural background to the world of the Old Testament can help us read it in a way that makes sense today. The laws and legal codes of the Old Testament make much more sense in the light of the surrounding cultures. Sometimes disturbing narratives concerning war, commerce or marriage are explained in the context of the ancient near east.

Drawing upon parallel literature, archaeology and contemporary scholarship *Time Travel to the Old Testament* is an interesting and entertaining read that will help even someone new to the Bible to feel much more at home in the ancient world. By starting to see things the way the ancient Hebrews did, the Bible becomes more than just history but reveals itself as entirely relevant to many of the issues we face today.

**Includes related bible studies, maps, images and index.**